# TOP 10
# MUNICH

ELFI LEDIG

DK

EYEWITNESS TRAVEL

Left **Deutsches Museum** Centre **Frauenkirche** Right **Alte Münze**

LONDON, NEW YORK,
MELBOURNE, MUNICH AND DELHI
www.dk.com

Produced by Dorling Kindersley Verlag, Munich

English-language adaptation produced by
International Book Productions Inc., Toronto

Reproduced by Colourscan, Singapore Printed
and bound in China by Leo Paper Products Ltd

First American Edition, 2005
10 9 8 7 6 5 4 3 2

Published in the United States by
DK Publishing, 375 Hudson Street, New York,
New York 10014

ISSN 1479-344X
ISBN 978-0-75664-096-5

Within each Top 10 list in this book, no hierarchy
of quality or popularity is implied. All 10 are, in
the editor's opinion, of roughly equal merit.
Floors are referred to throughout in accordance
with German usage; ie the "first floor" is the
floor above ground level.

> **We're trying to be cleaner and greener:**
>
> • we recycle waste and switch things off
> • we use paper from responsibly managed
>   forests whenever possible
> • we ask our printers to actively reduce
>   water and energy consumption
> • we check out our suppliers' working
>   conditions – they never use child labour
>
> **Find out more about our values and
> best practices at www.dk.com**

## Contents

### Munich's Top 10

**The information in this DK Eyewitness Top 10 Travel Guide is checked regularly.**
Every effort has been made to ensure that this book is as up-to-date as possible at the time of
going to press. Some details, however, such as telephone numbers, opening hours, prices,
gallery hanging arrangements and travel information are liable to change. The publishers
cannot accept responsibility for any consequences arising from the use of this book, nor for
any material on third party websites, and cannot guarantee that any website address in this
book will be a suitable source of travel information. We value the views and suggestions of
our readers very highly. Please write to: Publisher, DK Eyewitness Travel Guides,
Dorling Kindersley, 80 Strand, London, Great Britain WC2R 0RL.

Left **Antiquarium, Residenz** Centre **Schloss Nymphenburg** Right **Oktoberfest**

Left **Theatinerkirche** Right **Fischbrunnen (Fish Fountain) Marienplatz**

 *Following pages* **Munich, the Alps in the background**

# TOP 10
# MUNICH

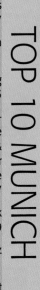

TOP 10 MUNICH

# Munich Highlights

*Of the city he lived in for many years, 20th-century writer Thomas Mann said that "Munich glows". And indeed, the sky is often a brilliant blue dotted with puffy white clouds in "Italy's northernmost city", where the relaxed, often Baroque lifestyle gives it a southern flair. Englischer Garten and the Isar meadows are right in the middle of the city; Starnberger See and the mountains are virtually on the doorstep. But Munich is also a city of art and culture with an abundance of historic buildings, museum treasures, and a lively cultural scene. Fine art, leisure, and la dolce vita make this a unique city.*

### Deutsches Museum
Renowned as the oldest and largest museum of science and technology in the world, the museum attracts more than 1.3 million visitors every year *(see pp8–11)*.

### Schloss Nymphenburg
Ludwig I's Gallery of Beauties features portraits of noblewomen and famous beauties, such as the tailor's daughter, Helene Sedlmayr *(see pp12–13)*.

### Museumsviertel
Three Pinakotheken (picture galleries) now lie side by side in the Museum District. The oldest, the Alte Pinakothek in a reconstructed building from 1836, is devoted to historic European painting – its collection boasts priceless treasures including panels by Albrecht Dürer *(see pp14–17)*.

### Olympia-gelände
In 1972, a large park, including an artificial hill, was created from World War II rubble for the Summer Olympics. At the time, the distinctive tent roof was considered an architectural innovation *(see pp18–19)*.

### Residenz
Dating back to 1385, the Residenz has been expanded by various wings and courtyards over the centuries *(see pp20–21)*.

Olympiapark

Olympiapark

LANDSHUTER ALLEE

DACHAUER STRASSE

SCHWERE-REIT

LEONROD-PLATZ

LEONRODSTRASSE

DACHAUER STRASSE

ACKERMANNSTRASSE

PLATZ DER FREIHEIT

NYMPHENBURGER STRASSE

MARS PLATZ

Max-vorsta

ARNULFSTRASSE

MAXESSTRASSE

LANDSBERGER STRASSE

Schwanthaler-höhe

SCHWANTHAL

THERESIENHÖHE

Theresienwiese

BAVARIARING

LINDWURM

### Oktoberfest
First held to celebrate the wedding of Ludwig I (1810), this is the largest folk festival in the world. Some six million visitors flock to the fairgrounds every year *(see pp22–3).*

### Beer Gardens
Locals are passionate about their beer garden tradition – bring your own food and pay only for a cool pint *(see pp24–5).*

### Around Marienplatz
Site of the Neues Rathaus (New Town Hall) Marienplatz is the main square. The historic carved figures of the Glockenspiel in the town hall tower come alive in a coopers' dance three times a day *(see pp26–7).*

Around Munich

### Schloss Neuschwanstein
Ludwig II's most famous castle was inspired by his admiration of Wagner's operas *(see pp28–31).*

### Starnberger See
This lovely scenic lake on Munich's doorstep is surrounded by picturesque towns, royal summer palaces, and the popular Buchheim Museum *(see pp32–3).*

With 1.3 million inhabitants, Munich is Germany's third-largest city.

# 🔟 Deutsches Museum

*The Deutsches Museum, founded by Oskar von Miller in 1903, is housed on an island in the Isar River in a building dating from 1925. The world's largest museum of technology and engineering is a tour de force – only a fraction of the exhibits can be viewed in a single day. The best approach is to plan your visit in advance.*

*The museum on Museums-Insel in the Isar River*

🍴 A good alternative to the museum cafeteria is Café im Volksbad in the Müller Baths, a splendid Art Nouveau building across from the museum.

🛍 The museum shop sells model kits (including robots), games, building sets, instruments, posters, and books.

• Museumsinsel 1
• S-Bahn: Isartor (all lines), U1/U2: Fraunhoferstraße, Tram: 17, 18
• Map M6
• (089) 21 79-1
• www.deutsches-museum.de
• Open 9am–5pm daily (some departments until 8pm Thu)
• Closed 1 Jan, Shrove Tue, Good Fri, 1 May, 1 Nov, 21 Dec, 24–25 Dec, 31 Dec
• Adm €8.50 (reduced €3 and €7), Wed after 4pm €3, family ticket €17, children ages 6–15 €3, children under 6 free; combined ticket with branch museums €15

## Top 10 Sights

1. Galileo's Workshop
2. Pharmaceuticals
3. Enigma Machine
4. Zeiss Planetarium
5. Mining
6. Musical Instruments
7. Aviation and Space Travel
8. Power Machinery
9. Telecommunications
10. Marine Navigation

### 1 Galileo's Workshop
In the Physics section, a reconstruction of Galileo's workshop *(above)* features a large collection of equipment used by the famous astronomer and physicist.

### 2 Pharmaceuticals
The highlight of this section, opened in 2000, is a model of a human cell magnified 350,000 times *(below)*.

### 3 Enigma Machine
The Enigma encoding machine *(above)*, built during World War II, is a fine example of early information technology.

### Floorplan of the Deutsches Museum

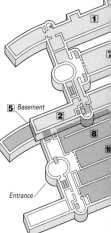

5 Basement

Entrance

### 4 Zeiss Planetarium
Projected onto the 15-m (49-ft) dome of the sixth floor are the sun, the moon, the planets, constellations, and nebulae, as well as the more than 5,000 fixed stars visible to the naked eye.

➡ *Laser shows are presented in the Zeiss Planetarium on the sixth floor; tickets for these events are sold separately.*

### 7 Aviation and Space Travel

Dozens of airplanes are on display, including an original by the Wright brothers and the famous Junkers *JU-52*. You can even board some planes. More exhibits on travel are housed at *Flugwerft Schleißheim*, a branch museum.

### 9 Telecommunications

Superb exhibits such as the first 19th-century telegraph, Thomas Edison's gramophone, and a 1913 AEG transmitter are displayed here, along with the latest in communications technology.

### 5 Mining

Exhibits on mining technology over five centuries are featured in the mining section *(above)*.

### Key to Floorplan

- Ground floor
- First floor
- Second floor
- Third to sixth floors

### 10 Marine Navigation

Along with countless model ships, the vast exhibition hall features several original sail- and steamboats, such as the 1932 steam tugboat *Renzo* and the wooden fishing vessel *Ewer Maria (above)*.

### Museum Guide

The museum's 17,000 exhibits are displayed over six floors. The lower floors feature heavy vehicles and sections dealing with chemistry, physics, scientific instruments, and aviation. The middle floors are dedicated to the decorative arts, and the upper floors are devoted to astronomy, information technology, and microelectronics. The Zeiss Planetarium is located in the dome on the sixth floor.

### 6 Musical Instruments

Sounds for Hitchcock's *The Birds* were created on the trautonium *(below)*.

### 8 Power Machinery

Steam engines, motor engines, and turbines are to be found here. Some of these colossal machines, like the Alban high-pressure steam engine *(above)*, are veritable works of art.

*For details on Deutsches Museum branch museums See p11*

Left **Aviation Hall** Centre **Zeiss Planetarium** Right **Model of the Seine Bridge at Neuilly**

# 🔟 Deutsches Museum Collections

### 1 Physics & Astronomy
The physics section features mechanical aids such as pulleys, pumps, and measuring and observation devices – including Foucault's pendulum, which featured in Umberto Eco's eponymous novel. A sense of the size and age of our universe is conveyed in the astronomy section.

### 2 Clocks, Chemistry, Pharmaceuticals & Environment
Examples of traditional craftsmanship are on display in the extensive clock and watch exhibit. In the chemistry section, famous experiments and a reconstruction of Justus von Liebig's laboratory fascinate visitors. Rooms dedicated to pharmaceuticals show the evolution of drug research. Ecological issues are dealt with in the environment exhibit.

### 3 Mining, Metallurgy, & Agriculture
In the basement, a re-created mine is complemented by exhibits on the more than 12,000-year-old history of metallurgy. The agriculture section demonstrates the cultivation of cereals and grain, brewing, and sugar refining.

### 4 Glass Ceramics, & Machine Tools
In this section, materials and production techniques used in a variety

Azimuth quadrant, by
G F Brander, 1760

of industries are on display. These include exhibits demonstrating glass and paper manufacture; the range of ceramics manufacture, from bricks to fine china; and tools from Stone Age drills to computer-controlled lathes.

### 5 Energy Technology
From original windmills to plasma- and fusion-technology, this section features inventions that facilitate everyday life. The huge steam engines and high-voltage experiments are not to be missed.

### 6 Communications
In addition to telegraph and radio equipment, this department includes sections on printing technology, photography, and film. Visitors can marvel at room-sized computers from the 1940s and 1950s.

### 7 Marine Navigation
Numerous models of ships illustrate several millennia of marine navigation. The rescue cruiser *Theodor Heuss* is displayed in the open-air exhibition space to the south of the museum.

### 8 Aviation and Space Travel
In the vast hall, 220 years of aviation history are re-created – from the Montgolfier brothers'

*This selection represents a fraction of the highlights – there are many more, such as a reconstruction of the Altamira cave.*

hot-air balloons to modern jets. The space travel section includes a replica of the Spacelab.

### Civil Engineering

An authentic suspension bridge dominates the exhibition hall; wall-mounted screens track the oscillations as visitors venture onto and then cross over this swaying bridge.

### Kid's Kingdom

Reserved exclusively for children and accompanying adults, this section is designed for young scientists, ages three and up. Interactive exhibits let children experience phenomena such as communication, energy, optics, and acoustics. The Technical Toys section offers welcome relaxation after all the hands-on research.

### Top 10 Aviation & Transportation

1. Fokker D VII, fighter aircraft (World War I)
2. Douglas DC-3, commercial aircraft, 1943
3. Heinkel He 111, bomber aircraft (World War II)
4. Lockheed F-104 Starfighter
5. Dornier Do31, vertical lift-off aircraft
6. Puffing Billy (first locomotive in the world)
7. Drais wheel
8. Benz motorcar (first automobile in the world)
9. Rumpler "Tropfenwagen" (aerodynamic car, 1921)
10. NSU Delphin III motorcycle, 1956

**Transportation Centre Exhibition Hall**
The automobile collection in the transportation centre exemplifies the stellar quality of the exhibits.

# The Branch Museums

**Exhibition hall, Flugwerft Schleißheim**

*Flugwerft Schleißheim, the Deutsches Museum's branch museum on the history of aviation, is located in an old airplane hanger on a historic airfield in Schleißheim (Effnerstraße 18, Oberschleißheim; 089/31 57 14-0). In addition to the old buildings and the airfield itself, this site offers 7,800 sq m (84,000 sq ft) of exhibition space housing over 50 airplanes, helicopters, and hang-gliders, as well as instruments and equipment. There are special exhibitions, children's tours, and expert-guided tours. The museum also has a shop and a restaurant – Pegasus – that serves as a year-round venue for exhibitions by young artists.*

*The Verkehrszentrum, or Transportation Centre, was opened in 2003 on the Theresienhöhe (Theresienhöhe 14a; (089) 500 80 61 40). Three heritage-protected halls, once home to the Munich Fair, now house historic locomotives, automobiles, carriages, and bicycles. With this branch museum, the Deutsches Museum has created the largest transportation museum in the world, offering a detailed and comprehensive exploration of urban transportation, travel, mobility, and transportation technology. Special exhibitions and lectures round out the programme.*

*For detailed information on the branch museums, visit* **www.deutsches-museum.de**

# Schloss Nymphenburg

*To celebrate the birth of their son in 1664, the Elector Ferdinand Maria and his wife Henrietta Adelaide of Savoy commissioned Agostino Barelli to build a summer palace to the west of Munich. The wings and annexe buildings were added from 1701 onwards. The historic gardens to the rear of the palace beckon for a pleasant stroll. Over the course of 300 years, the original ornamental garden was expanded into a vast ensemble comprising a Baroque garden, a system of canals, and small pavilions scattered throughout the park.*

*The canal in the gardens of Schloss Nymphenburg*

⬤ The Palmenhaus café is a perfect spot to relax over a cup of coffee (089-17 53 09).

✪ Audio guides are available for a fee. Theme tours of the grounds are also offered.

- Schloss Nymphenburg
- Tram 12, 16,17, Bus 51
- Map A2 –A3 & B2–B3
- (089) 179 08-0
- Schloss, pavilions & Marstallmuseum: Open Apr–mid-Oct: 9am–6pm daily; mid-Oct–Mar: 10am–4pm daily
- closed 1 Jan; Shrove Tue; 24, 25 & 31 Dec
- Adm: (includes Schloss, pavilions, and the Marstallmuseum) €10 (reduced €8); in winter €8 (reduced €6)
- Schlosspark: Open daily Jan–Feb, Nov: 6:30am–5pm; Mar: 6am–6pm; Apr–Sep: 6am–8:30pm; May–Aug: 6am–9:30pm; Oct: 6am–7pm; Dec: 6:30am–5:30pm
- Park adm free
- Free park tours in spring and autumn

## Top 10 Sights

1. The Palace
2. Gallery of Beauties
3. Steinerner Saal
4. Lackkabinett
5. Palace Gardens
6. Marstallmuseum
7. Amalienburg
8. Pagodenburg
9. Badenburg
10. Magdalenenklause

### The Palace
Maximilian II Emanuel and Karl Albrecht expanded the original 1664 villa by adding buildings designed by Enrico Zucalli and Joseph Effner. Arcaded galleries connect them to the main building, contributing to the harmony of the ensemble *(right)*.

### Gallery of Beauties
Ludwig I commissioned Joseph Stieler to create a gallery of beauties – a collection of portraits of noblewomen, townswomen, and dancers – such as Helene Sedlmayr, a beautiful tailor's daughter *(above)*.

### Steinerner Saal
The Rococo embellishment in the spacious ballroom was created by Johann B Zimmermann and Cuviliés the Elder during the reign of Maximilian III Joseph.

### Lackkabinett
Exquisite Chinese motifs in black laquer on wood panelling are reprised in the Rococo ceiling fresco *(below)*.

*The Porcelain Factory museum, located in an annexe, documents the history of the Nymphenburger Porzellan factory since 1747.*

### 5 Palace Gardens

Symmetrically laid-out French gardens to the rear of the palace give way to an English-style landscaped park, which was established using the existing forest. The gardens feature pavilions, lodges, fountains, ornamental ponds, and other park installations.

**Plan of the Palace Gardens**

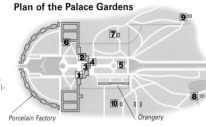

*Porcelain Factory*   *Orangery*

### 6 Marstallmuseum

This building houses carriages and sleighs that once belonged to the Bavarian rulers. Ludwig II's gilded state coach *(below)* is one such example.

### 8 Pagodenburg

In this 18th-century pavilion with an unusual octagonal floorplan, Western and Eastern ornamentation is beautifully combined *(above)*. The ground floor is decorated with Delft tiles.

### 7 Amalienburg

Built by Cuvilliés the Elder between 1734 and 1739 for Electress Amelia, this small hunting lodge is a masterpiece of European Rococo *(right)*.

### 9 Badenburg

Featuring a ballroom and a two-storey bathing hall containing a heated pool – making it one of Europe's first – this pavilion is definitely worth a visit. Three of the pavilion's rooms are lined in costly Chinese wallpaper.

### 10 Magdalenen-klause

Grottoes and follies were an expression of 18th-century romantic yearnings. This folly contains rooms of monastic severity, which served as a peaceful retreat for Maximilian Emanuel, along with a chapel located in a grotto.

### From Formal Garden to Palace Park

In 1664, the site featured an ornamental garden. This was enlarged in 1701 and a canal was added. Its transformation into a formal Baroque garden began in 1715 under the direction of Dominique Girard and Joseph Effner, who built a system of canals, fountains, hedged gardens, and a forest-like park. Pavilions and lodges were added over the course of the 18th century. In the 19th century, Friedrich L von Sckell reconfigured the park in the style of an English landscape garden.

*The Museum Mensch und Natur in the right wing of the palace features exhibits on natural science. Visit www.musmn.de*

# 📖10 Museum District – Alte Pinakothek

*The Museum District comprises three major museums: the Alte Pinakothek, the Neue Pinakothek, and the Pinakothek der Moderne (see pp16–17). Nearby is the Glyptothek, the State Collection of Antiquities, and Lenbachhaus. The Alte Pinakothek was founded by Ludwig I, designed by Leo von Klenze, and opened in 1836. It houses the collections of Bavarian dukes, electors, and kings, as well as the treasures of dissolved monasteries. Today, the museum holds priceless masterpieces of 14th- to 18th-century art.*

*Lion at the entrance to the Alte Pinakothek*

🄲 The English-style Café Klenze opened in 2005 in the Alte Pinakothek. It serves cakes and gateaux.

🄲 Audio guides are sometimes included in the admission price.

• **Alte Pinakothek:** *Barer Str. 27, (089) 23 805 216* • *Open 10am–6pm Tue–Sun (until 8pm Tue); closed some hols* • *Adm: €5.50 (reduced €4); Sun €1*
• **Neue Pinakothek:** *Barer Str. 29, (089) 23 805 195* • *Open 10am–6pm Wed–Mon (until 8pm Wed); closed some hols* • *Adm: as above*
• **Pinakothek der Moderne:** *Barer Str. 40, (089) 23 805 360* • *Open 10am–6pm Tue–Sun (until 8pm Thu & Fri); closed some hols* • *Adm: €9.50 (reduced €6); Sun €1*

• *Map K2*
• *U2: Theresienstraße, Tram 27*
• *www.pinakothek.de*

## Top 10 Paintings
1. Battle of Alexander at Issus
2. Deposition from the Cross
3. Land of Cockaigne
4. Pietà
5. Portrait of Karl V
6. The Rape of the Daughters of Leukippos
7. Portrait of Willem van Heythuisen
8. Disrobing of Christ
9. Four Apostles
10. Adoration of the Magi

### 1 Battle of Alexander at Issus
Altdorfer's 1529 painting depicts the decisive moment of Alexander the Great's victory over the Persian King Darius *(below)*.

### 2 Deposition from the Cross
Dramatic lighting characterizes Rembrandt's 1633 masterpiece. It is exhibited in the Dutch painting collection, which also features landscapes and other works.

### 3 Land of Cockaigne
Breughel, the most famous representative of the Flemish School, offers a satirical depiction of gluttony and idleness *(above)*. This piece is part of a section also housing a large collection of Rubens' paintings.

### 4 Pietà
Sandro Botticelli's 1495 painting captivates the viewer with its rich red hues and strong contrasts. It is one of the masterpieces in the Italian painting section.

### 5 Portrait of Karl V
In 1548, the Italian painter Titian created this portrait of Emperor Karl V on the occasion of the Reichstag of Augsburg (1547).

*An annual pass for all three Pinakothek museums costs €70 (a €40 saving).*

**The Rape of the Daughters of Leukippos**
Rubens' 1618 high Baroque masterpiece *(above)*.

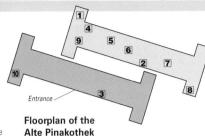

**Floorplan of the Alte Pinakothek**

Entrance

### Key to Floorplan

| | Ground Floor |
|---|---|
| | First Floor |

### Four Apostles
The Albrecht Dürer collection documents the development of the artist from his *Self-Portrait in Fur Coat* (1500) to the *Four Apostles* (1526), painted two years before his death.

### Adoration of the Magi
The late Gothic work by Holbein the Elder from 1502 is one part of the *Eight Scenes* from the Kaisheimer altar.

### Disrobing of Christ
El Greco created this sombre work *(below)* between 1585 and 1608. It is part of the small yet exquisite collection of Spanish paintings.

### Portrait of Willem van Heythuisen
Hals' magnificent painting *(above)* (1625–30) is an outstanding example of Dutch portraiture. The collection includes landscapes and other works.

### Museum Guide

The Alte Pinakothek's collections are housed on two floors. German painting up to 1500 is located on the ground floor. On the first floor, German painting after 1500, Old Dutch Masters, Italian Renaissance painting, 17th-century French, Flemish, and Dutch painting, and a somewhat smaller Spanish collection are on display. More than 700 works of art are on view in the museum's 19 main rooms and 47 side galleries. The cafeteria and a bookshop are also located on the ground floor.

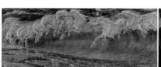

Left *Neptune's Horses,* Crane Centre *The Poor Poet,* Spitzweg Right *Play of the Waves,* Böcklin

# 🔟 Neue & Pinakothek der Moderne

### 1 Neptune's Horses
In this 1892 painting, Walter Crane fuses Pre-Raphaelite expression with Art Nouveau and Symbolist influences.

### 2 The Poor Poet
Carl Spitzweg's famous 1839 painting captures the spirit of the Biedermeier period.

### 3 Boys on the Beach
Dating from 1898, this work by Max Liebermann exemplifies the preoccupation of German Impressionists with capturing the play of light in their work.

### 4 Breakfast in the Studio
Edouard Manet's painting from 1868 – a seminal work of strong light and dark contrasts that heralds the beginning of Impressionism – is one of the highlights of the Neue Pinakothek.

### 5 Play of the Waves
Arnold Böcklin's oeuvre was heavily inspired by classical mythological themes. This work from 1883 depicts water

Manet's *Breakfast in the Studio*

nymphs, mermaids, and sea gods in a subtly erotic Neo-Baroque manner.

The Design Collection

### 6 The Classic Modern Collection
The museum's collection is divided into two principal sections. The Classic Modern encompasses the period up to 1960 and features works by Kirchner, Nolde, Braque, Picasso, Klee, Beckmann, and others.

### 7 The Contemporary Art Collection
This section documents the art scene from 1960 onward and includes works by Beuys, Baselitz, Warhol, de Kooning, Twombly, and others.

### 8 The Graphic Arts Collection
A wide range of works from the Old Masters (Rembrandt, Titian) to Cézanne are some of the highlights of this collection, along with modern graphic works by Baselitz and Wols, and Franz

On this list numbers 1–5 are in the Neue Pinakothek; 6–10 are in the Pinakothek der Moderne.

Marc's pen-and-ink drawing *The Tower of the Blue Horses* (1912). Over 45,000 drawings and roughly 350,000 prints are shown in rotating exhibitions.

Olaf Metzel's *Journey to Jerusalem* (2002)

on the ground floor of the Pinakothek der Moderne.

## 9 The Architecture Collection

Some 350,000 architectural drawings and plans, roughly 100,000 photographs, and approximately 500 models are presented in rotating exhibits

## 10 The Design Collection

Modern utilitarian objects are the theme of this nearly 60,000-strong collection. The exhibits range from chairs (Thonet room), to 1960s Pop furniture, to objects from the world of aerodynamics and computer design.

### Top 10 Events in Construction of the Pinakothek der Moderne

1. 1990: Planning begins
2. 1992: Stephan Braunfels wins design competition
3. 1993: Bavaria asks that donations cover 10 per cent of building costs
4. 1994: The PDM Foundation raises 30 million DM
5. 1995: Decision is made to build the museum
6. 1996: Turning the sod
7. 1998: Raising-of-the-roof ceremony
8. 2000: Dispute over extra costs (30 million DM)
9. Structural damage on roof
10. 2002: Museum opens

# Museum & Art District

*Founded by Ludwig I, the Neue Pinakothek was opened in 1853; it was destroyed in 1944. The new structure, designed by Alexander von Branca, was inaugurated nearly four decades later, in 1981. With a permanent collection of over 4,500 paintings and 300 sculptures, the Neue Pinakothek is one of the most important museums of 19th-century art.*

*The spacious building designed by Stephan Braunfels for the Pinakothek der Moderne was inaugurated in 2002 as a site for art of the 20th and 21st centuries. With over 20,000 sq m (215,300 sq ft) of floor space, the museum provides ample room for both permanent and special exhibitions. All galleries are grouped around a central rotunda and linked via a network of stairs. At first criticized because of the exorbitant building costs (€121 million), the museum has since been acknowledged as one of the most impressive art collections in the world. It is also the biggest art museum in Germany.*

*The three Pinakotheks in the Museum District are*

*soon to be joined by additional museums such as the Brandhorst collection, which is opening in early 2009.*

*The Glyptothek, the Museum of Antiquities, and the Lenbachhaus are within easy walking distance of each other and constitute the nexus of the Art District. The Museum District is also home to dozens of private galleries.*

**Rotunda, Pinakothek der Moderne**

*For an excellent introduction to the Pinakothek der Moderne, visit* www.pinakothek-der-moderne.de

# ☆10 Olympiapark

*In preparation for the 1972 Olympic Games, a former airfield and parade ground were transformed into an Olympic park. The park features landscaped hills, an artificial lake, a communications tower, and sports facilities. Designed by the firm of Behnisch & Partners, the elegant, airy ensemble derives its character chiefly from the transparent tensile roof designed by Frei Otto. Tent-shaped, it covers part of the stadium, the hall, and the pool, and is considered a masterpiece of modern architecture.*

*Aerial view of Olympiapark*

🍴 The Revolving Restaurant offers excellent food and a fantastic view.

🧗 Book a climb on the tensile roof in summer – complete with rope and hooks (089-30 67 24 14).

---

- U3: Olympiazentrum
- Map D1–E1
- (089) 30 67 24 14
- *Olympic Tower:* 9am–midnight daily (last trip 11:30pm); adm: €4.50 (reduced €2.80)
- *Roof tour:* Apr–Oct: 4pm Fri–Sun, adm: €45 (children 10–15 years: €35)
- *Adventure tour* (grounds): Apr–Oct: 2pm daily, adm: €8 (children 6–15 years: €5.50)
- *Info:* www.olympia park-muenchen.de
- *BMW Welt:* 9am–8pm daily • *Sea Life:* 7am–10pm daily; adm: €14 (children €8.75) •
- *Olympic Aquatic Centre:* 7am–11pm Mon, Wed & Fri–Sun, 7am–5.15pm & 8.30–11pm Tue & Thu; adm: €3.60 (children 6 years and over €2.60); combination ticket for Sauna Paradise €12.80

## Top 10 Sights

1 Olympic Tower
2 BMW Welt
3 Olympic Stadium
4 Olympic Hall
5 Lake & Park
6 Olympic Skating Rink
7 Sea Life
8 Olympic Aquatic Centre
9 Father Timofej's Chapel
10 Theatron & Other Facilities

### 1 Olympic Tower

A high-speed elevator transports visitors to the observation platform and revolving restaurant of this 290-m- (900-ft-) high Olympic Tower *(right)*. From here there are fabulous views: when the famous Föhn winds are blowing, you can even see the Alps. The restaurant serves bistro food at lunch and gourmet fare in the evening.

### 2 BMW Welt

This futuristic building, with its striking Double Cone entrance, embodies the qualities of dynamism and elegance. It celebrates the BMW brand and hosts exhibitions on related topics.

### 3 Olympic Stadium

Seating almost 67,000 spectators, this stadium *(right)* was home to the FC Bayern football club for years. The club has now moved and the stadium is used for a variety of other events.

### 4 Olympic Hall

Conceived from the outset as a multipurpose venue, the Olympic Hall holds up to 14,000 spectators. Covering the hall is a large section of the spectacular tent-shaped tensile roof, suspended from 58 pylons. Used for a wide variety of sports events, the Olympic Hall also serves as a venue for concerts, conferences, and fairs.

➡️ *Many types of combination tickets are available for the Olympic Tower and various sports facilities.*

### Lake & Park

Piled-up war rubble served as the base for the small hills on the grounds. After they were landscaped, boulevards and an artificial lake were added, creating a perfect park for walking. Climb to the top of the Olympia-berg for a spectacular view of the park and city.

**Plan of Olympiapark**

### Theatron & Other Facilities

The many attractions in Olympiapark include tennis courts, an indoor cycling racetrack, a beach volleyball court, a basketball court, rowboats on the lake, and summer curling. The Theatron *(above)*, an amphitheatre with seating for 5,000, is used as a venue for free open-air concerts in summer.

### Olympic Skating Rink

The skating rink is a perfect place to practise skating or ice-dancing to music. Skates are available for hire.

### Sea Life

Visitors to this attraction come face to come with Mediterranean and tropical fish. The glass tunnel is a highlight.

### Olympic Aquatic Centre

One of the largest in Europe, this aquatic centre *(right)* offers diving pools, saunas, a steam grotto, sunbathing lawns, exercise rooms, and wellness programmes.

### Father Timofej's Chapel

This Russian Orthodox chapel *(above)*, built (without a permit) by Russians Timofej and Natasha in 1951 on the Olympic grounds, still stands today.

### 5 September 1972

A black day for Munich: Palestinian terrorists, members of the Black September group, infiltrated the Olympic Village at 4am, shot two members of the Israeli team, and took nine athletes hostage. Police efforts to free the hostages at Fürstenfeldbruck airport failed. Nine Israeli hostages, five Palestinians, and one policeman died. Despite these tragic events, the decision was made to carry on with the Games after a brief break.

*The Olympiapark is the largest fitness complex in the city. For more information, visit www.olympiapark-muenchen.de*

# Residenz

*Located in the heart of the city, this former residence of Bavarian kings and home of the Wittelsbach dynasty until 1918 was gradually transformed from a moated castle (1385) into an extensive complex with seven courtyards. Highlights include the largest secular Renaissance building (the Antiquarium), interiors from the 17th century and the Rococo period, and Leo von Klenze's Classicist Königsbau. The complex also houses special collections such as the silver and church vestments collection, and porcelain from the 18th and 19th centuries.*

*View into the Grottenhof of the Residenz*

The historic Café Tambosi in the Hofgarten offers light meals. The Pfälzer Residenzweinstube (Residenzstr. 1) offers heartier fare.

There are numerous guided tours in and around the Residenz.

- Residenzstr. 1
- U3/U6: Odeonsplatz
- Map L3–M3
- (089) 29 06 71
- Residenz: Open Apr–mid-Oct: 9am–6pm daily; mid-Oct–Mar: 10am–5pm daily (one section of the Residenz is open mornings, one afternoons)
- Closed 1 Jan; Shrove Tue; 24, 25 & 31 Dec
- Adm: €6 (reduced €5); Combined adm to the Residenz and Schatzkammer: €9 (reduced €8, under-18s free)
- Cuvilliés-Theater: Open Apr–mid-Jun & Oct: 2–6pm Mon–Sat, 9am–6pm Sun; mid-Jun–Sep: 9am–6pm daily; Nov–Mar: 2–5pm Mon–Sat, 10am–5pm Sun
- Adm: €3 (reduced €2)
- Not wheelchair accessible

## Top 10 Sights

1. Antiquarium
2. Cuvilliés Theater
3. Schatzkammer
4. Hofkapelle
5. Courtyards
6. Reiche Kapelle
7. Reiche Zimmer
8. Egyptian Art Museum
9. Coin Collection
10. Hofgarten

### Antiquarium
Commissioned by Albrecht V, this Renaissance jewel was built between 1568 and 1571. Allegoric frescoes, grotesques, and Bavarian landscape scenes embellish the 69-m- (225-ft-) long barrel vault. The Antiquarium was restored between 1995 and 2000 *(centre)*.

### Cuvilliés Theater
Built between 1751and 1755, this beautiful Rococo theatre by Cuvilliés the Elder is widely regarded as Europe's finest *(below)*.

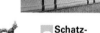

### Schatzkammer
The 16th-century Schatzkammer contains worked gold, porcelain, the Wittelsbach dynasty's crown jewels, and many other treasures *(left)*.

### Hofkapelle
This elaborately stuccoed chapel was built by Krumpper in 1601–14.

*The Coin Collection and the Egyptian Art Museum have separate opening hours and entrance fees.*

### Courtyards
You enter Kaiserhof through the northern Renaissance doorway; the southern doorway leads into the Mannerist Grottenhof. Brunnenhof has an octagonal shape. Apothekenhof is the largest courtyard, the Cuvilliés Theater court-yard the smallest.

**Plan of the Residenz**

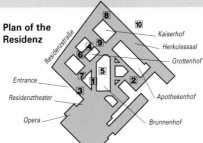

Residenzstraße

Entrance

Residenztheater

Opera

Kaiserhof

Herkulessaal

Grottenhof

Apothekenhof

Brunnenhof

### Reiche Kapelle
With its ebony altar and silver bas-reliefs, Maximilian I's private chapel (1607) is a prime example of Mannerist architecture *(below)*.

### Reiche Zimmer
Walk through the Rittersaal to reach this series of rooms done in the early Rococo style. The Reiche Zimmer, designed in 1730 by François Cuvilliés, and the Grüne Gallerie *(right)*, are but two of the stunning rooms.

### Egyptian Art Museum
This museum, opened in 1970 in a wing of the Residenz along-side the Hofgarten, houses a fine collection of pieces from ancient Egypt and the Coptic period *(above right)*.

### Coin Collection
Here the largest coin collection in the world can be found, along with exhibits of weights and measures.

### Hofgarten
Bordered by formal flowerbeds and hedges, and shaded by linden trees, this Renaissance garden on the north side of the Residenz has an Italian air. The Temple of Diana, a small pavilion lined with seashells designed by Heinrich Schön the Elder, marks the centre of a network of paths, which criss-crosses the garden. To the east lies the Bavarian State Chancellery, a much-debated modern structure incorporating the ruin of the former army museum.

### Destruction and Reconstruction
Bavaria's rulers built the Residenz over hundreds of years; in just a few hours during World War II, large sections of it were destroyed. Reconstruction began immediately after the war ended. Many of the art treasures stored elsewhere during the war were returned safely – sometimes by circuitous routes. Visitors can view some 130 rooms documenting princely culture from four centuries.

*The Herkulessaal in the Residenz, formerly a throne hall, is a popular concert venue because of its excellent acoustics.*

# Oktoberfest

*With more than six million visitors, over five million litres of beer, 200,000 pairs of pork sausages, and 100 spit-roasted oxen – Munich's Oktoberfest is the largest folk fair in the world. At the foot of the Bavaria statue, a huge field, the Theresienwiese (Wiesn for short), is transformed into a fairground with beer tents operated by traditional breweries, rides, and a variety of vendors selling gingerbread hearts, roast chicken, and fresh pretzels. For 16 days, visitors and locals, some in traditional costume, indulge in Bavarian revelry.*

Souvenir or love token – Wiesn hearts

For those who prefer alcohol-free beverages, the Wiesn features coffee kiosks.

Discounts are available on certain dates for some attractions.

- Theresienwiese
- U3/U6: Goetheplatz, U1: Theresienwiese
- Map D5
- 16 days mid-Sep–early Oct
- Hours: 10am–11:30pm Mon–Fri, 9am–11:30pm Sat, Sun & hols (some beer tents even longer). Last orders are at 10:30pm daily.
- free
- For large groups, reserve tables well in advance of the fair's start
- www.oktoberfest.de

## Top 10 Features

1. Grand Entry
2. *O'zapft is!*
3. Beer Tents
4. Oxen Roast
5. *Steckerlfisch*
6. Beim Schichtl
7. Flea Circus
8. Rides
9. Memorial
10. Statue of Bavaria

### Grand Entry
Since 1925, the Wiesn opening is signalled by the Saturday morning Grand Entry of the Oktoberfest landlords. Draught horses decked in festive harnesses pull flower-decorated brewery wagons *(below)* through the city. They are accompanied by brass bands and brewery owners, families, and workers in traditional costume.

### O'zapft is!
The Grand Entry is followed by the opening ceremony in the oldest Wiesn beer tent, Schottenhamel. At noon, Munich's mayor taps the first beer barrel and says "O'zapft is!" – the barrel is tapped.

### Beer Tents
Beer is king in the large tents, where patrons link arms and sway to the music of brass bands, and challenge each other to drink yet another *Maß* or litre *(above)*. The motto is: "Everyone has a right to his or her own beer heaven." For a less beery ambience, visit one of the smaller tents, such as Fischer Vroni

*In addition to beer, wine is available at tents such as the Weinwirt or Käfer's wine bar.*

### Oxen Roast
Entire oxen are roasted on a spit right before your eyes. A portion of roast oxen or a pork hock with crackling are just two of the traditional and hearty Bavarian treats served up at the Oktoberfest. Some 100 oxen are slaughtered for the Wiesn every year.

### Flea Circus
Another old-time tradition: the tiny trained creatures and their lord and master have entertained spectators for over half a century. The flea circus is an absolute must for all fans of yesteryear.

### Memorial
On 26 September 1980 at about 10:30pm, a bomb exploded near a Wiesn exit. Thirteen people were killed and more than 200 were injured. A stele *(left)* stands as a reminder of the attack carried out by a neo-Nazi.

### Statue of Bavaria
In 1843, Ludwig I commissioned Leo von Klenze to build the Ruhmeshalle (Hall of Fame) on the Theresienhöhe; today, it houses the busts of famous Bavarians. The colossal statue of Bavaria by Ludwig Schwanthaler (cast in ore by Ferdinand von Miller) rises in front of the hall. A platform inside the statue's head offers a spectacular view of the Wiesn *(below).*

### Steckerlfisch
The air is not only filled with the smell of beer but also with the tantalizing aroma of grilled fish – *Steckerlfisch* (fish on a stick) – prepared on a charcoal grill *(right).*

### Beim Schichtl
Welcome one and all to this cabaret – a Wiesn fixture since 1871. Today you can still watch acts such as the "beheading" of a living person on the guillotine *(below).*

### Rides
With traditional amusement rides such as the merry-go-round, clay-pigeon shooting, and the sedate Crinoline, or the latest thrilling attractions such as Euro-Star, Freefall, and several roller-coasters – there's something for everyone, from children to adrenaline addicts. The slowly rotating giant Ferris wheel offers a spectacular view of the scenery.

### The History of the Oktoberfest

The marriage of Crown Prince Ludwig and Therese von Sachsen-Hildburghausen on 12 October 1810 was celebrated with a five-day festival on Theresienwiese, named in honour of the bride. A horse race capping the festivities was slated to be repeated the following October. It became an annual event, quickly growing into a major fair with rides and beer stalls. The first "beer palaces" appeared in 1896. Today, the fair attracts millions of tourists and is famous worldwide.

# ⭐ Beer Gardens

*In summer, Bavaria's "liquid food" is served in beer gardens. And summer unofficially begins during Lent in March, when the breweries market their bock beers such as Salvator, Maximator, or Triumphator. No matter what you drink – ale, light beer, or Weißbier (wheat beer) from Augustiner, Löwenbräu, or Paulaner – if you haven't sat on a wooden bench beneath the chestnut trees on a mild summer's night and sipped a Maß (a litre) of beer while enjoying the aroma of pork sausage or grilled fish, you simply don't know Munich.*

Bavarian waitresses carry heavy loads

🚫 All beer gardens also serve non-alcoholic beverages.

🍺 Beer gardens are divided into full-service and self-service areas. In the latter, people are allowed to bring their own picnics.

• Daily in season, usually mid-May–late Sep, from 10 or 11am to 11pm, sometimes later. Last orders usually 10:30pm
• It is best to use public transit when you visit a beer garden

## Top 10 Beer Gardens

1. Augustiner-Keller
2. Löwenbräukeller
3. Flaucher
4. Hirschgarten
5. Chinesischer Turm
6. Seehaus
7. Sankt-Emmerams-Mühle
8. Paulaner
9. Muffathalle Beer Garden
10. Hofbräukeller

### Augustiner-Keller
This vast beer garden shaded by ancient chestnut trees, near a former place of execution, has existed since the 19th century. Two hundred decorated tables for regular patrons add a whimsical note *(above)*. On beautiful summer evenings, this beer garden is packed. Don't miss the special Augustiner brew from wooden barrels. 🔊 *Arnulfstr. 52*
• 5,000 seats (2,000 full-service) • playground

### Löwenbräukeller
A quintessential Munich beer garden. The historic building – near Löwenbräu brewery – hosts annual carnival balls and the tapping of the first Triumphator barrel. 🔊 *Stiglmaierplatz • 1,300 seats*

### Flaucher
Located on the banks of the Isar beneath a mature stand of trees, this lovely beer garden has a park-like feel. Popular in the daytime with cyclists, sunbathers, volleyball players, and families with children, it is romantic in the evenings by candlelight. 🔊 *Isarauen 8 • 2,000 seats • large playground*

### Hirschgarten
Munich's largest beer garden – which features deer in an enclosure after which the beer garden is named – lies near Nymphenburg Palace. The golden Augustiner brews flow from a huge "stag" barrel. 🔊 *Hirschgarten 1 • 8,000 seats • large playground*

There are more than 100 beer gardens in Munich and surroundings: together, they can hold over 100,000 people.

### 5 Chinesischer Turm

In the Chinese Pagoda, an Englischer Garten landmark *(right)*, brass bands play on the second floor on weekends. It is frequented mainly by students, tourists, and local characters.
⊗ *Englischer Garten • 7,000 seats • playground and antique carousel nearby*

### 9 Muffathalle Beer Garden

On a prime site beside the Isar, Munich's newest beer garden sports umbrellas instead of traditional chestnut trees. The Muffathalle menu is well-suited to the beer garden – both are varied and full of surprises.
⊗ *Zellstr. 4 • 300 seats*

### 10 Hofbräukeller

Across the Isar in Haidhausen, the Hofbräukeller, once also the site of the brewery and its beer cellar, has attracted patrons since 1892. The canopy of chestnuts *(below)* is so dense that patrons remain dry and comfortable even on rainy days. ⊗ *Innere Wiener Str. 19 • 1,700 seats (400 full-service) • playground*

### 6 Seehaus

A place to see and be seen, this popular beer garden lies in the centre of the Englischer Garten on a small lake. The terrace overlooking the lake is more stylish, but the beer garden has a cosy atmosphere *(above)*.
⊗ *Englischer Garten • 2,000 seats (400 on the terrace) • playground, boat rentals at the lake*

### 7 Sankt-Emmerams-Mühle

A beer garden that is both trendy and pastoral.
⊗ *St. Emmeram 41 • 700 seats, plus 450 seats with self-service • playground*

### 8 Paulaner

The brewery's beer garden on the Nockerberg is rather small, but famous for its beer. In March, the brewery hosts a highly original annual event, the Salvator-tapping. There is much laugher as prominent politicians meet, submit to an evening of ribbing, and savour the new bock beer *(left)*. ⊗ *Hochstr. 77 • 4,000 seats • historic garden pavilion in the beer garden • playground*

### Purity Law for Bavarian Beer

Munich is home to many brewery dynasties. Locals often choose their favourite pubs and beer gardens based on the brews they serve rather than location or food. Personal preferences aside, the Purity Law, which dates back to 1516, is strictly applied to all local beers. According to this law, beer is pure only when it is brewed exclusively from malt (which is germinated grain, usually wheat, barley or spelt), hops, yeast, and water. No additives are allowed.

# 🔟 Around Marienplatz

*Henry the Lion transformed Marienplatz into the centre of Munich – and it remains the heart of the city today. This is where the Neues Rathaus (New Town Hall) stands, major public transit lines meet, and locals and visitors alike stroll past street entertainers, or sit at the restaurant and café patios lining the square. A pedestrian zone begins at the western end of the square; the elegant Weinstraße and Theatinerstraße lead off from the north; toward the east are the Isartor and Maximilianstraße, and to the south the Viktualienmarkt.*

Façade of the Neues Rathaus

🍴 There are numerous cafés and restaurants on and around Marienplatz.

🔭 For excellent views visit the Neues Rathaus tower, the Peterskirche tower, or the south tower of the Frauenkirche.

• U3/U6: Marienplatz, all S-Bahns • Map L4
• Neues Rathaus, Marienplatz 8; Tower: Open 9am–7pm Mon–Fri, 10am–7pm Sat, Sun & hols (Nov–Apr: 10am–5pm Mon–Fri, 10am–7pm Sat, Sun & hols)
• www.muenchen.de
• Frauenkirche, Frauenplatz 1; Tower (South tower, West Entrance), there are a few stairs to the elevator: Open Apr–Oct: 10am–5pm Mon–Sat; Adm
• Peterskirche, Rindermarkt 1; Tower: Open 9am–6pm daily (from 10am Sun & hols; In summer to 7pm depending on the weather); Adm
• Visitors cannot view churches during services

## Top 10 Sights

1. Marienplatz
2. Neues Rathaus
3. Altes Rathaus
4. Pedestrian Zone
5. Peterskirche
6. Frauenkirche
7. Asamkirche
8. Viktualienmarkt
9. Feldherrnhalle
10. Theatinerkirche

### Marienplatz

Dominated by the Neues Rathaus, the square *(centre)* features a golden statue of the Virgin Mary from 1638, and the 19th-century Fischbrunnen (Fish Fountain). On Ash Wednesday, the mayor and town councillors wash their wallets there so that the city's coffers will always be full.

### Neues Rathaus

Built between 1867 and 1908, the Neo-Gothic Neues Rathaus (New Town Hall) is topped by the Münchner Kindl (Munich Child), the city's symbol. At 11am, noon, and, from May to October, also at 5pm, people gather on Marienplatz to enjoy the town hall's famous Glockenspiel – a chiming clock with dancing figures.

### Altes Rathaus

Now home to a toy museum, the Gothic Altes Rathaus (Old Town Hall) of 1474 has been rebuilt often, but the hall on the ground floor and the tower, once a city gate, are original.

### Pedestrian Zone

Munich's most popular traffic-free shopping zone begins at the western end of the square and stretches to Karlsplatz. Be sure to see the late Renaissance Michaelskirche.

### Peterskirche

At the highest point of the Old Town stands the 13th-century St Peter's, Munich's oldest parish church. Its tower, affectionately called Old Peter *(left)*, commands a fine view.

### 6 Frauenkirche
Topped by onion domes, the Frauenkirche is Munich's best-known symbol. Built in record time (1468–88), the church is the largest Gothic basilica in southern Germany. Highlights include choir figures by Erasmus Grasser and the tomb of Ludwig IV of Bavaria.

**Plan of Marien- platz**

### 10 Theatinerkirche
Munich's "Italian mile" begins with the Theatinerkirche (1663–1768) – an exuberant blend of large Baroque domes, flowing volutes, a gigantic cupola, and Rococo façades *(above)*.

### 7 Asamkirche
Bequeathed to the city by the Asam brothers, this church (1733–46) is a jewel of the late Baroque – a soaring natural stone façade on the outside and an exquisitely ornamented grotto on the inside. Egid Quirin Asam paid for the church *(below)*, which was built near his home.

### 8 Viktualienmarkt
Since 1807, this colourful food market has thrived here. A stroll past the 140 market stalls is a treat not to be missed *(above)*.

### 9 Feldherrnhalle
Modelled on Loggia dei Lanzi in Florence, Friedrich von Gärtner built the Feldherrnhalle in 1844 as a monument to Bavaria's military heroes. It marks the boundary between Old Town and Schwabing.

### Münchner Kindl

Perched atop the Town Hall tower, grasping the gospel in its left hand and its right hand raised in a gesture of benediction, the Münchner Kindl in its monk's habit is a reminder of the city's monkish origins. Dressed in black and yellow, the colours of the city, it accompanies all official processions – including the Oktoberfest – on horseback. It is also found on postcards, beer bottles, and even sewer covers. The "child's" gender remains a mystery. The live stand-in is always a woman.

*The Schrannenhalle was once located on the southern end of the Viktualienmarkt. It was saved and has been reconstructed.*

# 🔟 Neuschwanstein and Ludwig II

*An idealized vision of a knight's castle on the outside and a homage to Wagner's operas on the inside, Neuschwanstein was Ludwig II's most ambitious project. During the same period, he commissioned Linderhof and Herrenchiemsee, two castles in the French style. More than 50 million visitors have admired these fairy-tale castles since they were built by the shy and world-weary king. At Neuschwanstein, in particular, there seems to be no low season. A daytrip from Munich toward Füssen in the Schwangau is an unforgettable experience.*

Hohenschwangau in the hills below Neuschwanstein

🍴 Refreshments are available in the cafeteria located on the castle grounds; and there are several restaurants nearby.

🎫 Guided tours are mandatory; tickets show the tour number and precise time of entry.

- Schwangau bei Füssen
- Map Q4
- Tourist Office Schwangau (0 83 62) 81 980
- Neuschwanstein Castle • (0 83 62) 93 98 80 • www. neuschwanstein.de
- Tickets at Ticketcenter Hohenschwangau (0 83 62) 93 08 30
- Open Apr–Sep: 9am–6pm daily (ticket office hours 8am–5pm), Oct–Mar: 10am–4pm daily (ticket office hours 9am–3pm)
- Closed 1 Jan; Shrove Tue; 24, 25 & 31 Dec
- Adm: €9 (reduced €8); combined admission with Hohenschwangau €17 (reduced €15)
- Call ahead to book a special tour held Wed for those in wheelchairs

## Top 10 Features

1. The Building
2. Throne Hall
3. Bedroom
4. Chapel
5. Study
6. Minstrel's Room
7. Grotto
8. Dining Room
9. Winter Garden
10. Hohenschwangau

### The Building
The foundation stone was laid in 1869, the gatehouse was completed in 1873, and the castle in 1884 *(centre)*. Work continued, with the king constantly altering the plans, until his death in 1886. The keep and Ritterbad (knight's bath) were never completed.

### Throne Hall
Gold, saints, and a touch of Byzantium: the throne hall is modelled in part after Munich's All Saints Church and the Hagia Sophia in Istanbul. Originally, the throne was to stand – like an altar – in the apse *(below)*.

### Bedroom
In contrast to the romanticism of the living quarters, the bedroom was designed in a Gothic style complete with elaborately carved oak panelling. Scenes from Wagner's *Tristan and Isolde* decorate the walls.

### Chapel
Altar and murals depict Ludwig IX, the beatified king of France and namesake of the fairy-tale king of Bavaria.

### Study
Ludwig's study is filled with pictures from Wagner's opera *Tannhäuser*. On his desk is a fanciful pen-and-ink set in the shape of *Lohengrin*.

*Two alternatives to reaching the castle on foot are a bus service, or, for a romantic experience, a horse-drawn carriage.*

### Grotto

**7** Going between the living room and study, visitors pass through a grotto, where a small waterfall flowed during the king's lifetime *(left)*. The larger Venus grotto, complete with an artificial lake, is located in the park of Linderhof Castle *(see p30)*.

### Winter Garden

**9** Adjoining the grotto, the winter garden affords a spectacular view of Allgäu *(above)* through a large window.

### Hohenschwangau

**10** Ludwig spent part of his childhood and youth in this summer palace, which is located in wildly romantic scenery. His father, Maximilian II, restored the palace fully in 1832. Hohenschwangau's coat of arms bears a swan – later often depicted as Lohengrin's swan, which is a constantly recurring motif throughout Neuschwanstein.

### Minstrel's Room

**6** Influenced by the ceremonial hall of the Wartburg in Eisenach, this is the castle's largest room. The walls are decorated with scenes from the legend of Parzival and his quest for the Holy Grail *(below)*.

### Dining Room

**8** Dishes were transported in an elevator from the kitchen three stories below to the dining room, where the shy king took most of his meals on his own. Murals depict the tradition of the minstrel's song.

### New Technology in an Old Castle

Despite the medieval ambience, Neuschwanstein is full of high-tech features from its era. The dining room was equipped with a serving hatch and elevator that went up three floors. The kitchen had warm running water and automatic roasting spits. Forced-air central heating kept the rooms warm. Toilets were fitted with an automatic flush mechanism. An electric intercom was used to communicate with servants, and the second and third floors were linked by a telephone.

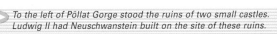

*To the left of Pöllat Gorge stood the ruins of two small castles. Ludwig II had Neuschwanstein built on the site of these ruins.*

Left **Grotto at Linderhof** Centre **Linderhof Castle Park** Right **Moorish Hall, Schachen Alm**

# Linderhof & Herrenchiemsee

### 1 Linderhof Castle

Linderhof's history began as a hunting lodge of Maximilian II that Ludwig II had dismantled and reassembled in the park in 1872. Originally planned as a second Versailles, the castle turned out to be far more modest in scale, albeit designed in a delightful and whimsical neo-Rococo style.

### 2 Castle Park

Set in a landscape garden, the park is a French-style formal garden created from 1870 onwards using designs by Carl von Effner. Its parterres are reminiscent of the Baroque style, its terraces of the Renaissance.

### 3 Fountain of Neptune With Cascades

On the north side of the castle, cascades flow across 30 steps

**Herrenchiemsee Castle**

bounded by the Fountain of Neptune at the bottom and the music pavilion at the top. Arcades flank the two sides of the waterfall.

### 4 Grotto of Venus

Designed to emulate the Hörselberg in Wagner's opera, *Tannhäuser*, this artificial grotto, complete with stalactites, features a lake on which the king was rowed about in a gilded barge.

### 5 Moorish Kiosk

Created for the Paris World's Fair in 1867, Ludwig II acquired the pavilion for Linderhof in 1876.

### 6 Chapel

This is the oldest structure of the castle complex, built in 1668 as the chapel of St Anna.

### 7 Herrenchiemsee Castle

On the island of Herrenchiemsee in Lake Chiemsee, Ludwig II finally began to build his "New Versailles" in 1878. Seven years later, he ran out of funds after completing 20 magnificent rooms, which are open to visitors today.

### 8 King Ludwig II Museum

The museum is housed in the south wing of the New Castle and documents the life of "Kini", a Bavarian nickname for the king, in a series of 12 rooms.

### 9 Hall of Mirrors

With its 90-m (290-ft) length, the Hall of Mirrors surpasses its

*For further information on Linderhof Castle, visit* **www.linderhof.de**

predecessor at Versailles. The lavish ceiling frescoes depict Louis XIV, the French "Sun King."

### Castle Gardens
Another homage to Versailles are the gardens on the west side of the castle, where water features enchant visitors from May to October. With a picturesque view of the castle and Lake Chiemsee, this is a wonderful place for a stroll. Horse-drawn carriages run from the ferry dock to the castle.

**The Hall of Mirrors at Herrenchiemsee**

### Top 10 Events in the Life of Ludwig II

1. 25 August 1845: Birth
2. 1864: Ascends throne
3. 1864: First encounters Richard Wagner
4. 1866: Defeated by the Prussians
5. 1867: Engaged to and unengaged from Sophie
6. 1869: Start of construction at Neuschwanstein
7. 1870–71: Franco-Prussian War
8. 1873: Purchases Herrenchiemsee Island
9. 9 June 1886: Declared unfit to rule
10. 13 June 1886: Drowns in Lake Starnberg

# Ludwig II and His Castles

"Kini's" building mania began in 1867. At first, he concentrated his efforts in Munich, where he redesigned his private palace apartments. But he was already planning his fairy-tale castles. In 1868, he developed the plans for Linderhof – the only castle to to be completed. After work started at Neuschwanstein in 1869, Ludwig focused entirely on the Hohenschwangau region. Construction on Herrenchiemsee Castle began in 1878; Ludwig spent a mere nine days there. Projects were planned for Munich, too, including a festival hall for Wagner operas (of which a smaller version was built in Bayreuth in 1876). By 1886, Ludwig was in debt by 14 million marks. With bankruptcy looming, the King was removed from power, and died shortly thereafter.

**Ludwig II by F. von Piloty**

**Fountain with gilded statues, Linderhof Park**

For further information on Herrenchiemsee Castle, visit www.herren-chiemsee.de

# 🔟 Starnberger See

*Of all the lakes in Munich's lake region, Starnberger See is the most popular, being practically on the city's doorstep. It is also the largest body of water in the region – 21 km (13 miles) long, 5 km (3 miles) wide, and up to 125 m (415 ft) deep – and offers attractive spots for bathing, sailing, and surfing. Members of the nobility built their summer residences here; Empress Elisabeth (Sisi) spent her summers at Possenhofen, while her cousin Ludwig II resided at Berg. The best way to experience the lake is to take a steamboat trip.*

Bavarian Steamboat Company tour boat on the lake

🍴 Zum Häring (Midgardhaus) in Tutzing lies directly on the lake and offers scrumptious homemade strudel. (Midgardstr. 3–5, 081 58 12 16)

🚤 The "Weißblaue Flotte" offers various themed boat tours.

---

- S6: Starnberg, Possenhofen, Feldafing, Tutzing
- Map S3
- www.starnberg.de
- Buchheim Museum: Bernried, Am Hirschgarten 1, (081 58) 99 700, www.buchheimmuseum.de
- Open Apr–Oct: 10am–6pm Tue–Sun; Nov–Mar: 10am–5pm Tue–Sun;
- Adm: €8.50 (reduced €3.50); children under 5 free
- Bayerische Seenschiffahrt (Bavarian Steamboat Company): docks in Starnberg, Bernried (Museumslinie), Berg, Tutzing; historical, adventure, and gourmet tours are offered
- (08 151) 80 61
- www.bayerische-seenschifffahrt.de

## Top 10 Sights

1. Starnberg
2. Possenhofen
3. "Weißblaue Dampferflotte"
4. Roseninsel
5. Schloss Tutzing
6. Buchheim Museum
7. Seeshaupt
8. Schloss Ammerland
9. Schloss Berg
10. Commemorative Cross for Ludwig II

### 1 Starnberg

In the 19th century, this former fishing village developed into a popular summer resort *(centre)*. Over the past decades, Munich's elite has settled here, building on land that can make access to the lake difficult. A walk on the promenade is still a very pleasant experience and there is a good golf course not too far from the town.

### 2 Possenhofen

Possenhofen boasts a beautiful beach and many old villas. The castle Possenhofen, with its four battlement towers built in 1536 and reconstructed in the 17th century, was a refuge for Sisi – Empress Elisabeth.

### 3 "Weißblaue Dampferflotte"

The fleet of the Bavarian Steamboat Company offers theme tours and excursions, as well as providing public transportation.

### 4 Roseninsel

A romantic destination for daytrips, this small island off the town of Feldafing was settled as far back as prehistoric times. In 1853 Peter J Lenné and Franz J Kreuter built a casino with a park and a formal rose garden on the island *(below)*.

You can circumnavigate Starnberger See by car, bicycle, or on foot. The distance is 55 km (34 miles).

### Schloss Tutzing

This horseshoe-shaped palace surrounded by a landscaped park is home to the Protestant Academy *(right)*. From Tutzing station, it is just a short walk to the Ilkahöhe *(see p70)* and a restaurant of the same name. On clear days, the view of the Alps is magnificent.

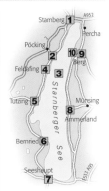

**Starnberger See**

### Buchheim Museum

Nestled in a park north of Bernried, Buchheim Museum houses an impressive collection of Expressionist art as well as folklore and ethnological exhibits, more than 3,000 paperweights, African masks, and much more.

### Seeshaupt

Attractively located at the southern tip of Lake Starnberg, with a harbour full of yachts and a lovely lakeside promenade, Seeshaupt has managed to preserve its rural character. From here, it is just a short trip to the Osterseen nature reserve.

### Schloss Ammerland

King Ludwig I bequeathed this castle *(below)* to the musician, author, and illustrator Franz von Pocci. Built between 1683 and 1685, it is beautifully located on the eastern shore of the lake,

### Schloss Berg

Berg is the birthplace of author Oskar Maria Graf. The palace served as the summer residence of the Wittelsbach dynasty and of Ludwig II, the fairy-tale king who died in the nearby lake.

### Commemorative Cross for Ludwig II

A cross on the shore of the lake marks the spot where Ludwig II was found dead in the water. Fans of the "Kini" meet here every year on the anniversary of his death.

### The Mysterious Death of Ludwig II

Was it a murderous plot, suicide, or a heart attack in the frigid waters? On the evening of 13 June 1886, Ludwig II set out for a walk with Dr von Gudden, his personal physician. Later, both were found floating dead in the lake – von Gudden bore scratch marks on his face. Conspiracy theories have abounded ever since, a posthumous confirmation of Ludwig's remark: "I wish to remain an everlasting mystery to myself and to others."

*In good weather, hot-air balloon rides depart from Starnberg-Landstetten; for information call (0 81 57) 91 04.*

Left **Otto I** Centre **Ludwig the Bavarian** Right **Hitler signing the Munich Agreement**

# TOP 10 **Historic Events**

### 1 1158: Foundation of the City
Welf Henry the Lion, Duke of Bavaria, tore down the old salt bridge in 1157–8 and erected a new crossing over the Isar River, a short distance to the south. There, the small town of Munichen developed into the royal residence city of Munich. The day on which the Hohenstaufen Emperor Friedrich Barbarossa awarded the town the right to hold a market and mint coins, 14 June 1158, is still celebrated as Munich's birthday.

### 2 1240–1918: The Wittelsbach Dynasty
From 1240 onward, the Wittelsbach dynasty was instrumental in defining the evolution of the city. They graduated from simple dukes to electors and finally to kings. Ludwig I commissioned the erection of Classical public buildings in Munich; Ludwig II built larger-than-life fairy-tale castles; the last member of the Wittelsbach dynasty, Ludwig III, had to flee Bavaria after World War I.

### 3 1328: Ludwig the Bavarian – German Emperor
In 1314, Duke Ludwig IV (the Bavarian) was elected king of Germany; in 1328, he was crowned emperor of the Holy Roman Empire.

### 4 1442: Expulsion of the Jews from Munich
Following pogroms against the Jews in the 13th and 14th centuries, Duke Albrecht III gave the order to expel all Jews from Upper Bavaria in 1442. Jewish culture did not return to Munich until the 18th century.

### 5 1806: Capital of the Kingdom of Bavaria
In the wake of the Napoleonic redrafting of Europe, the Electorate of Bavaria was elevated to a kingdom, with Munich as the capital and royal residence of the much-enlarged new state. The boundaries of Bavaria at that time were already roughly the same as they are today.

### 6 1848: March Revolution – Abdication of Ludwig I
In March of 1849, revolutionary uprisings reached Munich, culminating in the storming of the Zeughaus (the treasury, currently the Stadtmuseum). Having lost the confidence of the court and the bourgeoisie, (in part because

The Wittelsbach dynasty's family tree

*The crown jewels of the Holy Roman Empire were kept in Munich between 1328 and 1350.*

of an affair with the notorious dancer Lola Montez), Ludwig I was forced to abdicate.

### 7 1918–19: November Revolution and Räterepublik

On the night of 8 November 1918, the socialist Kurt Eisner proclaimed the "Free State of Bavaria" in the Mathäserbräu (today a cinema with a commemorative Eisner column). Eisner became president for a brief period. Following his assassination on 21 February 1919 by a monarchist extremist, *Räterepubliken* (Soviet republics) emerged in Munich and other Bavarian cities. These were quickly suppressed by government troops.

### 8 1935–45: "Capital of the Movement"

Hitler's party, the NSDAP, grew out of a small cell that began in Munich. As early as 1923, Hitler attempted his first coup *(Hitlerputsch)* against the Weimar Republic. As a sign of thanks, Munich was given the title "Capital of the Movement" in 1935, after the Nazis seized power.

### 9 1962: Schwabinger Riots

In the summer of 1962, harmless buskers were a catalyst for violent clashes between youths and the Munich police forces that lasted for several days. These events inspired the the city and the police to rethink their hardline policy on police intervention.

### 10 1972: Olympic Games

Munich and environs hosted the 20th Olympic Games in 1972. A terror attack on 5 September against the Olympic team from Israel, resulting in the deaths of nine athletes, overshadowed the Games *(see p19)*.

## Top 10 Famous Citizens

### 1 Asam Brothers
Cosmas Damien (1687–1739) and Egid Quirin (1692–1750) Asam were the chief proponents of Bavarian Rococo.

### 2 Maximilian Joseph von Montgelas
Montgelas (1759–1838) is the acknowledged creator of the modern Bavarian state.

### 3 Ludwig I
Numerous magnificent buildings were built by King Ludwig I (1786–1868). In 1826, he transferred the university from Landshut to Munich.

### 4 Lola Montez
As the mistress of Ludwig I, Lola Montez (1818–61) is said to have had great influence on the sovereign.

### 5 Ludwig II
"Kini" Ludwig II (1845–1886), has gone down in history as the "fairy-tale king."

### 6 Franz von Lenbach
The "Painter Prince" (1836–1904) greatly influenced Munich's art scene.

### 7 Franz von Stuck
Stuck (1863–1928) was co-founder of the Munich Secession. His Art Nouveau villa is now a museum.

### 8 Thomas Mann
In 1933, the Nobel Laureate of Literature (1875–1955) left his hometown, never to return.

### 9 Karl Valentin
Satirist, actor, comedian, and a well-known character in the city, Valentin (1882–1948) performed for many years with his sidekick Liesl Karlstadt.

### 10 Scholl Siblings
Hans (1918–43) and Sophie (1921–43) were active in the "White Rose" resistance group. They were denounced in 1943 and executed.

*Stattreisen München (089 544 042 30) offers historic city tours. Visit www.stattreisen-muenchen.de*

35

Left & Centre **Lenbachhaus, interior and exterior** Right **Farmhouse room, Nationalmuseum**

# 🔟 Museums & Galleries

### 1 Museum District– Pinakotheken

Together, the Alte and Neue Pinakothek and the Pinakothek der Moderne house the city's major painting collections *(see pp14–17)*.

### 2 Deutsches Museum

The largest museum of science and technology in the world *(see pp8–11)*.

### 3 Bayerisches Nationalmuseum

One of the largest museums in Europe for art, crafts, and folklore. In its wide-ranging collection are Gothic sculptures, precious wall hangings, watches, and Christmas cribs. ◊ *Prinzregentenstr. 3 • Map N3 • Open 10am–5pm Tue–Sun (to 8pm Thu) • Adm • wheelchair accessible • www. bayerisches-nationalmuseum.de*

### 4 Münchner Stadtmuseum

Documenting the history and culture of the city, there are sections on puppetry, musical instruments, photography, and film *(see p54)*. ◊ *St-Jakobs-Platz 1 • Map L5 • Open 10am–6pm Tue–Sun • closed Shrove Tue & some hols • Adm (Sun & hols free) • wheelchair accessible*

### 5 Glyptothek and Staatliche Antikensammlungen

This exquisite collection of Greek and Roman sculptures and bas-reliefs includes 2,500-year-old Archaic figures, whose original colouring has been recently restored. Antique jewellery, bronzes, and Greek ceramics are on display in the Antikensammlungen. ◊ *Königsplatz 1 & 3 • Map K2 & J3 • Glyptothek: Open 10am–5pm Tue–Sun (to 8pm Thu) • closed Shrove Tue & some hols • Adm (€1 on Sun) • wheelchair accessible • Antikensammlung: Open 10am–5pm Tue–Sun (to 8pm Wed) • Adm (€1 on Sun)*

**Morris Dancer, Stadtmuseum**

### 6 Städtische Galerie im Lenbachhaus

Lenbachhaus – the villa of painter Prince Franz von Lenbach – enjoys worldwide renown thanks to its collection of works from the Blue Rider group. The north wing houses the art collection, while the preserved living quarters offer insight into the domestic culture of the Gründerzeit (Foundation Period). In 1994, an underground exhibition space was added. ◊ *Luisenstr. 33 • Map J2 • Open 10am–6pm Tue–Sun • Adm • www.lenbachhaus.de*

**The Neo-Classical façade of the Glyptothek on Königsplatz**

*The No. 100 bus route includes stops at the Villa Stuck, National-museum, Schack-Galerie, and Haus der Kunst.*

*Vase with Sunflowers* (1888) by Vincent van Gogh, Neue Pinakothek

### Jüdisches Museum
Aiming to provide a forum for open discussion, this museum also reflects the breadth of Jewish history, art and culture. ✆ St-Jakobs-Platz 16 • Map L5 • Open 10am–6pm Tue–Sun • Adm

### Museum Villa Stuck
Preserved in its original Art Nouveau style, the villa of Secessionist Franz von Stuck (1863–1928) houses a permanent Art Nouveau exhibition. ✆ Prinzregentenstr. 60 • Map P4 • Open 11am–6pm Tue–Sun • Adm • www.villastuck.de

### Haus der Kunst
Today, Adolf Hitler's pompous monumental building (1932–7) is a venue for international art exhibitions. ✆ Prinzregentenstr. 1 • Map M3 – N3 • Open 10am–8pm daily (to 10pm Thu) • Adm • www.hausderkunst.de

### Staatliches Museum für Völkerkunde
Ethnological exhibits from around the world – from North America's oldest kayak to a Shiva temple. ✆ Maximilianstr. 42 • Map M4 • Open 9:30am–5:30pm Tue–Sun • closed some hols • Adm (€1 on Sun) • www. voelkerkundemuseum-muenchen.de

## Other Museums & Galleries

### Archäologische Staatssammlung
Prehistoric, Roman, and medieval exhibits.
✆ Lerchenfeldstr. 2 • Map N3

### Staatliches Museum Ägyptischer Kunst
Art from Egypt, land of the pyramids (see p21). ✆ Residenz, Hofgartenstr. 1 • Map L3

### Deutsches Theatermuseum
History of German theatre. Large specialist library.
✆ Galeriestr. 4a & 6 • Map M3

### Paläontologisches Museum
*Archaeopteryx bavarica*, a prehistoric bird, is a highlight at this dinosaur museum. ✆ Richard-Wagner-Str. 10 • Map J2

### Valentin-Musäum
Curios relating to Karl Valentin; excellent café. ✆ Isartor tower, Im Tal 50 • Map M5

### Schack-Galerie
Featuring 19th-century German painting (Böcklin, Spitzweg, Schwind, and others), this is a museum for romantics. ✆ Prinzregentenstr. 9 • Map N3–P3

### Alpines Museum
A museum dedicated to mountains. ✆ Praterinsel 5 • Map N5

### Deutsches Jagd- und Fischereimuseum
Large dioramas of wild beasts are featured here.
✆ Neuhauser Str. 2 • Map K4

### Kunsthalle der Hypo-Kulturstiftung
Outstanding contemporary art exhibitions.
✆ Theatinerstr. 8 • Map L4

### lothringer 13
Multimedia art.
✆ Lothringer Str. 13 • Map G6

Left **Eisbach, Englischer Garten** Centre **Thai pagoda, Westpark** Right **Botanischer Garten**

# 🔟 Gardens & Parks

### 1 Schloss Nymphenburg
Enclosed by a wall, this 2-km- (1-mile-) wide park extends west from the palace 1.5 km (1 mile). Picturesque pavilions and follies are scattered throughout the park, which has been declared a nature reserve to protect the 300-year-old trees *(see pp12–13)*.

### 2 Englischer Garten
With 373 hectares (922 acres), the Englischer Garten is the largest urban park in Germany and the green lung of the city. It serves as a leisure paradise in summer, when thousands lounge in the sun on the expansive meadows, and cyclists, joggers, and roller-bladers zoom along the paths. The surface of the Kleinhesseloher See is dotted with boats, while surfers try their luck on the Eisbach near the Haus der Kunst. For a welcome refreshment, try a cool beer in one of the beer gardens *(see pp24–5)* at the Chinesischer Turm, the Seehaus, the Hirschau, and the Aumeister. An American, Benjamin Thompson, known as Count Rumford (1753–1814), conceived the idea of the park, which was designed by Ludwig von Sckell as a prime example of classical landscape park design. In 1837, the Monopteros, a mock Greek temple, was built on an artificial hill. ⊗ *Map G4–H1*

### 3 Botanischer Garten
This is one of the most important botanical gardens in the world. Created in the park at Nymphenburg in 1914, some 14,000 plant species from around the globe are cultivated here. In the greenhouses, visitors can embark on journeys to tropical rainforests or arid deserts.
⊗ *Map A2 • Open Apr & Sep: 9am–6pm; May–Aug: 9am–7pm; Feb, Mar & Oct: 9am–5pm; Nov–Jan: 9am–4:30pm • Adm*

### 4 Westpark
An expanse of 72 hectares (178 acres) has been landscaped with numerous artificial hills, paths, a lake, and ponds. Created for the International Garden Exhibition in 1983, the western section of the park features an impressive East Asian ensemble with Chinese and Japanese gardens, and Thai and Nepalese pagodas. Concerts, plays, and open-air film screenings are presented on the lakeside stage in summer. ⊗ *Map B6–C6*

**The Monopteros in the Englischer Garten**

➡ *In winter, the Kleinhesseloher See in the Englischer Garten is used for ice-skating and curling.*

### 5 Hofgarten

In the 17th century, the Hofgarten was laid out on the north side of the Residenz in the style of Renaissance gardens. It is bounded on two sides by long arcades. Rows of mature linden, chestnut, and maple trees provide welcome shade for *boule* players in summer. Tango aficionados meet at the Temple of Diana – a polygonal pavilion with a shallow dome – for dances on mild summer evenings *(see p20)*.

**Temple of Diana, Hofgarten**

### 6 Alter Botanischer Garten

During the 19th century, the former botanical garden was located in this small park. Today, it serves as the perfect oasis to relax in after a shopping spree in the nearby pedestrian zone and city centre. § *Map J3*

### 7 Bavariapark

This park lies directly behind the statue of Bavaria and the Ruhmeshalle, and stretches westward on the Theresienhöhe. It was designed by order of Ludwig I and received its current name after the Bavaria statue was completed in 1850. It is an ideal place to take a break from the hustle and bustle of the Oktoberfest. § *Map D5*

### 8 Luitpoldpark

Created on the occasion of Prince Regent Luitpold's 90th birthday, the park was expanded in 1950 by a hill built out of rubble, the Luitpoldhügel, which commands a fine view of the city. On clear days, you can see all the way to the Alps. § *Map F1*

### 9 Hofgarten Schleißheim

Stretching between the Neues Schloss in Schleißheim and Schloss Lustheim, this is one of the few gardens from the Baroque era that has retained most of its original form. Enrico Zuccalli (1642–1724) created the basic layout with canals in 1684. Domenique Girard added parterres and a cascade from 1715 onward, creating the tremendous illusion of depth that characterizes the principal axis. The cascade, located in front of the Neues Schloss, was renovated in 1999. § *Oberschleißheim, Neues Schloss*

### 10 River Meadows along the Isar (Isarauen) and Rose Garden

The long stretch of the Isarauen serves as the city's other green lung. South of the Wittelsbacher Bridge is the rose garden. In addition to many rose species, it features a large collection of exotic trees and shrubs, as well as a small teaching garden with poisonous plants. § *Map E6*
• *Open Summer: 7am–6:30pm daily; Winter: 7am–4:30pm Mon–Fri*

**Neptune Fountain, Alter Botanischer Garten**

Two cemeteries, the Alte Nördliche and the Alte Südliche Friedhof, also serve as green oases with mature trees.

Left **Emperor's tomb, Frauenkirche** Centre **St Maria in Ramersdorf** Right **Frauenkirche**

# Churches & Houses of Worship

### Frauenkirche
Munich's 15th-century cathedral dominates the city silhouette with its twin towers *(see p27)*.

### Asamkirche
Dedicated to St Johann-Nepomuk, this late Baroque church built by the Asam brothers features ceiling frescoes depicting the saint *(see p27)*.

### Peterskirche (Old Peter)
Although this is the oldest parish church in the city (13th century), the interior is a mix of Gothic (altar by Schrenk), Baroque (baptismal font), and Rococo (side altars). Climbing the 302 steps to the top of the Renaissance tower is worth the effort *(see p26)*.

**Putto, Asamkirche**

### Ludwigskirche
Friedrich von Gärtner built this church, which is flanked by two towers, in the style of Italian Romanesque (1829–43). The glo-

**The Romanesque-Byzantine Ludwigskirche**

rious fresco *Judgement Day* by Peter von Cornelius is the second-largest church fresco in the world. ◎ *Ludwigstr. 20 • Map M2 • 7:30am–8pm daily*

### Michaelskirche
An important structure in many ways, this is the largest late Renaissance church north of the Alps. Construction began in 1583. It features the second-largest barrel vault in the world, after St Peter's in Rome, and was built for the Jesuits. The crypt contains the sarcophagi of Elector Maximilian I and Ludwig II. Not to be missed is the bronze figure of St Michael battling the dragon (1585). ◎ *Neuhauser Str. 6 • Map K4 • Open 7am–9pm daily*

### Theatinerkirche
Construction of this church, which is also called St Cajetan, was begun in 1663 to mark the birth of the heir to Elector Ferdinand. It is the most Italianate of all Munich's churches *(see p27)*.

### Klosterkirche St Anna
The Lehel district is home to Munich's earliest Rococo church, built by Johann Michael Fischer from 1727 to 1733, with an interior designed by the Asam brothers. Construction of the nearby neo-Romanesque parish church of St Anna began in 1887. ◎ *St-Anna-Platz 21 or 5 • Map M4 & N4 • Open 6am–7pm or 8am–6pm daily*

*Visitors should view church interiors only when no services are taking place.*

**High altar, Asamkirche**

### Heiliggeistkirche

The beginning of the 13th century saw the creation of a hospital church at this site, followed in 1392 by a Gothic basilica. In 1724, the existing structure was remodelled in the Baroque style. The interior is characterized by a blend of Gothic and late Baroque. Stucco work is by the Asam brothers. ⊗ Im Tal 77 • Map L5 • Open 7am–noon & 3pm–6pm daily

### Damenstift St Anna

St Anna was originally a monastery of Sisters of the Salesian Order. Today, it is a school. he façade and interior of this late Baroque church were designed in the 18th century by the Asam brothers. Frescoes destroyed in World War II have been reconstructed in sepia. ⊗ Damenstiftstr. 1 • Map K4 • Open 8am–8pm daily

### Ohel Jakob Synagogue

Munich's new main synagogue was inaugurated in 2006, 68 years after Hitler ordered the destruction of its predecessor. An imposing stone structure, with a raised glass roof, it is part of the recently opened Jewish Centre on St-Jakobs-Platz (see p80). ⊗ St-Jakobs-Platz • Map K5

## Top 10 Other Houses of Worship

**Dreifaltigkeitskirche**
Late Baroque church (1711–16) with Asam ceiling fresco. ⊗ Pacellistr. 6 • Map K4

**Salvatorkirche**
Cemetery church adjoining the Frauenkirche (1494) in Bavarian brick Gothic. Greek-Orthodox. ⊗ Salvatorplatz 17 • Map L3

**St Paul's**
Basilica with twin-tower enclosure and domed tower in Rhineland Gothic (1892–1906). ⊗ St-Pauls-Platz 11 • Map E5

**St Bonifaz**
Benedictine church and abbey (1835–50) begun under Ludwig I, who is buried in the crypt. ⊗ Karlstr. 34 • Map K3

**St Elisabeth**
Rococo church (c. 1760). Interior by Ignaz Günther. ⊗ Mathildenstr. 10 • Map J5

**Allerheiligen am Kreuz**
Built in 1478 as a cemetery church, with many subsequent changes. Baroque sections. ⊗ Kreuzstr. 10 • Map K5

**St Lukas**
Historic Protestant church across from the Paternsel. Church concerts. ⊗ Mariannenplatz 3 • Map N5

**St Georg**
Rococo village church. Many artists are buried in the cemetery. ⊗ Bogenhauser Kirchplatz 1

**St Michael in Berg am Laim**
Former court church in Bavarian Rococo style. ⊗ Clemens-August-Str. 9a

**St Maria in Ramersdorf**
Late Gothic building with Baroque interior. Pilgrimage church. ⊗ Aribonenstr. 9

Left & Centre **Interior and exterior, Münchner Kammerspiele** Right **Cuvilliés-Theater**

# Opera, Concerts & Theatre

### 1 Bayerische Staatsoper

Built in 1811, the neo-Classical national theatre was reconstructed (1823–5) after a fire. It grew into one of the most important music stages, and premieres of Wagner operas were held here in the presence of Ludwig II. Closed for many years after the end of World War II, the theatre re-opened in 1963. Noted for its impressive repertoire, the theatre boasts an auditorium with five balconies resplendent in royal gold and purple. ⬡ Max-Joseph-Platz 2 • Map L4 • (089) 21 85 19 20 • www.staatsoper.de

### 2 Bayerisches Staatsschauspiel

In 1951, the Neues Residenztheater opened its doors next to the Opera House. Stark on the outside, the interior is lavish and monumental thanks to refurbishment in 1988–91. Artistic director Dieter Dorn presents a wide range of dramatic works. The Theater im Haus der Kunst

**Bayerische Staatsoper**

(see p34) is also part of the Bayerische Schauspielhaus. ⬡ Max-Joseph-Platz 1 • Map L4 • (089) 21 85 19 40 • www.bayerisches staatsschauspiel.de

### 3 Cuvilliés-Theater

Time seems to have stood still in this breathtakingly beautiful Rococo theatre. Furnishings and decor were packed away in crates for safe storage during World War II. After the original building was destroyed by bombing, the theatre was rebuilt, reopening in 1958. It is a stage for performances by the Bayerische Staatstheater (see p20).

### 4 Münchner Kammerspiele

Built by Richard Riemerschmid in 1901 and now restored, this theatre became the home of the Münchner Kammerspiele in 1926. Inside, Art Nouveau rules, with intertwining ornamentation and dozens of lighting fixtures in the shape of flower buds. During the 1920s, the Kammerspiele was considered the most important stage outside Berlin and caused quite a stir staging works by Bertolt Brecht and others. Even today, you are sure to be treated to innovative theatre. ⬡ Maximilianstr. 28 • Map M4 • (089) 23 39 66 00 • www.muenchner-kammerspiele.de

### 5 Staatstheater am Gärtnerplatz

Lovers of traditionally staged operas, operettas, and musicals will feel right at home in this

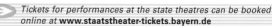

Tickets for performances at the state theatres can be booked online at **www.staatstheater-tickets.bayern.de**

intimate theatre. Built in 1865 as a bourgeois equivalent to the royal theatre houses, it has remained a popular venue to this day. ◈ *Gärtnerplatz 3 • Map L6 • (089) 21 85 19 60 • www. staatstheateramgaertnerplatz.de*

### Gasteig
An unwieldy brick structure on the outside, this theatre is a venue for more than 1,700 events per year – from concerts by the Munich Philharmonic to a film festival. Seating 2,500, the Philharmonie has excellent acoustics. This large hall is complemented by other smaller auditoriums. ◈ *Rosenheimer Str. 5 • Map N6 • (089) 48 09 80 • www.gasteig.de*

### Herkulessaal
Perfect for classical concerts, this vast hall in the Residenz, with over 1,200 seats, is popular with the Bayerischen Rundfunk Symphony Orchestra, the Münchner Symphoniker, and the Münchner Kammerorchester, which stage sell-out concerts here.
◈ *Residenzstr. 1 (Entrance Hofgarten) • Map L3 –M3 • (089) 29 06 71*

### Prinzregententheater
Built in 1901 as a Wagner festival theatre, the space, conceived as an amphitheatre, is

**Gasteig**

chiefly used as a performance venue for the Bayerische Theaterakademie August Everding.
◈ *Prinzregentenplatz 12 • Map H4 • (089) 21 85 28 99 • www.prinzregententheater.de*

### Münchner Volkstheater
What you experience here is by no means simple folk theatre but a sophisticated repertory of entertaining, popular plays. ◈ *Brienner Str. 50 • Map J2 • (089) 523 46 55 • www.muenchner-volkstheater.de*

### Deutsches Theater
This large theatre is the city's main venue for international stars and musicals. During Fasching (carnival), it is transformed into a glittering ballroom. ◈ *Schwanthalerstr. 13 • Map J4 • (089) 55 23 44 44 • www.deutsches-theater.de*

*Most theatres close at the start of the summer holidays (end of July). The new season usually begins at the end of September.*

Left **Pasinger Fabrik** Right **Blutenburgtheater**

# Small Theatres & Cabarets

### 1 Pasinger Fabrik
Theatre Much Noise About Nothing is the name of the largest stage of this alternative cultural centre, located next to the U-Bahn station in Pasing. The centre includes a space for children's and youth theatre, a venue for musical performances, and a cafeteria, which serves delicious food. ◈ *München-Pasing, August-Exter-Str. 1 • (089) 82 92 90 79 • www.pasinger-fabrik.com*

### 2 Komödie im Bayerischen Hof
Comedies, musicals, and revues, often with well-known stars, are the mainstays of this elegant and luxurious theatre in the famous Bayerischer Hof. ◈ *Promenadeplatz 6 • Map K4–L4 • (089) 29 16 05 30 • www.komoedie-muenchen.de*

### 3 Theater 44
This intimate space in Schwabing is home to Munich's oldest, privately operated theatre. Close proximity to the actors ensures patrons enjoy a special experience. ◈ *Hohenzollernstr. 20 • Map F2 • (089) 3 22 87 48 • www.theater44.de*

### 4 TamS-Theater
You'll find the TamS in a rear courtyard in the heart of Schwabing. Founded in 1970 by Philip Arp, it gained fame with his *Valentinaden* evenings, which continued

the tradition of the great comedian and his droll and scurrilous humour. TamS continues to stage unusual and paradoxical productions. ◈ *Haimhauserstr. 13a • Map G2 • (089) 34 58 90 • www.tamstheater.de*

### 5 TeamTheater
Teamtheater Tankstelle is the name of the larger stage, and Teamtheater Comedy is its smaller sister. Enjoy the spectacle on stage while savouring culinary delights. ◈ *Am Einlass 2a or 4 • Map L5 • (089) 260 43 33 &. 260 66 36 • www.teamtheater.de*

### 6 Schauburg
One of the most renowned stages for young people's theatre yet equally enjoyable for adults. Set up in a converted cinema, Schauburg is celebrated for its innovative work with new theatrical forms. ◈ *Elisabethplatz • Map F3 • (089) 23 33 71 55 • www.schauburg.net*

**Exterior of Schauburg**

*Tickets for many theatre and music performances are available from München Ticket. Visit www.muenchenticket.de*

**Theater 44**

### Blutenburgtheater

"Germany's first stage for mysteries" lives up to its name. Mysteries make up this theatre's highly entertaining and gripping programme. ◈ Blutenburgstr. 35 • Map D3 • (089) 1234300 • www.blutenburg-theater.de

### Metropol

Characterized by a 1950s aesthetic, this former cinema was converted into a theatre and has gained an excellent reputation for distinguished performances, frequently accompanied by music. ◈ München-Freimann, Floriansmühlstr. 5 • (089) 32 19 55 33 • www.metropoltheater.com

### Lach- und Schieß gesellschaft

This cabaret gained fame in the 1950s under the direction of Dieter Hildebrandt and became even more popular later when a TV series was made of it. The cast has changed but the programme has remained the same – political cabaret with a bite. ◈ Ursulastr. 9 (near Haimhauserstr.) • Map G2 • (089) 391997 • www.lachundschiess.de

### Theater im Fraunhofer

This down-to-earth pub offers not only hearty Bavarian treats but also a small stage for music, cabaret, and satire in the back. ◈ Fraunhoferstr. 9 • Map L4 • (089) 26 78 50 • www.fraunhofertheater.de

## Top 10 Stars of Music & Theatre

**1 Richard Strauss**
The composer (1864–1949) was born in Munich.

**2 Frank Wedekind**
In 1896, the playwright and author (1864–1918) founded a satirical journal, *Simplicissimus*, in Munich.

**3 Otto Falckenberg**
Falckenberg (1873–1947), artistic director of the Münchner Kammerspiele (1917–44).

**4 Karl Valentin**
Still a popular figure, the comedian who turned things upside down and inside out was a Munich native (1882–1948).

**5 Weiß Ferdl**
Ferdinand Weisheitinger (1883–1949) was artistic director of the Am Platzl cabaret for 20 years.

**6 Liesl Karlstadt**
Fondly remembered as Karl Valentin's congenial onstage sidekick (1892–1960).

**7 Carl Orff**
Famous for *Carmina Burana*, the Munich composer (1895–1982) taught at the Conservatory of Music.

**8 Bertolt Brecht**
Originally from Augsburg, the playwright's (1898–1956) career began at the Münchner Kammerspiele.

**9 August Everding**
Munich's music scene was dominated for decades by August Everding (1928–99), dramatist and artistic director of the Staatsoper.

**10 Rainer Werner Fassbinder**
He won international fame with his films *(see p55)* but his career began in the Bavarian capital, where he founded the "antitheater" in 1968.

Up-to-date performance programmes are posted on all advertising pillars and are also found in daily newspapers.

Left **Nationaltheater** Right **Munich Biennale logo**

# 🔟 Festivals & Open-Air Events

### 1 Munich Biennale

This music theatre festival was founded in 1988 by composer Hans Werner Henze. The city of Munich commissions young composers to write their first full work for the festival. Now a biannual event, the festival has become an established highlight in the cultural life of the city, with a broad programme. 🔊 *biannual, 2 weeks in May (even-numbered years) • www.muenchenerbiennale.de*

**Löwenbräu lion, Oktoberfest**

### 2 Blade Nights

As many as 300,000 in-line skaters take advantage of Blade Nights, held between May and September since 1999. Roads are closed to traffic on Monday nights along five alternating routes – meaning no holds barred. 🔊 *May–Sep: every Mon • www.muenchnerbladenight.de*

### 3 Filmfest München

Smaller than the Berlin film festival and not quite as star-studded, Munich's festival has made a name for itself as a festival of the people. There are screenings of international films in several cinemas throughout the city. Gasteig is the festival centre, and free open-air screenings are held here in the evenings. 🔊 *8 days at the end of Jun • www.filmfest-muenchen.de*

### 4 Tollwood

This lively festival is held twice a year, in summer and winter with music, dance, and theatre in tents. Formerly an alternative event, it has matured into a major festival with a wide-ranging programme of performances, vendors, and beverage and food stalls. 🔊 *Summer festival (Jun–Jul) in south Olympiapark, Winter festival (Nov–31 Dec) in Theresienwiese • www.tollwood.de*

### 5 Opern-Festspiele

Under Ludwig II, Munich grew into a centre of music, and was the site of premieres of Wagner's operas and of a major Mozart festival. In 1910, the Richard Strauss festival week was launched, a tradition continued in the Opern-Festspiele, which features both classic works and contemporary pieces, accompanied by the innovative Festspiele + programme. 🔊 *late Jun–late Jul • www.bayerische.staatsoper.de*

**Open-air film festival**

*Bibliophiles can forage for reading material at the Münchner Bücherschau at the Gasteig in November/December.*

### 6 Königsplatz Open Air

The pompous backdrop of the Königsplatz (Royal Square) seems tailor-made for open-air events. In summer, usually in July, you can enjoy classic concerts and even opera performances. To round out the programme, the large square is also used as a stage for rock and pop concerts and film screenings. ❀ *Jul • www.kinoopenair.de*

### 7 THEATRON MusikSummer and PfingstOpenAir

According to *The Guinness Book of Records*, MusikSummer is the longest open-air festival in the world. It boasts 24 days of free musical entertainment under the open skies in the Olympiapark amphitheatre. Concerts range from rock and pop to classical music. A weekend festival, PfingstOpenAir, is staged in May. ❀ *Aug & late May • www.theatron.de*

### 8 Oktoberfest

More than six million visitors make the pilgrimage to the world's largest popular fair, the Wiesn, which takes place over 16 days in September *(see pp22–3)*.

### 9 Dance

An innovative dance festival organized by the city of Munich, in collaboration with local and international partners. Many of the productions are multidisciplinary – and always beyond the ordinary. ❀ *biannual late Oct–early Nov (2008, 2010–) • www.dance2006.de*

### 10 SpielArt

Munich's "Window on the World of Theatre" presents theatre productions from around the world at various venues, usually with a focus on one country each season. ❀ *biannual mid-Nov–early Dec (2009–) • www.spielart.org*

## Top 10 Other Events

### 1 Ballet Week
Staatsballett and guest performances. ❀ *mid-Apr • www.bayerisches.staatsballett.de*

### 2 Frühlingsfest
Little sister to the Oktoberfest, the Springfest is also held on the Theresienhöhe. ❀ *mid-Apr–early May*

### 3 Internationales Dokumentarfilmfestival
International documentaries, premieres, and films by up-and-coming new filmmakers. ❀ *May • www.dokfest-muenchen.de*

### 4 Stadtgründungsfest
Cultural events between Marienplatz and Odeonsplatz. ❀ *1st weekend in Jun*

### 5 Brunnenhofkonzerte
Classical music, but also tango, movie scores, and many other genres are presented in free concerts in the Brunnenhof of the Residenz on warm summer nights. ❀ *Jul • www.muenchen.de*

### 6 Klaviersommer
High-calibre stars and international concerts, from classic to funk. ❀ *Jul*

### 7 Christopher Street Day
Gay street parade, shows. ❀ *Jul • www.muenchen.gay-web.de/csd*

### 8 Fantasy Filmfest
Horror films, trash, and more for B-movie fans. ❀ *Sep • www.fantasyfilmfest.com*

### 9 Comicfest
Three days of comics, the New Art: pictures, books, and action on Praterinsel. ❀ *biannual Jun (2009–) • www.comicfest.de*

### 10 Lange Nächte
Late nights for music, theatres, museums, bookstores, and so on. ❀ *www.muenchen.de*

*Following pages* **Karlsplatz and Justizpalast (Ministry of Justice)**

Left **Hofbräuhaus** Centre **Augustinerbräu** Right **Weißes Bräuhaus**

# 🔟 Traditional Pubs

### 1 Hofbräuhaus
Anyone visiting Munich should make the pilgrimage to this venerable beer hall *(see p80)* – symbolic of all Bavarian pubs and the most famous pub in the world. Locals, too, simply can't stay away. Brass bands play daily at noon and again after 6pm.
Ⓝ Am Platzl 9 • Map M4 • (089) 22 16 76 • www.hofbraeuhaus.de

### 2 Augustinerbräu
Here in this historic building, thirsty travellers will find a beer hall and a restaurant with spectacular decor (including the Muschelsaal, a shell-lined room). The fare is typically Bavarian, the beverage, the famous Augustiner beer. In summer, choose between a table on the patio in the pedestrian zone, or in the stunningly beautiful Arkadenhof to the rear.
Ⓝ Neuhauser Str. 27 • Map K4 • (089) 23 18 32 57 • www.augustiner-restaurant.com

### 3 Löwenbräukeller
Stiglmairplatz, a busy square not far from the city centre, is dominated by this historic 1883 building. It has a beautiful pub, several halls, a ballroom, and a large beer garden *(see p24)*. In March, the pub hosts the tapping of the first Triumphator barrel, ringing in the "fifth season" – the bock beer

season. The stone lion perched above the entrance is the symbol of the Löwenbräu brewery.
Ⓝ Stiglmaierplatz • Map E4 • (089) 52 60 21 • www.loewenbraeukeller.com

### 4 Weißes Bräuhaus
Here you'll sample Munich cuisine prepared to perfection: *Pfannkuchensuppe* (clear broth with pancake strips), *G'schwollene* (fried veal sausage), *Schweinsbraten* (pork roast). The meals are inexpensive, and experienced staff are renowned for keeping up with the onslaught of orders from clamouring customers. A wheat ale is the most common brew served here; or try a pint of delicious Schneider Weiße.
Ⓝ Im Tal 10 • Map L4 • (089) 29 98 75 • www.weisses-braeuhaus.de

### 5 Nockherberg
In 1999, this traditional beer haven high above the Isar burned to the ground. Since 2003, however, politicians have once again gathered in the reconstructed Paulaner pub for the annual Salvator beer tapping. When this star-studded event has ended, "ordinary" patrons flock to the pub on the mountain for a taste of dark bock beer, which has an 18 per cent alcohol content.
Ⓝ Hochstr. 77 • Map G4 • (089) 45 99 13-0 • www. nockherberg.com

**Löwenbräukeller, Stiglmairplatz**

Munich serves up culinary treats, from haute cuisine to traditional fare; for restaurants See pp64–5, 85, 93, 103, 111

**Arkadenhof in the Augustinerbräu**

### 6 Beim Sedlmayr
This rustic pub, serving traditional Bavarian cuisine, was founded by the popular Bavarian comedian Walter Sedlmayr. ✆ Westenriederstr. 14 • Map L5 • (089) 22 62 19

### 7 Franziskaner Fuchsenstuben
Known for dishing up the best *Weißwürste* (veal sausages) and *Leberkäse* (minced meat loaf) in the city, this pub has been in business for 200 years. ✆ Perusastr. 5 • Map L4 • (089) 23 18 12 10

### 8 Augustinerbräustuben
Come to this pub during the Oktoberfest to admire the draught horses, and true Bavarian ambience in the former beer cellars and horse stalls of the brewery. ✆ Landsberger Str. 19 • Map D4 • (089) 50 70 47

### 9 Fraunhofer
This authentic pub has an interior from the turn of the 19th century. Frequented by students and big in the alternative scene, the pub features a cabaret stage in the rear courtyard. ✆ Fraunhoferstr. 9 • Map L6 • (089)26 64 60

### 10 Paulaner Bräuhaus
Extremely cosy pub thanks to the reconstructed dark-wood interior and fittings. On tap is the homebrew of the traditional Paulaner brewery. Venison is a highlight of the menu. ✆ Kapuzinerplatz 5 • Map E6 • (089) 5 44 61 10

## Top 10 Munich Beers

### 1 Augustiner
Brewed since 1328 in the monastery near the cathedral, Augustiner is widely regarded as the champagne of beers.

### 2 Franziskaner Weißbier
Franciscan friars have brewed this beer since 1363 in the former monastery on Residenzstraße. Now part of the Spaten-Löwenbräu Group.

### 3 Paulaner
Pauline monks in the Au began to brew beer as far back as 1634. Salvator beer is still made using monk Barnabas Still's 18th-century recipe.

### 4 Löwenbräu
Traditional brew with a history going back to the 14th century. Since the 19th century, the brewery has been the largest in Munich.

### 5 Hofbräu
Duke Wilhelm V founded his own court brewery in 1589. A new fermenting site was set up on Platzl in 1607 (today Hofbräuhaus).

### 6 Spaten
Dating from the 14th century, the brewery is named after the 16th-century Spatt family.

### 7 Unertl Weißbier
To some, Unertl from Haag in Upper Bavaria is the Weißbier *par excellence*.

### 8 Erdinger Weißbier
High on the scale among the nearly 1,000 different types of Bavarian wheat beers.

### 9 Ayinger
A small village brewery in Aying, home of a dozen world-famous beers.

### 10 Andechser
Beer has been brewed at this Benedictine abbey on the "sacred mountain" since the Middle Ages.

Left & Centre **Viktualienmarkt** Right **Market stall**

# Markets & Fairs

### 1 Viktualienmarkt

For a special experience, be sure to visit the Viktualienmarkt *(see p27)*, founded in 1807. Formerly a farmers' market, it has evolved into a shopping destination for gourmets. From Monday to Saturday, you will find daily offerings of fresh fruit and vegetables, meat, eggs, honey, and flowers, as well as exotic spices and other speciality foods. The market also features a small beer garden under the maypole and several fountains with sculptures portraying popular characters from Munich's history. ⊗ *Map L5*

### 2 Markt am Elisabethplatz

Located in Schwabing, Elisabethplatz was named after the Austrian empress Elisabeth (Sisi). This market, which is closed on Sundays, has been here since 1903 and is the second-largest one in Munich. Along with fruit, vegetables, cheese, sausage, and wine, market stalls offer many homemade specialities. The small market café is especially attractive. ⊗ *Map F3*

### 3 Markt am Wiener Platz

Many made-for-TV films shot in Munich use the permanent market stalls on Wiener Platz in Haidhausen as a backdrop. Local tradespeople and office workers drop by on their coffee breaks for a quick snack at one of the kiosks. ⊗ *Map P5*

### 4 Großmarkthalle

Munich's indoor *Großmarkt* (wholesale market) has a vibrant atmosphere. Opened in 1912, the complex features four large halls. Several excellent restaurants and pubs have established themselves in and around the market. ⊗ *Thalkirchnerstr.*

### 5 Auer Dulten

Church festivals, held here from the 14th century onward, evolved into popular annual fairs *(Dulten)*, and eventually into three nine-day fairs: Maidult, in late April; Jakobidult, starting 25 July; and Herbstdult, in late October. As aromas of roasted almonds and grilled fish waft through the air, vendors loudly proclaim the virtues of their wares – dishes, candles, patent medicine, and, of course, knick-knacks. ⊗ *Mariahilf-platz • Map F6–G6 • www. auerdult.de*

### 6 Antikmärkte

For antique furniture, head to Antikpalast (Rosenheimer Straße 143). The flea and antique market in Daglfing (Traberstraße 1) has a large selection of glass, silver, porcelain, paintings, rustic furniture, and more. Many treasures can also be found at the flea and antique market in Munich-Freimann (Lilienthalallee 29). ⊗ *www. antikpalast-muenchen.de • www.flohmarkt-daglfing.de • www. zenith-die-kulturhalle.de*

**Snuff box found at a flea market**

 *Farmers' markets are held on specific weekdays throughout Munich.*

**Statue of Roider Jackl, Viktualienmarkt**

## 7 Second-Hand & Flea Markets

Perfect for rummaging and strolling are the giant flea market on the Theresienwiese in April and the largest open-air flea market in Bavaria, on the grounds of the Neue Messe (Alfons-Goppel-Straße 3). ✎ www.muenchen.de

## 8 Second-Hand Stores

Perhaps a sign of the times, second-hand has gone mainstream, and "vintage" stores are springing up overnight.
✎ *Städtisches Gebrauchtwarenhaus, Sachsenstr. 25 • Cindy's Second Hand, Lindwurmstr. 56, Map E6 • List of stores: www.jiz-muenchen.de*

## 9 Weihnachtsmärkte

Christmas markets are a long-standing and utterly charming tradition here. The largest is held on Marienplatz, while those located in Schwabing and Haidhausen offer the best atmosphere.
✎ *Marienplatz, Map L4 • Münchner Freiheit, Map G2 • Weißenburger Platz, Map P6*

## 10 Magdalenenfest

Fair and market around the feast of St Mary Magdalene in July. ✎ *Hirschgarten • Map B4*

## Top 10 Munich Characters

1 **Julius Thannhauser** Carnival entertainer (1860–1921), whose fame reached far beyond Munich.

2 **Elise Aulinger** Popular actress (1881–1965), a pioneer of radio programming and creator of the *Ratschkathl* character.

3 **Hans Blädel** Trained as a shoemaker, he became a popular comedic music virtuoso (1871–1937).

4 **Minna Reverelli** Born Hermina Knapp (1892–1941), Minna was the Queen of Yodeling at Platzl.

5 **Ratschkathl** Cabaret artiste Ida Schumacher (1894–1956) was the best *Ratschkathl*. She created the tram-track-crack-cleaning-lady character.

6 **Roider Jackl** A farmer's son (1906–75) famous for his spirited performances of *Gstanzln* – satirical rhymes set to music – and a master of barbed humour.

7 **Blasius** Pseudonym of Sigi (Siegfried) Sommer (1914–96), author of a popular column in the *Münchner Abendzeitung*.

8 **Bally Prell** Decked out in colourful costumes, she recited rhymes to delighted fans (1922–82).

9 **Walter Sedlmayr** A home-grown talent and local favourite (1926–90), he was a successful stage actor and adman for Paulaner beer.

10 **Helmut Fischer** Munich actor (1926–97), best remembered for his role as Monaco-Franze in the TV series of the same name.

Left **Poster for documentary film festival** Centre **Arri Kino cinema** Right **Mathäser cinema**

# 🔟 Munich – the Bavarian Hollywood

### 1 Geiselgasteig & Bavaria Filmstadt

Second only to Berlin's film industry, Geiselgasteig has been a centre for film since 1910. Major productions have been shot here well into the modern era, including Petersen's *Das Boot*, and films by Bergman and Fassbinder. Today, Bavaria Filmstadt presents screenings and live shows on the back lot. ✆ *Geiselgasteig, Bavariafilmplatz 7 • (089) 64 99 23 04 • mid-Mar–Oct: 9am–4pm; Nov–Feb: 10am–3pm daily • www.bavaria-filmstadt.de*

### 2 Filmfest München

Since 1983, the largest German public film festival has been screening the latest international films at the end of June. Movie buffs love the Indies event, a series on independent American

**Filmfest München programme from 1991**

film. Gasteig is the festival centre, and screenings are held at various cinemas throughout the city. An offshoot of the film festival, the International Festival of Film Academies is in November. ✆ *www.filmfest-muenchen.de*

### 3 Academy for Television and Film

A training ground for film professionals since 1967, the academy's famous graduates include Wim Wenders and Roland Emmerich. Regular film screenings are held in the academy's in-house cinema. ✆ *Frankenthaler Str. 23 • (089) 68 95 70 • www.hff-muenchen.de*

### 4 Münchner Filmmuseum im Stadtmuseum

This dream theatre for cinephiles has been newly renovated and equipped with the latest projection technology for all movie formats. For 40 years, it has been showing foreign films, series, films from the museum's archives, and famous silent-film reconstructions, often with live music. ✆ *St-Jakobs-Platz 1 • Map L5 • (089) 23 32 23 48 • wheelchair accessible*

### 5 International Documentary Film Festival

May is the month of documentary film in Munich. The programme includes documentary, topical, and Bavarian films, forum discussions with filmmakers, and a best-of-programme event. ✆ *(089) 51 39 97 88 • www.dokfest-muenchen.de*

*For an overview of cinemas, current screenings, and other film-related events, visit* **www.artechock.de/film**

### Fantasy Filmfest
A penchant for the eerie and gruesome is a prerequisite for this festival of horror films and thrillers, held in July and August.
⊕ www.fantasyfilmfest.com

### Mathäser
Munich's former film palace was re-opened in 2003. This ultra-modern multiplex cinema is also used for film premieres.
⊕ Bayerstr. 5 • Map J4 • (089) 51 56 51 • wheelchair accessible

### Arri Kino
Designed by Arnold & Richter, this is a cinema rich in tradition, with a large lobby and bar. ⊕ Türkenstr. 91 • Map L1 • (089) 38 89 96 64 • not wheelchair accessible

### Maxim
This discriminating cinema is operated by Munich cinephile Sigi Daiber. It screens independent films and documentaries, including films by Tarkovsky.
⊕ Landshuter Allee 33 • Map D3 • (089) 16 87 21 • wheelchair accessible

### Werkstattkino
This cinema, tucked away in the basement of a rear courtyard building is dedicated to films beyond the mainstream.
⊕ Fraunhoferstr. 9 • Map L6 • (089) 2 60 72 50 • not wheelchair accessible

**Stunt show, Bavaria Filmstadt**

## Top 10 Munich Filmmakers

### Percy Adlon
Adlon (1935–) worked in Hollywood following the success of *Out of Rosenheim*.

### Herbert Achternbusch
Born in Munich, Achternbush (1938–) creates anarchic Bavarian films in the tradition of Karl Valentin.

### Michael Verhoeven
Verhoeven (1938–) belongs to a prominent, talented family of actors and directors, and is married to actress Senta Berger.

### Joseph Vilsmaier
Successful director (1939–) of biopics, among others the 1997 *Comedian Harmonists*.

### Helmut Dietl
Dietl (1944–) portrayed the Munich scene in TV series such as *Monaco Franze* (1983) and *Kir Royal* (1985).

### Rainer Werner Fassbinder
Famous prodigy of the New German Cinema, Fassbinder (1945–82) directed more than 40 films.

### May Spils
With the 1967 *Zur Sache Schätzchen (What Gives, Sweetheart?)*, starring Werner Enke and Uschi Glas, Spils created the film that captured the spirit of Schwabing in the 1960s.

### Doris Dörrie
Director and author Dörrie (1955–) became known for her 1985 film *Männer (Men)*.

### Caroline Link
In 2002, Link (1964–) won the Oscar for Best Foreign Film for *Nirgendwo in Afrika*.

### Florian Gallenberger
Gallenberger (1972–), who was born in Munich, received an Oscar in 2001 for his short film *Quiero ser*.

Following pages **Lenbachhaus**

Left **Optimolwerke** Centre & Right **Kultfabrik München**

# 🔟 Nightlife

### 1 The Atomic Café
With its bright orange 1960s decor, the Atomic has been a popular club for years. You'll find a broad spectrum of live music here, from Brit pop, indie, and hip-hop, to rock and soul. 🔊 *Neuturmstr. 5 • Map M4 • (089) 2 28 30 52 • Open 9pm Tue–Sat; closed Sun–Mon.*

### 2 Pacha
Formerly the renowned Nachtcafé, Pacha offers the complete sprectrum of house music and top DJs. Its large terrace makes it one of the most beautiful clubs in the city. 🔊 *Maximiliansplatz 5 • Map K3 • (089) 30 90 50 850 • Open from 10pm Fri, Sat & before public holidays; from 6:30pm Thu • www.pacha-muenchen.com*

### 3 Zerwirk
Built in 1264 as a bathhouse, this building (the second-oldest in Munich) has been a falcon house, a brewery and a theatre. It is now a vegan restaurant, a literary salon and a club. It is currently very popular with the trendy Glockenbach crowd. 🔊 *Ledererstr. 3 • Map L4 • (089) 23 23 91 91 • Club: Open Fri & Sat • www.zerwirk.de*

### 4 Volksgarten Club & Garden
The name gives it away: this club has a large garden with palm trees, water and a sand beach that makes it a popular choice in the summer. Come for Friday's black beat and house night ("Das Volksbegehren") or Saturday's "Die Macht der Nacht". 🔊 *Ramersdorf, Rosenheimer Str. 145 • Map H6 • (089) 36 81 45-0 • Open from 10pm Tue, Wed, Fri & Sat • www.volksgarten.de*

### 5 Muffathalle
A former heating plant, this large hall opens only for scheduled events such as concerts, theatre, dance performances, and readings. The café is open daily except Sundays. This is one of the most beautiful venues in the city, located right behind the Müller'sche Volksbad, and has a lovely beer garden that beckons in summer. 🔊 *Zellstr. 4 • Map N5 • (089) 45 87 50 10 • www.muffathalle.de*

**Bar at the Café Muffathalle**

### 6 P1
Hangout of FC Bayern football club players and other celebrities, with a rep-

**Note:** *Unless otherwise specified, an admission fee is charged for all concerts, clubs, and discos.*

utation that reaches far beyond Munich. Extremely strict doormen are infamous for refusing entry to "ordinary folk." On weekdays, P1 feels like a lounge rather than a nightclub. ◈ *Prinzregentenstr. 1 • Map M3 • (089) 21 11 14 10 • Open daily (until 4am Sun–Thu; later Fri & Sat) • www.p1-club.de*

### Night-Club (Bayerischer Hof)

With live jazz, funk, and soul, this is a club where music lovers can experience the real thing. ◈ *Promenadeplatz 2–6 • Map K4–L4 • (089) 212 09 94 • Open 10pm–3am daily • Adm (sometimes free) • www.bayerischerhof.de*

### Club Morizz

One of Munich's chicest meeting places for the gay community, but equally popular with other partygoers *(see p62).*

### Kultfabrik München

The *Kultfabrik* (cult factory), is a vast entertainment district, with over 20 bars, clubs and discos. ◈ *Grafinger Str. 6 • Map H6 • (089) 49 00 90 70 • www.kultfabrik.de*

### Optimolwerke

With 13 discos, clubs, and a *Spiegelzelt* (mirrored tent), the Optimolwerke complex is located next door to the Kultfabrik. ◈ *Friedenstr. 10 • Map H6 • (089) 45 06 920 • www.optimol werke.de*

**Live act at the Night-Club**

## Top 10 Singles Bars & Cafés

**1 Café Glockenspiel**
An evening meeting place for the 30- to 40-year-old crowd. Heated patio. ◈ *Marienplatz 28 (enter through the passage, elevator to the 5th floor) • Map L4*

**2 Negroni**
Intimate bar in Haidhausen with a classic atmosphere, its own kitchen and a vast range of cigars. ◈ *Sedanstr. 9 • Map P6*

**3 Café Lotter-Leben**
Café-bar located on Viktualienmarkt with an extravagant ambience. ◈ *Frauenstr. 4 • Map L5*

**4 Villa Flora**
This villa complete with beer garden is the hangout of a fun-loving crowd. ◈ *Hansastr. 44 • Map C5*

**5 Sausalitos**
Popular with young people seeking a Mexican ambience in the cactus-studded interior. ◈ *Türkenstr. 50 • Map L1*

**6 Lenbach**
Trendy VIP bar. ◈ *Ottostr. 6 • Map K3*

**7 Hit the Sky**
Bathed in pink and deep red, the interior of this club inspires flirtation. ◈ *Baaderstr. 33 • Map L6*

**8 Baader Café**
Reasonable prices and a gregarious student clientele. ◈ *Baaderstr. 47 • Map L6*

**9 Vorstadt-Café**
Open from breakfast to the cocktail hour. ◈ *Türkenstr. 83 • Map L1*

**10 Interview**
Café with Philippe Starck design and outdoor tables (open 9.30am–1am). ◈ *Gärtnerplatz 1 • Map L5*

A huge nightlife complex – Kunstpark Nord in Fröttmaning – is due to be completed near Allianz Arena in 2009.

Left **Schumann's** Centre **Tambosi** Right **Bar Centrale**

# 🔟 Bars & Cafés

### 1 Schumann's
Munich's top bar since 1982, now in a new location on the Hofgarten. Most tables are reserved for regulars, so be sure to book one in advance. Although the menu is limited, every item on it is delicious. Charles Schumann's fried potatoes and steak are famous. ⊕ *Odeonsplatz 6 & 7 • Map L3 • Open evenings daily • www.schumanns.de*

### 2 Toshi-Bar
Next door to the elegant Hotel Vierjahreszeiten, former celebrity watering hole L-Bar is now the stylish Japanese Toshi-Bar. The generous lounge area has comfy sofas. Dishes from the linked restaurant's menu are served here. ⊕ *Wurzerstr. 18 • Map M4 • Open evenings daily*

### 3 Hong Kong Bar
Sip an exotic drink at the 40-m- (130-ft-) long bar while enjoying the Far Eastern atmosphere. Imaginatively pre-

**Pusser's**

pared Asian dishes are the mainstay in the adjoining dining room. Mixed clientele. ⊕ *Kapuzinerstr. 39 • Map E6 • Open evenings*

### 4 Julep's
Rustic American ambience with barkeepers who are trained to mix some 200 cocktails, although you can also simply stand at the counter and drink a beer straight out of the bottle. Classics such as lobster and Tex-Mex dishes characterize the menu in the dining area. ⊕ *Breisacher Str. 18 • Map H5 • Open evenings*

### 5 Pusser's
One of the latest American-style bars in Munich, with a maritime decor. Cocktail highlights are the various rum-based creations. In addition, there's a wide selection of whiskies, Guinness, and Ayinger beer. Drop in to the piano bar for classic bar food and Caribbean dishes. ⊕ *Falkenturmstr. 9 (near Platzl) • Map M4 • Open evenings*

### 6 Bar Centrale
Italian bar open day and night. At the front, where there are also a few tables on the pavement, the air is filled with the heady aroma of espresso, while 1960s decor dominates the area at the rear. Outstanding cocktails, pasta dishes and bar snacks. ⊕ *Ledererstr. 23 • Map L4 • No credit cards*

*Munich no longer has a closing time for bars; many stay open until 3am or later.*

**Café Luitpold**

**Tambosi**
Historic coffee house in the Hofgarten, open morning to night. Take a seat inside and be transported back to the 1800s. In summer, there are two patios, one on Odeonsplatz, the other beneath linden trees on the Hofgarten side. Live music is occasionally performed by music students.
Ⓢ Odeonsplatz 18 • Map L3

**Café Ruffini**
A Munich institution – wholesome breakfasts should be this delicious everywhere. Bread and cakes are made in the café's own bakery. Tables on the roof patio are highly sought. There are nightly concerts or literary readings.
Ⓢ Orffstr. 22 • Map D3 • Open Tue–Sun

**Café Luitpold**
Traditional daytime café offering homemade pralines and cakes, as well as tasty meals. The kitchen closes at 7pm. Pretty courtyard and stunning conservatory. Ⓢ Brienner Str. 11 (Luitpoldblock) • Map L3 • Open Mon–Sat (also Sun in winter)

**Café Frischhut**
A favourite with hungover night owls, this café opens at 5am and serves fresh, deep-fried baked goods, doughnuts, and other goodies. Ⓢ Prälat-Zistl-Str. 8 • Map L5 • Closed Sun & hols

## Top 10 Bars, Cafés & Pubs with Live Music

**1 Jazzbar Vogler**
Fabulous blues and jazz venue. Mon–Sat. Ⓢ Rumfordstr. 17 • Map L5

**2 Waldwirtschaft Großhesselohe**
Popular Bavarian pub with beer garden. Live jazz. Ⓢ Pullach–Großhesselohe, Georg-Kalb-Str. 3 • (089) 74 99 40 30

**3 Café am Beethovenplatz**
Munich's oldest café; genteel atmosphere, live classical or jazz music. Ⓢ Goethestr. 51 • Map E5

**4 The Big Easy**
New Orleans-style bar and restaurant. Great ambience. Jazz brunch on Sundays. Ⓢ Frundsbergstr. 46 • Map C3

**5 Night-Club**
Tucked away in the Bayerischer Hof's basement, this club has top-notch jazz and funk headliners. Ⓢ Promenadeplatz 2–6 • Map K4 –L4

**6 Podium**
Featuring rock, oldies, and jazz, this is a 30-year-old institution. Ⓢ Wagnerstr. 1 (near Siegesstr.) • Map G2

**7 Unterfahrt**
This pub is in a cellar of the Einstein Kulturzentrum; venue for world-class jazz concerts. Ⓢ Einsteinstr. 42 • Map H5

**8 Atomic Café**
A club featuring many live music acts (see p58).

**9 Kaffee Giesing**
This renowned café was founded by songwriter Konstantin Wecker. Live music from 9pm. Ⓢ Bergstr. 5

**10 Hofbräuhaus**
A Bavarian brass band performs most days in Hofbräuhaus. Ⓢ Am Platzl 9 • Map M4

*Several museums feature attractive cafés, including the Glyptothek, the Kunsthalle (Hypo Kulturstiftung), and the Lenbachhaus.*

Left **Deutsche Eiche** Centre **The bar at Club Morizz** Right **Internet café Kr@ftAkt**

# Gay & Lesbian Hangouts

### Deutsche Eiche

Once frequented by renowned filmmaker Fassbinder and friends, this is a well-established gay pub with a hotel and bathhouse. Both Bavarian and international cuisine are on the menu. The bathhouse occupies four floors in the rear building, with steam bath, whirlpool, and roof garden. ⊙ *Reichenbachstr. 13 • Map L5 • (089) 23 11 66-0 • www.deutsche-eiche.de*

### Club Morizz

With its elegant ambience, witty decor, beautiful bar counter, and red club chairs, the Morizz is one of chicest meeting places – and not only for the gay community. The food (European cuisine and many Thai-inspired dishes) and drinks are excellent. Several

**Club Morizz**

times a week, a DJ gets the beat going; the house parties are extremely popular. ⊙ *Klenzestr. 43 • Map L6 • (089) 201 67 76 • www.club-morizz.de*

### Iwan's Bar

A friendly bar and restaurant in the quiet Glockenbachviertel area, with outdoor tables in the summer. You'll enjoy European-Asian cuisine, which is offered at a lower price during lunchtime. Iwan's is known for excellent cocktails and friendly service. During the day, the crowd is mixed, but at night you'll encounter the gay scene's in-crowd. Whether you're gay or not, you'll feel comfortable and be entertained. ⊙ *Hans-Sachs-Str. 20 • Map L5 • (089) 20 00 90 90 • www.cafe-iwan.de*

### Bau

A haven for fans of jeans, leather, latex, and uniforms, this huge bar offers moderate prices. The two floors alternate between brightly lit and darker, more intimate areas. This is definitely a place for tough guys – and for those drawn to them. ⊙ *Müllerstr. 41 • Map K6 • (089) 26 92 08 • www.bau-munich.de*

### Café Glück

Originally a trendy gay and lesbian hangout, Café Glück has now been colonised by Munich's straight population. With its mixed clientele, the atmosphere is by no means camp. It is a

*Old Mrs Henderson is a legendary drag club (Müllerstr. 1, 089-26 01 99 46) with transvestite shows at the weekend.*

good spot to enjoy coffee and a cake in the afternoon, or a drink and some excellent food in the evening. ◈ *Palmstr. 4 • Map F6 • (089) 201 16 73*

### Moro

Formerly a seedy corner pub, the Moro has reinvented itself as a trendy pub bar with a rustic interior. Attracting clientele from all walks of life, the menu ranges from Bavarian to Mediterranean to Asian cuisine. ◈ *Müllerstr. 30 • Map L5 • (089) 23 00 29 92 • www. moro-munich.com*

### Kr@ftAkt

Munich's gay Internet café with a bar and outdoor patio located at the gateway to the gay district, Sendlinger Tor. Cocktails and small dishes are served to a mixed public in daytime, which gives way to a predominantly gay crowd at night. ◈ *Thalkirchner Str. 4 • Map K5 • (089) 21 58 88 81*

### Inges Karotte

This is the oldest lesbian hangout in the city. Gays and straight friends are equally welcome. Many regulars and Saturday night disco with a DJ. ◈ *Baaderstr. 13 • Map M5 • (089) 201 06 69 • Open Sun–Fri*

### Bei Carla

Little known to foreign visitors, Bei Carla has been well known in Munich as a women's cafe for many years. The homely, rustic ambience attracts a crowd mainly aged from their late 20s to

**The colourful exterior of Bau**

their early 40s. Despite Bei Carla's long-standing reputation as a lesbian hangout, men are also welcome. ◈ *Buttermelcher Str. 9 • Map F5 • (089) 22 79 01 • www.bei-carla.de*

### C-Club

Gays and lesbians hit the dance floor to the sounds of the 1980s and the pop charts in this super party venue. Transvestite shows at weekends. ◈ *Müllerstr. 1 • Map L5 • (089) 26 34 69*

Munich's gay bookshop Max & Milian is located at Ickstattstr. 2 (089-2 60 33 20).

Left **Tantris** Centre **Entrance to Lenbach** Right **Königshof**

# 🔟 Fine Dining

### 1 Tantris
Arguably one of the best restaurants in the world, Gault Millau awards Tantris its highest score – 19 points. Hans Haas' philosophy of gastronomic pleasure is unequalled anywhere. This is a place for celebrating special occasions, revelling in top-notch cuisine, perfect service, and the expert recommendations of sommelière Paula Bosch. 🚫 *Johann-Fichte-Str. 7 • Map G1–G2 • (089) 36 19 59-0 • Open noon–3pm & 6:30pm–1am Tue–Sat • www.tantris.de • €€€€€*

### 2 Königshof
Located on the second floor of the Königshof hotel, this elegant restaurant has one Michelin star and 18 Gault Millau points. Out-of-this-world cuisine and a fantastic selection of over 800 wines. 🚫 *Karlsplatz 25 • Map J4 • (089) 55 13 60 • Open Tue–Sat • www. koenigshof-muenchen.de • €€€€€*

### 3 Ederer
Star chef Karl Ederer works his magic on the second floor of a palace in the Fünf Höfe arcades. Served in spacious and elegant

**The runway at the Lenbach**

rooms, all items on the menu are prepared with organic ingredients, which are transformed into delectable creations. 🚫 *Kardinal-Faulhaber-Str. 10 • Map L4 • (089) 24 23 13 10 • €€€€–€€€€€*

### 4 Lenbach
Opened in 1997, Lenbach is located in the restored Bernheimer Palais on Lenbachplatz. British design guru Sir Terence Conran based the interior on the seven deadly sins – a runway, symbolizing vanity, goes through the middle of the dining room. Ali Güngörmüs – Gault-Millau discovery of 2004 – conjures up creative magic with his fusion cuisine. Outdoor patio. 🚫 *Ottostr. 6 • Map K3 • (089) 54 91 30–0 • Open Mon–Sat • www.lenbach.de • €€€€–€€€€€*

### 5 Vinaiolo
Characterized by a unique apothecary-style decor, this restaurant in Haidhausen is a blend of osteria, bistro, and vinothèque, serving up inspired Italian cuisine. When selecting the reasonably priced wines, be sure to ask the padrone, a wine merchant, for recommendations. 🚫 *Steinstr. 42 • Map P6 • (089) 48 95 03 56 • Open noon–3pm & 6:30pm–1am Tue–Sun, 6:30pm–1am Mon • www.vinaiolo.de • €€€–€€€€*

### 6 Landersdorfer & Innerhofer
Top culinary standards in the heart of the city – Hans Landersdorfer's Austrian-inspired cuisine

Many top-notch restaurants offer lunch menus at reasonable prices. For price categories **See p85**

**Geisel's Vinothek in the Hotel Excelsior**

satisfies even the most discerning palate. His potato bread, served with appetizers, is justly famous. Robert Innerhofer is in charge of the wine cellar. ⓢ *Hackenstr. 6–8 • Map K5 • (089) 26 01 86 37 • Open Mon–Fri • €€€–€€€€*

### Kleinschmidtz
A congenial bistro-style place in the Glockenbach district. Seasonal menus are inventive and always delicious. ⓢ *Fraunhoferstr. 13 • Map L6 • (089) 260 85 18 • Open 6pm–1am daily • No credit cards • €€€*

### Geisel's Vinothek
Tucked away in the Hotel Excelsior, Geisel's offers a selection of 400 wines and fine cuisine. ⓢ *Schützenstr. 11 (Hotel Excelsior) • Map J4 • (089) 55 13 71 40 • Open noon–1am daily (from 5pm Sun) • €€€*

### Südtiroler Stuben
The gastronomic temple of Bavarian celebrity chef Alfred Schuhbeck. Refined Alpine cuisine. ⓢ *Platzl 8 • Map M4 • (089) 216 69 00 • Open 6–11pm Mon, noon–2:30pm & 6–11pm Tue–Sat • €€€€€*

### Rue des Halles
Parisian bistro ambience with an understated interior. Outstanding French cuisine; the *mousse au chocolat* is divine. ⓢ *Steinstr. 18 • Map P5 • (089) 48 56 75 • Open 6pm–1am • €€€*

## Top 10 All-Day Breakfasts & Brunches

**1 Kaffee Giesing**
Sunday brunch with live music. Patio. ⓢ *Bergstr. 5 • (089) 692 05 79*

**2 Ruffini**
Breakfast from early morning until 4pm weekends. ⓢ *Orffstr. 22 • Map D3 • (089) 16 11 60*

**3 Vorstadt-Café**
Café near the university serving breakfast until 4pm. ⓢ *Türkenstr. 83 • Map L1 • (089) 272 06 99*

**4 Café im Volksbad**
Art Nouveau café in Müllersche Volksbad with outdoor tables and a breakfast menu until 5pm. ⓢ *Rosenheimer Str. 1 • Map N5 • (089) 44 43 92 50*

**5 Interview**
Brunch until 5pm, when the bar opens. Patio. ⓢ *Gärtnerplatz 1 • Map L5 • (089) 202 16 49*

**6 Café Neuhausen**
Rich selection of breakfast dishes available until 4pm. ⓢ *Blutenburgstr. 106 • Map D3 • (089) 18 97 55 70*

**7 Café Altschwabing**
Stucco and *fin-de-siècle* atmosphere. Breakfast served until 5pm. ⓢ *Schellingstr. 56 • Map L2 • (089) 273 10 22*

**8 Aroma-Kaffeebar**
Breakfast buffet, coffee blends, and homemade cakes. ⓢ *Pestalozzistr. 24 • Map K6 • (089) 26 94 92 49*

**9 Café am Beethovenplatz**
Classic jazz brunch on Sundays. Patio. ⓢ *Goethestr. 51 • Map E5 • (089) 552 91 00*

**10 Rothmund**
Large selection until 3pm (theme brunches on Sundays). Outdoor tables. ⓢ *Rothmundstr. 5 • Map J6 • (089) 53 50 15*

Munich is a city that worships fine dining. For inexpensive restaurants in individual districts **See pp85, 103, 111, 50–51**

Left **Fünf Höfe** Centre & Right **Boutiques along Maximilianstraße**

# 🔟 Shopping

### Pedestrian Zone
Munich's central pedestrian zone stretches along Kaufinger-straße and Neuhauser Straße to Karlsplatz/Stachus. Here you will find all the major European chains and many department stores. Estimates show that Germany's largest retail turnover per minute happens right here. Beyond Stachus, there are more stores in Sonnenstraße, Schützenstraße, and in the Elisenhof at the main railway station. ✆ Map K4–L4

### Theatinerstraße
Affluent shoppers head to Munich's most elegant shopping street, which starts at Marienhof behind the Town Hall. The number of fashion boutiques and high-end stores has swelled since the classy Fünf Höfe shopping arcades opened. ✆ Map L4

Munich's pedestrian zone

### Fünf Höfe
Historic buildings and contemporary architecture, arcades, courtyards, stores (Manufaktum, Emporio Armani), culture (Kunsthalle of the Hypo-Kulturstiftung), and fine gastronomy (Schumann's daytime bar, Ederer, Barista, Café Kunsthalle) – this award-winning jewel of urban design by architects Herzog and de Meuron covers the area between Theatiner-, Kardinal-Faulhaber-, Maffei- and Salvatorstraße. ✆ Map L4

### Odeonsplatz & Brienner Straße
Luxury stores and boutiques line this square and the exclusive boulevard that runs off it. Here, you will also find an exemplary piece of urban renewal – the 19th-century Luitpoldblock with luxury shops, galleries, and Café Luitpold (see p61) with its palm garden. ✆ Map L3

### Maximilianstraße
Maximilian II laid out this elegant boulevard in the mid-19th century. Extending between the Nationaltheater and the Alt-stadtring, it has evolved into one of Europe's most exclusive shopping destinations. Bulgari, Armani, Chanel, and other shops beckon beneath the pointed arches designed by Friedrich Bürklein. The boulevard is also home to the Hotel Vierjahreszeiten, the Kammerspiele, and – since the autumn of 2003 – the Maximilianhöfe. ✆ Map M4

### Maximilianhöfe

The Maximilianhöfe is a complex encompassing a reconstructed Bürklein building on Maximilianstraße, a complex with offices and luxury boutiques (Gianfranco Ferré, Dolce & Gabbana, and others), and the state opera's new rehearsal stage, featuring a transparent curtain façade. At the centre of the ensemble, the historic colonnaded hall of the former stables of the royal riding school has been preserved. The restaurant Brenner is a hidden treasure. ✪ Map M4

In the Maximilianhöfe

### Sendlinger Straße

One of the oldest shopping streets, with several traditional stores. Growing increasingly chic, the strip still offers a colourful mix and great diversity of retail, from a fashion department store to leather goods to a teashop. ✪ Map K5

### Around Viktualienmarkt

Worth a stroll in its own right, Munich's oldest market is surrounded by speciality shops of all sizes. To the south, you'll find the shops of the Gärtnerplatz district, while many small antique shops and the city's largest supermarket for organic foods line the narrow streets leading to Isartor. On the west side, in the direction of Rindermarkt, a new shopping arcade has been created around the medieval Löwenturm. ✪ Map L5

### Around the University

Bounded by the Amalienstraße, Türkenstraße, and Adalbertstraße, the student quarter features not only many excellent bookshops but also boutiques of all kinds, including eccentric clothing stores, and jewellery and design shops. ✪ Map L1–L2

### Leopoldstraße & Side Streets

Schwabing's Leopoldstraße is lined with boutiques, restaurants, and cafés, starting at Giselastraße. Stroll along the side streets on the left side of the boulevard (heading north) for a wide variety of interesting shops. Hohenzollernstraße, especially, has evolved into a centre for small boutiques. ✪ Map F2–G2

For information on the modern arcades behind historic façades, visit www.fuenfhoefe.de and www.maximilianhoefe.de

Left **Rhinoceros, Tierpark Hellabrunn** Centre **Zirkus Krone logo** Right **Farmhouses, Glentleiten**

# Children's Attractions

### 1 Olympiapark

From beach volleyball and basketball or skiing and boat rides to climbing tours on the world-famous tent roof at the largest sport-, fun- and fitness complex in the city *(see pp18–19)*, the variety of activities at Olympiapark will keep the kids amused all day.

### 2 Deutsches Museum

Older children will be fascinated by many displays in the largest museum of technology in the world – from classic building block sets to full-size jet airplanes. Young children will delight in exploring the Kinderreich section. Devoted entirely to "scientists" aged three and up, children can experience physics first-hand through interactive exhibits. Equally fun for kids of all ages is the Technisches Spielzeug (Technical Toys) exhibit and a "planet walk" from the Sun to Pluto, which takes about an hour to complete *(see pp8–11)*.

### 3 Tierpark Hellabrunn

Extremely popular with children, the city's zoo includes highlights such as the jungle tent for big cats and the new primeval forest pavilion. For the little ones, there is a petting zoo. Be sure to ask about feeding times. ⊗ *Tierparkstr. 30 • Map E6 • Open 8am–6pm in summer, 9am–5pm in winter • Adm • www.zoo-muenchen.de*

### 4 Puppet Theatre

Munich's oldest puppet theatre, founded in 1858, is housed in a small, gabled, and colonnaded temple. Performances are enthusiastically received by young and old alike. ⊗ *Blumenstr. 32 • Map K5 • (089) 26 57 12 • Adm • www.muenchner-marionettentheater.de*

### 5 Bavaria Filmstadt

Film and television productions are still made in these studios, which offer guided tours. There are explosions and excitement at the stunt show; replicas and scenes from famous films; and, most thrilling of all, a 3D cinema, where your seats move in synch with the on-screen action. Children must be at least 120 cm (4 ft) in height to view the film. ⊗ *Geiselgasteig, Bavariafilmplatz 7 • (089) 64 99 23 04 • Open Mar–Oct: 9am–4pm daily; Nov–Feb: 10am–3pm daily • www.filmstadt.de*

**Fuchur, the famous movie dragon, Bavaria Filmstadt**

For suggestions about child-friendly city tours and adventure walks, visit **www.muenchen.kinder-stadt.de**

**LEGOLAND Germany**

### Zirkus Krone
**6** High-flying acrobats, tigers, and lions – this is a classic circus. It tours in summer and is permanently based here in winter.
◈ Zirkus-Krone-Str. 1–6 • Map D4 • (089) 545 80 00 • Open 25 Dec–31 Mar Tue–Sun • Adm • www.zirkus-krone.de

### Märchenwald im Isartal
**7** Amusement park with a flower-bud merry-go-round, an old-fashioned carousel, shooting-star swings, and fairy-tale buildings. ◈ Wolfratshausen, Kräuterstr. 39 • (0 81 71) 1 87 60 • Adm
• www.maerchenwald-isartal.de

### Freilichtmuseum Glentleiten
**8** Old farmhouses, a forge, and traditional artisans in this open-air museum. Children receive a colouring book as a guide (see p123).

### Sea Life
**9** The main attractions for young visitors to Sea Life are the resident seahorses and the walk-through tunnel in the aquarium (see pp18–19).

### LEGOLAND Germany
**10** This amusement park with over 40 attractions, rides, and shows offers a dazzling array of buildings, animals, and sculptures built from more than 50 million LEGO building blocks. Fun for children ages 3 to 13. ◈ Günzburg, Legoland-Allee 1 • (082 21) 700 700 211 • Adm • www.legoland.de

## Top 10 Child-Friendly Cafés & Restaurants

### Villa Flora
**1** Half-price Sunday brunch for kids aged five to ten (free for those younger than five).
◈ Hansastr. 44 • Map C5

### Seehaus
**2** Café and beer garden on the banks of the Kleinhesseloher See, where you can rent rowing boats and pedalos.
◈ Englischer Garten • Map G2

### Café Janosch
**3** Ideal for parents with children up to the age of six.
◈ Fürstenriederstr. 16 • Map C4

### Biergarten am Chinesischen Turm
**4** A beer garden surrounded by green areas and playgrounds. ◈ Englischer Garten • Map G3

### Zum Aumeister
**5** Traditional beer garden and restaurant, with an adventure playground. ◈ Sondermeierstr. 1

### Waldwirtschaft
**6** Swings, slides, and mini golf mean plenty of fun for young visitors. ◈ Pullach–Großhesselohe, Georg-Kalb-Str. 3

### Forsthaus Wörnbrunn
**7** The menu is a colouring book, which children can take home with them. ◈ Grünwald, Wörnbrunn 1

### Hofbräukeller
**8** Complimentary babysitting services all day. ◈ Innere Wiener Str. 19 • Map P5

### Mangostin Asia
**9** Inexpensive family buffet on Sundays and play area. Reserve ahead. ◈ Maria-Einsiedel-Str. 2 • (089) 723 20 31

### Hirschau
**10** The beer garden is next to an enclosed playground. ◈ Englischer Garten, Gyßlingstr. 15 • Map H2

*More and more restaurants are offering family-oriented service with children's menus, booster seats, and even babysitting.*

Left **Cyclist taking a break** Right **Nymphenburg Park**

# 🔟 Walks & Cycling Tours

### 1 Walk through the Englischer Garten

From the Haus der Kunst (see p37), walk north through the beautiful section of the park that was landscaped 200 years ago. At Kleinhesseloher See, a footbridge takes you over a highway into the newer section of the park and to your final destination, the utterly charming Zum Aumeister beer garden (see p69). 🕒 1.5–2 hrs • Zum Aumeister, Sondermeierstr. 1, (089) 32 52 24

### 2 Hiking along the Isar

Departing from the Deutsches Museum (see pp8–11), walk south upriver along the right bank of the Isar. At the halfway mark, it's worthwhile taking a short detour to see the rose garden (see p39). This walk goes all the way to the meadows in Thalkirchen, where you can also stop to visit the Tierpark Hellabrunn, a zoo (see p107). 🕒 1.5–2 hrs • Mangostin Asia, Maria-Einsiedel-Str. 2, (089) 723 20 31

### 3 A Walk in Westpark

Set off at the eastern end of Westpark at the corner of Hansastr and Baumgartnerstr. Walk west through the park grounds until you reach a footbridge, which links the eastern and western sections. Special features of the park include artful Asian garden landscapes and a restaurant (with beer garden) next to a rose garden. 🕒 1–1.5 hrs • Gasthaus am Rosengarten, Westendstr. 305, (089) 57 86 93 00

### 4 Walk through Nymphenburg Park

Before setting off from Schloss Nymphenburg (see pp12–13), take your bearings from one of the many park plans posted near the entrance. An attractive route is a pavilion circuit – Pagodenburg, the cascades, the Temple of Apollo, Badenburg, and Amalienburg – and back to the palace. Round out your walk with a visit to the Museum Mensch und Natur or the Botanical Gardens. 🕒 1–1.5 hrs • Schlosscafé im Palmenhaus, Schloss entrance 43, (089) 17 53 09

### 5 Hiking on the Ilkahöhe

Starting at the S-Bahn (S6) station in Tutzing, the trail to the Ilkahöhe is clearly marked by white triangles and climbs up a total elevation of some 150 m (500 ft), in part on narrow forest paths. The view from the top of the hill is magnificent. On clear days, you can see the entire chain of the Bavarian Alps. 🕒 1.5–2 hrs • Forsthaus Ilkahöhe, Tutzing, (08158) 82 42

**View from the Ilkahöhe**

For more tours and maps visit **www.muenchen.de**; for cyling tour maps, visit **www.adfc.de**

### Cycling Tour to Freising

From the Aumeister beer garden in the Englischer Garten, follow the Isar cycling path in the direction of Freising, about 40 km (25 miles) away. At the bridge across the Isar in Freising, turn left toward Weihenstephan. This former Benedictine monastery is the oldest brewery in the world. Return to Munich by S-Bahn (S1), which departs from Freising station, 2 km (1 mile) away. ⊗ 2.5–3 hrs • Bräustüberl Weihenstephan, (08161) 130 04

Weihenstephan brewery, Freising

### Cycling Tour to Schloss Schleißheim

Some 200 m (650 ft) to the right of the S-Bahn train station in Milbertshofen, turn north at the small park and follow the cycling path, in part on an old streetcar track, in the direction of Oberschleißheim, where you can take a brief cultural break by visiting the Flugwerft Schleißheim and the Neues Schloß. Continue along the Schleißheim canal to Garching-Hochbrück and return by U-Bahn (U6). ⊗ 2–2.5 hrs • Schlosswirtschaft Oberschleißheim, Maximilianhof 2, (089) 315 15 55

Mask, Schloss Schleißheim

### Cycling Tour: Olympiapark to Schloss Blutenburg

From Olympiapark (see pp18–19), cycle along Nymphenburg canal to the palace and then continue west along the southern park wall (cycling is prohibited in the park) until you reach an underpass. The rest of the cycling path to Schloss Blutenburg, home to the International Youth Library, is clearly marked. ⊗ 1.5–2 hrs • Schlossschänke Blutenburg, (089) 811 98 08

### Cycling Tour: Along the Isar to Schäftlarn Monastery

From the Deutsches Museum (see pp8–11), follow the Isar cycling path in a southerly direction. Take a break at Grünwald to visit the fortress and continue on to Schäftlarn monastery. A note of caution – there are several bumpy stretches through forests and some hilly sections. Returning to Munich is easy – take the S-Bahn (S7) from Hohenschäftlarn station, 3 km (2 miles) away. ⊗ 2–2.5 hrs • Klosterbräustüberl Schäftlarn, Ebenhausen, (08178) 36 94

### Cycling Tour: Along the Würm to Lake Starnberg

Departing from Pasing S-Bahn station, the route begins with a short stretch along busy roads to the clearly marked Würm river cycling path. Follow the river south past Gauting to Leutstetten, where you can take a break in the beautiful castle restaurant with beer garden. The tour continues up a short incline past Mühltal station, past a golf course, and on to Starnberg. Again, there is an easy route home by S-Bahn (S6) from Starnberg station. ⊗ 2–2.5 hrs • Undosa Seerestaurant, Starnberg, (08151) 99 89 30

Left **Model of Allianz Arena** Right **Munich – a bicycle-friendly city**

# 🔟 Sport & Wellness

### 1 Hiking
There are many beautiful hiking trails in and around Munich that make for easy walking *(see p70)*. If you prefer a more extreme challenge, take a trip to the nearby Alps for mountain hiking. For information on hiking routes, contact the Deutscher Alpenverein (German Alp Association).
⊕ *www.alpenverein.de • (089) 14 00 30*

### 2 Inline Skating
The Englischer Garten is a fine place for inline skating, as are the specially marked paths in Olympiapark *(see pp18–19)*. For those who prefer a group dynamic, Munich's Blade Nights, held on selected city streets every Monday night from May to September – weather permitting – are a fun option.
⊕ *www.muenchner-blade-night.de*

### 3 Jogging
Munich boasts many small and large parks *(see pp38–9)* that are perfect for jogging. The most beautiful paths are to be found in the Englischer Garten and along the banks of the Isar. If you don't like to jog on your own, Road-Runners, a local organization, will put you in touch with a group of runners at your level.
⊕ *www.mrrc.de*

### 4 Cycling
Home to one of the best cycling-path networks in Europe, Munich has several "green lungs," where you can enjoy a bike ride without the nuisance of car exhaust fumes and noise *(see p71)*. Check with the ADFC (the German cycling association) for a wide selection of cycling tours in and around Munich. ⊕ *www.adfc-bayern.de • (089) 55 35 75*

### 5 Climbing
With the magnificent Alps on the doorstep, rock climbers have plenty of opportunities to indulge in their passion. Munich also offers several artificial climbing walls to practise on before heading off to try out a real rock face.
⊕ *www.ig-klettern.de*

### 6 Golfing
Golfing has become a popular sport in Munich and the surrounding area. Golf lovers can choose from among more than 40 golf courses that are located in the vicinity of the Bavarian capital. ⊕ *www.golf-eschenried.de*

---

**Allianz Arena**

The Allianz Arena in Fröttmaning, in the north of Munich, was built for the city's two football clubs. Designed by architects Herzog and de Meuron, the transparent façade can be illuminated in white, red, or blue (the colours of the clubs). Holding 66,000 spectators, the stadium includes an enormous food court with two club restaurants (each seating 1,500), a family restaurant, a self-serve restaurant, a press cafeteria, and a café bar. The stadium can be reached by underground line U6.

---

*For more information on the Allianz Arena, visit*
**www.allianz-arena.de**

**Golf course near Feldafing on Lake Starnberg**

### Beach Volleyball
Munich's several indoor facilities ensure that the ever-increasing number of enthusiasts can play, no matter what the weather.
🖰 www.robertobeach.de
• (089) 29 16 17 19

### Water Sports
Munich and the nearby lake region are a haven for anyone who enjoys water sports, from swimming, rowing, or sailing to canoeing. There are outdoor pools, reservoir lakes, small idyllic moor lakes, and countless other lakes dotting Upper Bavaria. 🖰 www.swm.de

### Winter Sports
The city and its environs attract all winter-sports fans, whether you like skiing, skating, snowboarding, or tobogganing. With such a wide variety of winter sports, there's something for everyone here.
🖰 www.muenchen.de

### Wellness
Munich offers a wide range of wellness facilities, from day spas to organic supermarkets to wellness centres. The Turkish bath in the Mathilden-Bad is a well-known and popular spot.
🖰 www.hamam.de
• www.olympiapark-muenchen.de

## Top 10 Sports Events

### Vierschanzen Tournee
The best-known ski jump tournament in the world, held New Year's week in Oberstdorf, Garmisch-Partenkirchen, Innsbruck, and Bischofshofen.
🖰 www.vierschanzen.org

### 6-Tage Rennen
Biggest cycling race of the year in Munich (6 days, mid-Nov), held at the Olympiahalle. 🖰 www.olympiapark-muenchen.de

### FC Bayern München
Munich's famous football club tries to stay a step ahead of their opponents, the "Lions."
🖰 www.fcbayern.de • (089) 69 93 10

### TSV München 1860
This Munich football club is called the "Lions" by their fans. 🖰 www.tsv1860.de
• (089) 64 27 85 100

### BMW International Open
Golf tournament (Aug) held at the Munich Nord-Eichenried club. 🖰 www.gc-eichenried.de
• (08123) 930 80

### Snowboard World Cup
In winter on the hills of the Olympiapark. 🖰 www.olympiapark-muenchen.de

### BMW-Open
This is a high-calibre tennis tournament in spring, put on by MTTC Iphitos e.V. 🖰 www.iphitos.de • (089) 322 09 03

### Munich Marathon
This media-sponsored marathon is held in Oct. 🖰 www.muenchenmarathon.de

### Horse-Racing
Held throughout the year at the racecourse in Munich Daglfing. 🖰 www.daglfing.de

### Winter Olympics Bid
If Munich wins its 2018 bid, it will be the first city to host summer and winter games.

*The canal at Schloss Nymphenburg is a popular spot in winter for curling and skating.*

Left **Corpus Christi Procession** Centre **Raising of the Maypole** Right **Leonhardi, Bad Tölz**

# 🔟 Traditions In & Around Munich

### Schäfflertanz
Every seven years, the Dance of the Coopers is performed to commemorate the end of the plague in the 1400s. The next one will take place in 2012. ✪ *Munich, during Fasching (carnival)*

### Dance of the Market Wives
Viktualienmarkt market women perform a dance in fancy dress. ✪ *Munich, Shrove Tuesday*

**Maypole ornament**

### Starkbier Season
Since "liquids don't count during fast-time," monks brewed a nourishing ale during the lenten fast, a tradition that has survived to this day. Bavaria's "fifth season" is launched by the ceremonial breaching of bock beer barrels, the most famous being the Salvator breaching on Nockherberg *(see p50)*. ✪ *Bavaria, 19 Mar–Easter*

### Maypole
Most Bavarian towns and communities raise decorated Maypoles on 1 May, a custom dating back to the Middle Ages when the "tree of life" was thought to bring success. Overnight, the Maypole is guarded by local youths: If a Maypole is stolen, it has to be ransomed with many barrels of beer. ✪ *Bavaria, 1 May*

### Corpus Christi Procession
Corpus Christi processions are held throughout southern Bavaria – the largest is in Munich – to mark this important Catholic feast day. ✪ *Thu after Trinity Sun*

### Kocherl Ball
Annual "Cook's Ball," where costumed couples dance a Bavarian waltz and polka at 6am at the

**Horses decked out in special harness for Leonhardi procession, Bad Tölz**

*On Shrove Tuesday, ski carnival is celebrated in the Alps. The best known is held at Firstalm – there's a prize for the best costume.*

**Folk costumes, Bad Tölz**

foot of the Chinese Tower in the Englischer Garten. This tradition harks back to an annual ball for Munich's domestic servants.
⊗ *Munich, Englischer Garten, Jul*

### Leonhardi Processions
Bad Tölz, Schliersee, Murnau, and many Bavarian towns stage processions on horseback or in painted carts in honour of St Leonard, the patron saint of horses.
⊗ *Oberbayern, 1st Sun in Nov*

### Christkindlmarkt
Wonderful Christmas markets with stalls, mulled wine, and treats. On Marienplatz and in many other areas of the city.
⊗ *Bavaria, Advent to 24 Dec*

### Alphorn, Yodeling & Schuhplattler
The Alphorn was a means of communication between cow-herders across long distances, as was yodelling, which evolved into a style of singing. Young men danced the Schuhplattler – a folk dance involving much slapping of shoe soles. These traditions are a mainstay at regional folk festivals.

### Folk Dress
Each region has its own distinctive folk dress, and folklore associations keep the tradition alive, parading regional costumes in processions and at festivals such as the Wiesn.

## Top 10 Holidays & Celebrations

### New Year's Eve
Best places to enjoy the spectacular fireworks: Bavaria statue, Olympiaberg, high-rises, and the highest banks of the Isar.

### Epiphany
During the week before 6 Jan, children dress up as the Three Magi and go door to door, collecting money for charity.

### Ash Wednesday
Carnival *(Fasching)* is followed by a fasting period and the start of the bock beer season.

### Easter
Easter egg hunts in Tierpark Hellabrunn and other locations.

### Labour Day
The raising of the Maypole and union marches are on 1 May.

### Corpus Christi
One of the most important days in the Bavarian Catholic calendar. Munich has a large procession.

### Thanksgiving
Thanksgiving and *Kirchweih* (consecration of churches) fall on the same day. The Auer Herbstdult *(see p52)* often begins on Thanksgiving, as does the *Almabtrieb*, when the cattle are driven from Alpine summer pastures.

### All Saints' Day
On 1 Nov, graves are decorated and lanterns lit. Halloween is celebrated the night before.

### St Martin's Day
Children carry lanterns in processions led by a rider dressed as St Martin. Roast goose is traditional at dinner.

### Christmas
Christkindl markets start on the first day of Advent. Midnight mass is held 24 Dec.

*Curling and a trial of strength called* **Fingerhakeln** *(finger wrestling) are traditional Bavarian sports.*

# AROUND TOWN

TOP 10 MUNICH

Left **Brunnenhof at the Residenz** Centre **Altes Rathaus** Right **Main post office, Maximilianstraße**

# Downtown & Old Town

MUNICH'S HISTORIC OLD TOWN *is also the downtown area. This is where you will find many historic buildings as well as Marienplatz, (the historic central square), and the Residenz. In the past, further expansion was hindered by the Englischer Garten to the northeast and the Isar River to the east. Within the boundaries of the old town gates – Karlstor, Isartor, Odeonsplatz, and Sendlinger Tor – lie the principal shopping districts. Here you will find the pedestrian zone, Theatinerstraße, and Maximilianstraße. However, Marienplatz remains the true heart of Munich for visitors and locals alike.*

Chiming clock, Neues Rathaus

## 🔟 Attractions

1 Marienplatz, Neues & Altes Rathaus

2 Frauenkirche

3 Alter Hof

4 Alte Münze

5 Maximilianstraße

6 Hofbräuhaus & Platzl

7 Sankt-Jakobs-Platz & Stadtmuseum

8 Sendlinger Straße & Sendlinger Tor

9 Residenz & Hofgarten

10 Odeonsplatz, Theatinerkirche & Feldherrnhalle

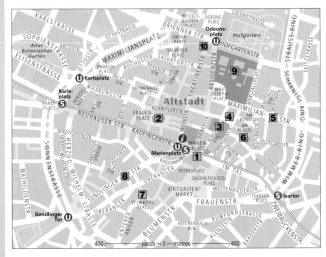

Some 20,000 visitors pass through Marienplatz and the adjacent pedestrian zone every hour.

## 1 Marienplatz, Neues & Altes Rathaus

The Mariensäule (Column of the Virgin), from 1590, and the 19th-century fish fountain on Marienplatz are popular meeting spots. Although the square is dominated by the ornate Neues Rathaus, or New Town Hall (1867–1908), the eastern side is bounded by the Gothic simplicity of the Altes Rathaus, or Old Town Hall, built during the 15th century. The Glockenspiel, a chiming clock, is not to be missed *(see pp26–7)*.

## 2 Frauenkirche

Weinstraße, a lane off Marienplatz, leads to the Frauenkirche (1468–88), a basilica designed by Jörg von Halsbach. A lack of funds forced him to abandon his idea of Gothic towers. The "Swiss bonnets" that top the towers were added later and are perhaps the forerunners of all the onion domes in Bavaria. Highlights are the emperor's tomb, Erasmus Grasser's carving, and the statue of St Christopher *(see p27)*.

## 3 Alter Hof

Built within the city walls between 1253 and 1255, the former residence of the Wittelsbach dynasty lies northeast of Marienplatz. Preserved in its original form, the west wing features a gatehouse embellished with the family's coat of arms. A bay window, known as the Affenturm, or Monkey Tower, is another original element. According to legend, a court monkey abducted young Ludwig IV, the future emperor

**Affenturm, Alter Hof**

**Gilded statue of the Virgin, Mariensäule**

of Germany, and climbed to the top of the tower with the boy before returning him safely to ground level. ◈ *Burgstr. 4 • Map L4 • 8am–4:30pm Mon–Thu (Fri to 2pm)*

## 4 Alte Münze

Northeast of the Alter Hof lies the Münzhof (1567), the former royal stables of the Bavarian rulers. This stunning Renaissance courtyard with arcades rising across three stories held the stables and coach houses, as well as the library and treasure chamber of Albrecht V. In the 19th century, the complex was converted into the state mint, hence the name Alte Münze, or Old Mint. Coins were minted here as recently as 1983. ◈ *Hofgraben 4 • Map L4–M4 • Courtyard open year-round*

**Renaissance triple-tier arcades in the Münzhof**

## 5 Maximilianstraße

Maximilian II built this monumental boulevard between 1852 and 1855. The stretch between Max-Joseph-Platz and Alstadtring *(see pp66–7)* is one of the world's most exclusive shopping streets. In the arcades, luxury boutiques such as Armani, Jill Sander, and Chanel offer their exquisite wares; the Hotel Vierjahreszeiten and the Kammerspiele are also found here, as is the new Maximilianhöfe complex *(see p67)*. At its far end, the boulevard is flanked with ornate public buildings. ◈ *Map M4*

Hofbräuhaus

especially for reconstructions of silent films. Ignaz-Günther-Haus – a late Gothic building that was the home and studio of the famous Rococo sculptor – stands on the west side of the square. ⓢ St-Jakobs-Platz 1 & 15 • Map L5 • www.juedisches-museum.muenchen.de; www.muenchen.de/stadtmuseum

### 6 Hofbräuhaus & Platzl

Munich's most famous pub dates from 1896 and was originally the royal court brewery, founded in 1598 by Wilhelm V. There is space for 1,000 patrons on the ground floor, where Hofbräu is, of course, the main beverage served – over 10,000 litres (2,600 gallons) per day. A barrel-vaulted banquet hall occupies the second floor and the complex also features a beautiful small beer garden. Walk through the winding lanes nearby, such as Burgstraße, to enjoy one of Munich's most historic districts.
ⓢ Am Platzl 9 • Map M4
• (089) 22 16 76 • www.hofbraeuhaus.de

Egid Quirin Asam

### 7 Sankt-Jakobs-Platz & Stadtmuseum

Since 2006 Sankt-Jakobs-Platz has been home to the new Jewish Centre. This comprises the Ohel Jakob Synagogue (see p41), the Jüdisches Museum (see p37), and a community centre. Six buildings on the square, including the Marstall (royal stables) and the former Zeughaus (arsenal), are occupied by the Stadtmuseum. It contains several permanent collections and exhibitions. The film museum enjoys international renown (see p36 & p54),

### 8 Sendlinger Straße & Sendlinger Tor

For a long time this was one of the oldest retail strips in the city, with shops owned by the same families for generations. In recent years, Sendlinger Straße has become more elegant – and more expensive. If you prefer a more eclectic experience, wander into the adjacent side streets and lanes, where you can browse in the many stores to your heart's content. Be sure to visit the two Rococo jewels of the district – the Asamkirche (see p27 & p40) and the Asamhaus at Sendlinger Straße No. 34. Egid Quirin Asam acquired the building (unfortunately closed to the public) and adapted it to his own needs. One of the windows affords a direct view of the high altar in the Asamkirche. A surviving element of the medieval

---

**Odeon**

The former Odeon at Odeonsplatz 3 was a glamorous concert hall financed by Ludwig I with funds taken from the defence fund, despite resistance from his cabinet. Built by Klenze in 1828, the building was destroyed in World War II. After the war, only the walls surrounding the inner courtyard were rebuilt to full height. The complex now houses the Ministry of the Interior.

Chancellery overlooking the Hofgarten

town fortifications, the vine-covered Sendlinger Tor marks the end of the street. ✺ *Sendlinger Str. 34 & 62 • Map K5*

### 9 Residenz & Hofgarten

Munich's largest historic complex, the Residenz *(see p39)*, lies adjacent to the Hofgarten, with its lovely plantings and arcades. To the north, the garden is bounded by the Bavarian Chancellery (1989–93), which incorporates the ruins of an army museum. Remnants of a 16th-century wall and garden are visible behind glass on one side. ✺ *Map L3–L4 & M3–M4*

### 10 Odeonsplatz, Theatinerkirche & Feldherrnhalle

Princely palaces once occupied the area between Residenz and Theatinerkirche *(see p27 & p40)*. From 1800, old fortifications here were dismantled to make way for the Ludwigstraße, which ends or begins – depending upon your viewpoint – with Odeonsplatz and the Feldherrnhalle. Statues of the Bavarian field marshals Tilly and Wrede are displayed in the niches of the loggia. ✺ *Map L3*

Feldherrnhalle with a view of the Residenz

➜ For information on the Feldherrnhalle and the beer hall Putsch of 1923, visit **www.shoa.de/hitlerputsch.html**

## An Old Town Stroll

### Morning

🕐 From Marienplatz walk through the pedestrian zone to Mazaristr., which will lead you to the **Frauenkirche** *(see p79)*. Continue north along Maffeistr. to the **Fünf Höfe** complex *(see pp66–7)* and stroll along Theatinerstr. to Odeonsplatz with **Theatinerkirche** and **Feldherrnhalle**. Enjoy an excellent cup of coffee with a view of the Hofgarten at **Café Tambosi**. You will need half a day to tour the **Residenz**, but you can explore the palace's many inner courtyards on your own. Cross the Residenzstr. to Max-Joseph-Platz and the opera and exclusive shops along Maximilianstr. Return to Marienplatz via Dienerstr., **Alter Hof**, and **Platzl**, just in time for the clock's chiming (at 11am or noon). Walk along Tal to the **Weißes Bräuhaus** at No.10 for a traditional Bavarian lunch.

### Afternoon

After lunch, climb to the top of **St Peter's** *(see p26)* and take in the glorious view of the Old Town. Then walk through the Rindermarkt with its medieval Löwenturm and right into Sendlinger Str. Although **Asamhaus** (No. 34) is closed to the public, the interior of the late Baroque **Asamkirche** (No. 62) will take your breath away. Keep left to reach St-Jakobs-Platz, the Stadtmuseum, and the impressive Ohel Jakob Synagogue. Drop into the **Stadtcafé** for an afternoon break. From **Viktualienmarkt**, just around the corner, go east to **Isartor** and the Valentin-Musäum *(see p82)* or south to the **Gärtnerplatz** district with its many pubs and bars.

Left **Gärtnerplatztheater on Gärtnerplatz** Centre **Karlsplatz** Right **Künstlerhaus**

# 📇10 Best of the Rest

### 1 Isartor & Valentin-Musäum

Dedicated to the city's favourite son, Karl Valentin (1882–1948), the Valentin-Musäum is situated in the south tower of the Isartor (14th century). A small room in the tower furnished in turn-of-the-19th-century style houses a café. ◈ *Im Tal 50 • Map M5 • 11am–5pm Mon–Tue & Fri–Sat, 10am–6pm Sun • Adm • www.valentin-musaeum.de*

### 2 Episcopal Palace & Palais Portia

The Episcopal Palace is the last remaining city palace (1733–7) by Franxçois Cuvilliés. Nearby is the Baroque Palais Portia. ◈ *Kardinal-Faulhaber-Str. 7 bzw. 12 • Map L4 • Closed to the public*

### 3 Literaturhaus

On Salvatorplatz stands the Literaturhaus, a former Renaissance school now used for literary gatherings. The famed coffee house Oskar Maria, a café and restaurant, is on the ground floor. ◈ *Salvatorplatz 1 • Map L3 • www.literaturhaus-muenchen.de*

**Isartor & Valentin-Musäum**

### 4 Wittelsbacher Platz

Brienner Straße leads from Odeonsplatz to Wittelsbacher Platz, which features a palace and statue of Maximilian I. ◈ *Map L3*

### 5 Promenadeplatz

In the Middle Ages, this long narrow square served as a salt market. On the north side is the famous Hotel Bayerischer Hof and Montgelas palace. ◈ *Map K4–L4*

### 6 Künstlerhaus

Meeting place for artists at the turn of the 19th century, the Künstlerhaus (1892–1900) on Lenbachplatz features a Mövenpick café and restaurant on the ground floor. ◈ *Map K3–K4*

### 7 Justizpalast

Dominating Stachus, the high court was completed by Friedrich Thiersch in 1898. ◈ *Map J4*

### 8 Karlsplatz

Also known as Stachus, this square with large fountains just past Karlstor marks the end of the pedestrian zone. ◈ *Map J4*

### 9 Gärtnerplatz

Pretty 19th-century hexagonal square with Gärtnerplatztheater in Munich's gay district *(see p42)*. ◈ *Map L5*

### 10 Max-Joseph-Platz

Square with Königsbau and Nationaltheater developed to the south of the Residenz from 1820 onward. ◈ *Map L4*

*Oskar Maria (see p84) in the Literaturhaus sells cups and saucers with quotes, in German, from Oskar Maria Graf.*

Left **Schrannenhalle** Centre **Alois Dallmayr** Right **Hugendubel**

# 🔟 Downtown Shopping Tips

### Schrannenhalle
The old market hall was recently restored and rebuilt. The 150-year-old glass-and-iron construction now plays host to an eclectic range of craft wares. ◈ *Viktualienmarkt 15 • Map L5*

### L Beck am Rathauseck
Department store with a great selection of fashion, lingerie, stationery, and music. ◈ *Marienplatz 11 • Map L4*

### Hugendubel, Marienplatz
Largest store for books in the city. There are branches on Stachus, in the Fünf Höfe, and in several other locations. ◈ *Marienplatz • Map L4*

### Alois Dallmayr
Not to be missed is this former supplier to the royal court. Gourmet delicacies and coffee are on the ground floor and an excellent restaurant is on the second floor. ◈ *Dienerstr. 14–15 • Map L4*

### Böhmler im Tal
Small but very fine furniture store, with home decor and gift departments. ◈ *Im Tal 11 • Map L4*

### Fan Shops for FC Bayern & TSV München 1960 Football Clubs
Team shirts and more. Stores selling souvenirs of the two local football clubs are located near Hofbräuhaus; they are almost directly opposite one another. ◈ *Orlandostr. 1 & 8 (near Platzl) • Map M4*

### Elly Seidl
You thought Belgians made the best chocolates? Then you haven't tried Elly Seidl's chocolate confections. ◈ *Maffeistr. 1 & Am Kosttor 2 • Map L4–M4*

### Sport Scheck
Sporting goods department store *par excellence*, selling every conceivable sports-related item and clothing in 4,000 sq m (43,000 sq ft) of retail space. ◈ *Sendlinger Str. 6 • Map L4*

### Kokon
Asian furnishings and crafts, including some antiques, many plants, and books. Decorative household utensils and other items in the basement. ◈ *Lenbachplatz 3 • Map K3–K4*

### Loden Frey
Loden is more than merely a fabric – it's a way of life. Loden cloth is prized all over the world for its hard-wearing quality. Now it is used both for traditional Bavarian costume and international fashion. ◈ *Maffeistr. 7–9 • Map L4*

*For additional information on the shopping districts and new retail plazas such as Fünf Höfe and Maximilianhöfe See pp66–7*

Left **Bar Centrale** Centre **Oskar Maria** Right **Courtyard, Stadtcafé**

# Cafés & Bars

### Café Rischart
Scrumptious jelly doughnuts, delicious pastries and cakes are served in this traditional daytime café. ◈ *Marienplatz 18 • Map L4*

### Oskar Maria
A café with a literary ambience: food is served on designer dishes decorated with quotes by Oskar Maria Graf. The most sought-after tables are in the gallery or, in summer, on the patio. ◈ *Salvatorplatz 1 • Map L3*

### Schumann's Tagesbar
This offshoot of legendary Schumann's is in the Fünf Höfe. Hip and modern. Daytime hours only. ◈ *Maffeistr. 6 • Map L4*

### Stadtcafé im Stadtmuseum
Frequented by museum visitors and the fashionable crowd, this café has one of Munich's most beautiful courtyard beer gardens. Alcoholic beverages and light meals are served, as well as coffee and cake. Excellent lunch choice. ◈ *St-Jakobs-Platz 1 • Map L5*

### Tambosi
Italian coffee specialties on the Hofgarten: This is Munich's oldest café, founded by Luigi Tambosi from Trento in Italy *(see p61)*. ◈ *Odeonsplatz 18 • Map L3*

### Bar Centrale
This chic Italian day-and-evening bar is perfect for morning espresso or a delicious cocktail at night. ◈ *Ledererstr. 23 • Map L4*

### Café Streiflicht
Hangout for journalists and shoppers in the building housing the daily newspaper, *Süddeutsche Zeitung*. The café is named after the long-running column in the paper. Daytime hours only. ◈ *Sendlinger Str. 8 • Map K5*

### Café Kreutzkamm
Delicious cakes and desserts make this atmospheric patisserie and café one of the best places in town to drop in on when you get that craving for a little sweet something. ◈ *Maffeistr. 4 • Map E3*

### Pusser's
This classic piano bar with a long-standing tradition offers more than 200 cocktails. ◈ *Falkenturmstr. 9 (near Platzl) • Map M4*

### Barista
Basement bar in the Fünf Höfe complex. Friendly daytime spot for lunches and light meals. Cocktail bar at night. ◈ *Kardinal-Faulhaber-Str. 11 • Map L4*

*For more bars, cafés, restaurants, pubs, and beer gardens*
**See pp24–5, 50–51, 58–65**

**Price Categories**

For a three-course meal for one with a glass of wine or beer (or equivalent meal), taxes, and service charges.

| | |
|---|---|
| € | under €30 |
| €€ | €30–40 |
| €€€ | €40–50 |
| €€€€ | €50–60 |
| €€€€€ | over €60 |

Above **Weinhaus Neuner**

# 🔟 Restaurants

**1 Altes Hackerhaus**
Hearty Bavarian cuisine in a former brewery building dating from 1832. Pretty courtyard with fountain. ⌖ Sendlinger Str. 14 • Map K5 • (089) 260 50 26 • Open 10am–midnight daily • €

**2 Braunauer Hof**
Traditional Bavarian cuisine served in a lovely garden patio setting near the Isator. ⌖ Frauenstr. 42 • Map L5 • (089) 22 36 13 • Open 10am–midnight, closed Sun • €–€€

**3 Andechser am Dom**
Original Bavarian atmosphere next to the basilica. Andechser beer is served here. ⌖ Weinstr. 7 • Map L4 • (089) 29 84 81 • Open 10am–1am daily • €

**4 Hundskugel**
Munich's oldest restaurant (1440) offers Bavarian cuisine with an international flair. Lunch dishes are reasonably priced. ⌖ Hotterstr. 18 • Map K4 • (089) 26 42 72 • Open 10am–midnight daily • €

**5 Paulaner im Tal**
Traditional eatery serving Bavarian dishes in large portions, with budget-friendly lunch menus. ⌖ Im Tal 12 • Map L4 • (089) 219 94 00 • Open 10am–1am daily • Not wheelchair accessible • €

**6 Buffet Kull**
Fine French cuisine in a relaxed bistro atmosphere. ⌖ Marienstr. 4 • Map M5 • (089) 22 15 09 • Open 6pm–1am daily • €€–€€€

**7 Conviva im Blauen Haus**
Light, freshly prepared lunch and dinner menus are the attraction here. ⌖ Hildegardstr. 1 • Map M4 • (089) 23 336 977 • Open 11am–1am Mon–Sat, 5pm–1am Sun • €–€€

**8 Weinhaus Neuner**
Munich's oldest wine restaurant (1852) offers creative cuisine and good-value lunch menus. ⌖ Herzogspitalstr. 8 • Map K4 • (089) 260 39 54 • Open 11:30am–2pm & 5:30pm–midnight Mon–Sat • Not wheelchair accessible • €–€€

**9 Sakura Sushi Bar**
Authentic sushi restaurant with just about every conceivable combination, as well as cooked dishes. ⌖ Prannerstr. 1 • Map L4–L5 • (089) 22 801 472 • Open 11am–3pm & 5pm–1am daily • €–€€

**10 Prinz Myshkin**
Outstanding vegetarian cuisine has been served here for over 20 years. ⌖ Hackenstr. 2 • Map K5 • (089) 26 55 96 • Open 11am–midnight daily • €–€€

**Note:** Unless otherwise specified, all restaurants accept major credit cards and are wheelchair accessible.

85

Left **Bayerische Staatsbibliothek** Right **Art Nouveau decoration, Ainmillerstraße house**

# Schwabing & University District

ENCOMPASSING SCHWABING, MAXVORSTADT, *and the fringes of Lehel, this district covers the entire area lying to the left and right of Ludwigstraße and Leopoldstraße. At the beginning of the 19th century, the expansion of the Old Town north and west of Odeonsplatz began with the development of Maxvorstadt, then a suburb. This is where you will find numerous museums, the university, polytechnics, colleges, and libraries. Schwabing, an idyllic suburb to the north, became a well-known bohemian district inhabited by artists and intellectuals toward the end of the 19th century. Even today, you can still feel the flair of this interesting area, the centre of Art Nouveau in Germany.*

Logo of Alter Simpl, a local artists' pub

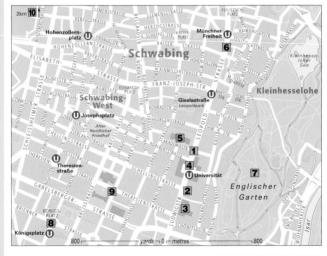

*For information on sights in Schwabing, visit www.muenchen.de*

### 1 Ludwigstraße & Siegestor

After the old town wall was pulled down, Ludwig I commissioned a monumental boulevard in the Italian Renaissance style – the Ludwigstraße (1815–50). This splendid street is bounded by the Feldherrnhalle to the south (see p81) and the Siegestor (Victory Gate) to the north. Based on the Arch of Constantine in Rome, the Siegestor is crowned by the figure of Bavaria riding a chariot drawn by four lions. Designed for victory parades in honour of the Bavarian army, the gate, damaged in World War II, has been restored. The 1958 inscription reads "Dedicated to victory, destroyed in war, an entreaty for peace." ✪ Map L3–M1

**Siegestor (Victory Gate)**

### 2 Ludwigskirche

Designed in the Italian Romanesque style, St Ludwig's Church (1829–43) is home to the second-largest church fresco in the world (see p40).

### 3 Bayerische Staatsbibliothek

The Bavarian State library is the second-largest municipal library in Germany, with more than 6 million volumes, 70,000 manuscripts, and valuable handwritten documents and prints. It has as its nucleus the 16th-century collections of Albrecht V and Wilhelm V. Today's building is the work of F von Gärtner (1832–43) in the style of Italian Renaissance palaces. ✪ Ludwigstr. 16 • Map M2 • www.bsb-muenchen.de

### 4 Ludwig-Maximilians-Universität

Ludwig I transferred the 15th-century university from Ingolstadt to Munich. The main assembly hall fronts on Geschwister-Scholl-Platz and is surrounded by faculty buildings. ✪ Geschwister-Scholl-Platz • Map M2 • www.uni-muenchen.de

### 5 Akademie der Bildenden Künste

The Academy of Fine Arts was built between 1808 and 1886 in the Italian Neo-Renaissance style. The list of students around 1900 is a who's who of modern art – Kandinsky, Klee, Kubin, Marc. ✪ Akademiestr. 2 • Map M1 • www.adbk.de

**Ludwig-Maximilians-Universität and fountain**

*Fragments of White Rose broadsheets are set into the courtyard of the main university building to commemorate this movement.*

*Walking Man, by J Borofsky, Leopoldstraße*

### 6 Leopoldstraße & Münchner Freiheit

Passing beneath the Siegestor, you will enter Schwabing and the district's principal promenade, the Leopoldstraße. Flanked by shops, pavement cafés, and fast-food outlets, the boulevard has lost some of its 1960s and '70s air, when a new generation of film-makers, students, and bohemians set the tone, but there are still some interesting pockets. One of the route's highlights is the Walking Man (1995), a 17-m- (55-ft-) high sculpture by Jonathan Borofsky at Ainmillerstraße 36. On the northern end of the Münchner Freiheit, in a café of the same name, tables are set out in summer beneath a larger-than-life statue of actor Helmut Fischer.

**Art Nouveau ornament**

### Jugendstil

Munich is the birthplace of Jugendstil, the German equivalent to Art Nouveau. In 1896, the first issue of the art journal *Jugend* (Youth) was published here, which gave the new movement – characterized by its decorative, linear style of undulating tendrils and plant stems – its name. Over 100 artists had joined forces to protest the "tyranny" of painter baron Franz von Lenbach.

Beautifully preserved Art Nouveau houses are to be found on several side streets off Leopoldstraße, notably Georgenstraße (Nos. 8–10) and Ainmillerstraße (Nos. 20, 22, 33, 34, 35, and 37). Take a detour onto Kaiserstraße for a glimpse of a pretty ensemble from the Foundation Period. Hohenzollernstraße and the section of Maxvorstadt bounded by Schelling-, Türken-, and Barerstraße, are packed with fun and eccentric boutiques (see p91). Nearly all side streets off the south side of Leopoldstraße lead to the Englischer Garten. Map F3–G2

### 7 Englischer Garten

Schwabing's "backyard" is Germany's largest urban park, offering a host of leisure opportunities – walks, beer gardens (Seehaus, Chinesischer Turm, Hirschau), jogging, boating, and – for the adventurous – surfing in the Eisbach, a small rocky stream with icy waters. The streets to the south of Münchner Freiheit lead almost directly to the Kleinhesseloher See and the Seehaus beer garden in the park (see p38).

### 8 Around Königsplatz

Munich owes its Royal Square, or Königsplatz, to Ludwig I and the vision of architect Leo von Klenze. The Propyläen (Doric) and the Glyptothek (Ionic), housing a magnificent sculpture collection, and the Antikensammlung (Corinthian), a collection of antiquities, were all built between 1816 and 1862 (see p36). Directly behind the Propyläen lies the Lenbachhaus (see p36); and one block farther down, the Paläontologische Museum (see p37). On the east side, the Königsplatz merges with the

88

*Examples of Art Nouveau can be seen in the Villa Stuck See p37.*
*For Art Nouveau tours, visit www.stattreisen-muenchen.de*

Leo von Klenze's Propyläen on Königsplatz

Karolinenplatz. The obelisk at its centre is a memorial to Bavarian soldiers who died in Napoleon's Russian campaign. During the Nazi era, Königsplatz was used for rallies and parades. Another relic of that era is today's Academy of Music and Theatre, then the so-called Führer-Bau, in which the infamous Munich Agreement was ratified in 1938. Today, this magnificent square is used for open-air events in summer.
◉ Map J2–J3

**9 Museum District**
Near Königsplatz on Barer Straße are the three large Pinakotheken (see pp14–17). Additional museums are planned for this district. ◉ Map K2–K3

**10 Olympiapark**
Completed for the 1972 Summer Olympic Games, this vast park and complex to the north has become Munich's main sports and amusement park complex (see pp18–19).

Pacelli-Palais – Art Nouveau Schwabing style

## A Day in the University District

### Morning

🕐 Begin your day in true bohemian style at the **Café Münchner Freiheit**. Afterward, stroll down **Leopoldstr.** and turn into Kaiserstr., with its pretty houses. Lenin lived at No. 46. At Kaiserplatz, follow Friedrichstr. to the corner of Ainmillerstr., with its Art Nouveau houses (Nos. 20–37). Continue along Friedrichstr. to Georgenstr. 8 and the **Palais Pacelli**, next door to the **Palais Bissing**. From here return to Leopoldstr. and the **Academy of Fine Arts** near the **Siegestor**. Walk to the **university** and cross the inner courtyard of the main building, which will bring you to the student district around Amalienstr., with its many cafés and restaurants. If you like French cuisine, try the excellent **Terrine** in Amalienpassage.

### Afternoon

Depending on weather and inclination, you can devote these hours to nature or culture. If you love the outdoors, take a walk in the **Englischer Garten** (see p70) and treat yourself to a beer-garden visit. Art lovers turn from Amalienstr. onto Schelling-str. and walk to the corner of Barer Str., which leads to the three **Pinako-theken** (see pp14– 17). Having feasted on art, take a break in one of the cafés (either at the Neue Pinakothek or the Pinakothek der Moderne). At the **Glyp-tothek** on Königsplatz, the cafe is also very pretty; if you prefer strolling, explore its sculpture collection and the adjacent **Antiken-sammlungen** (see p36).

Around Town – Schwabing & University District

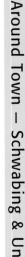

➤ In the 1920s, the artists Rilke, Gabriele Münter, Kandinsky, and Klee, to name but a few, lived in Ainmillerstraße.

Left **St Ursula's on Kaiserplatz** Centre **Market on Elisabethplatz** Right **BMW-Museum**

# 🔟 Best of the Rest

### 1 Erlöserkirche
This Protestant Art Nouveau church occupies the northern end of the Münchner Freiheit.
◈ *Münchner Freiheit • Map G2*

### 2 Wedekindplatz
Once the heart of rural Schwabing, the square on Feilitzschstraße is now somewhat rundown. It was the site, in 1962, of the local riots, known as "Schwabinger Krawalle" *(see p35)*. ◈ *Map G2*

### 3 Elisabethplatz
A piece of old Schwabing, this square is named after the Austrian empress. A market, the largest in the city after Viktualienmarkt, has been held here since 1903.
◈ *Map F3 • Market: 10am–6pm Mon–Fri, 7am–noon (sometimes later) Sat*

### 4 Alter Nördlicher Friedhof
There's nothing morbid about this park-like former cemetery that dates back to 1866 and has since been given over to the public for recreation and relaxation. Children play on the lawn among old tombstones while adults seek shade on the benches beneath the trees. ◈ *Zwischen Ziebland-, Arcis-, Adalbert- & Luisenstr. • Map F3*

### 5 Luitpoldpark
This park was created out of rubble from World War II. The restaurant in the Baroque Bamberger Haus features ornate dining rooms and a pretty terrace for outdoor dining during warm weather *(see p38)*.

### 6 Nikolaiplatz & Seidlvilla
At the corner of Sieges- and Josephstraße you'll come upon this tranquil square. The Seidlvilla (1905) houses a centre for readings, concerts, and exhibitions.
◈ *Map G2 • www.seidlvilla.de*

### 7 Kaiserplatz & Kaiserstraße
Russian Expressionist painter Vasili Kandinsky captured the silhouette of St Ursula's church on canvas. Ornate buildings from the Foundation Period flank the Kaiserstraße. In 1902, Lenin lived at No. 46. ◈ *Map F2*

### 8 BMW-Museum
The clover-leaf BMW-tower and the bowl-shaped museum at its base reopened in 2008 following major renovations. Exhibits focus on the history of automobile design and the old model BMWs on display will delight car buffs. ◈ *Petuelring 130 • Map E1 • Open 10am–10pm daily (to 8pm winter).*

### 9 Museum Reich der Kristalle
Next door to the Pinakothek der Moderne, this museum houses a large collection of crystals and minerals. ◈ *Map L2*

### 10 Museums on Prinzregentenstraße
The upper end of Prinzregentenstraße is home to the Haus der Kunst, the Bayerisches Nationalmuseum, and the Schack-Galerie *(see pp36–7)*.

*Elisabethplatz is also home to a small, cosy market café.*

Left **Buchhandlung Lehmkuhl** Right **Japanalia – new and old treasures from Japan**

# 🔟 Boutiques & Shops

**1 Buchhandlung Lehmkuhl**
This fine bookstore on Leopoldstraße has a distinguished inventory. Author readings are held here regularly. ◈ *Leopoldstr. 45 • Map G3*

**2 Natascha Müllerschön**
Understated and elegant designer fashion – and couture for those special occasions. Definitely worth a visit.
◈ *Franz-Joseph-Str. 21 • Map F3*

**3 Kandis & KandisMann**
Ann Dörr uses quality materials throughout her designer fashion collections. There are a few extravagant pieces too.
◈ *Hohenzollernstr. 29 • Map F2*

**4 Japanalia**
From Japanese teaware to crafts, kimonos, and furniture, Japanalia features a wide range of new, old, and antiquarian objects. ◈ *Herzogstr. 7 • Map F2*

**5 Autorenbuchhandlung**
As the name indicates, this bookshop was founded by authors who wanted to break free from the dictates of the book industry. Many author readings are held here. ◈ *Wilhelmstr. 41 • Map F2*

**6 Mashallah**
Oriental decor for the home. This subsidiary of Kokon *(see p83)* carries textiles and home accessories in an East-meets-West style. ◈ *Schellingstr. 52 • Map L2*

**7 Momento**
Arche shoes are among the popular labels sold here. Nearby, at Hohenzollernstr. 76, Fabri has last year's designs at a discount. ◈ *Hohenzollernstr. 40 • Map F2*

**8 Antiquariat Kitzinger**
A treasure chest located right next to the university's Institute of German Studies. Filled to the brim with books, the old-fashioned antiquarian shop is perfect for browsing. ◈ *Schellingstr. 25 • Map L2*

**9 Small Bag**
Take the time to rummage at Gisela Rädlein's shop. You will find the trendy and the antique, the bizarre and the practical, from delicate silver jewellery to old clocks and busts. ◈ *Herzogstr. 11 • Map F2*

**10 Silver & More**
Silver & More is one of the city's best boutiques for silver jewellery, lamps, *objets d'art*, and furnishings.
◈ *Türkenstr. 69 • Map L1*

*For details on Munich's principal shopping districts See pp66–7*

Left **Café Münchner Freiheit with sculpture** Centre **Dining area at Schmock** Right **Café Florian**

# 🔟 Cafés, Bistros & Bars

### 1 Café Münchner Freiheit
Multi-level café with large terrace on the north side of Münchner Freiheit. A larger-than-life statue of actor Helmut Fischer overlooks the outdoor tables. Perfect for lunch. ✎ *Münchner Freiheit • Map G2*

### 2 Café Reitschule
Located at the edge of the Englischer Garten, this traditional café boasts three patios, a beer garden, and a conservatory. From the inside, patrons have a view into the riding school. A great spot for a quick lunch. ✎ *Königinstr. 34 • Map N1*

### 3 Café Florian
Espresso bar with a small restaurant featuring Italian cuisine. In the evening, you can wander downstairs to the Coccodrillo cocktail bar, located in the basement. Pretty terrace. ✎ *Hohenzollernstr. 11 • Map F2*

### 4 Amaliencafé
Both students from the nearby university and the business crowd frequent this café. Ideal for a quick cappuccino or for a snack at lunch. ✎ *Amalienstr. 37 • Map L2*

### 5 Café an der Uni (Cadu)
Attractive small café hidden behind a wall on Ludwigsstraße. Excellent for a coffee break during a stroll through this area of the university district. ✎ *Ludwigstr. 24 • Map M2*

### 6 Terrine
This Art Nouveau bistro is an offshoot of Tantris, meaning fine French cuisine lunch to dinner. ✎ *Amalienstr. 89 (Passage) • Map L1*

### 7 Tresznjewski
Located near the three Pinakotheken, this café-bistro offers breakfast, coffee, lunch, and dinner, as well as cocktails, to patrons from all walks of life. ✎ *Theresienstr. 72 • Map K2 –L2*

### 8 Vorstadt-Café
There's something here for all palates, from "Love Breakfast" to lunch menus to Thai-Italian fusion at night. ✎ *Türkenstr. 83 • Map L1*

### 9 Schmock
Art Nouveau bar; its restaurant has a traditional Jewish (part kosher) menu. Hip clientele. ✎ *Augustenstr. 52 • Map J2*

### 10 Atzinger
The 1970s are alive and well at this student bar, which is usually packed with a colourful crowd. ✎ *Schellingstr. 9 • Map L2*

For more bars and cafés, gay and lesbian venues, fine restaurants, Bavarian pubs, and beer gardens See pp24–5, 50–51, 58–65

**Price Categories**

For a three-course meal for one with a glass of wine or beer (or equivalent meal), taxes, and service charges.

| | |
|---|---|
| € | under €30 |
| €€ | €30–40 |
| €€€ | €40–50 |
| €€€€ | €50–60 |
| €€€€€ | over €60 |

Max-Emanuel-Brauerei pub and beer garden

# 🔟 Restaurants

### Tantris
**1** Munich's top restaurant is the Mount Olympus of haute cuisine; the prices reflect this *(see p64)*.

### La Bouille
**2** French cuisine perfected by the Werneckhof team for over 20 years – now in a new location with a patio. ◈ *Neureutherstr. 15 • Map K1 • (089) 39 99 36 • Open noon–3pm & 7pm–midnight Mon–Fri, 7pm–midnight Sat, 6:30–11pm Sun • €€–€€€*

### Osteria Italiana
**3** The city's oldest Italian restaurant is tranquil and understated. Wonderful small courtyard. ◈ *Schellingstr. 62 • Map K1 • (089) 272 07 17 • Open noon–2:30pm & 6:30–11pm Mon–Sat • €€–€€€*

### Le Sud
**4** Good French restaurant with lots of ambience and a romantic patio. ◈ *Bismarckstr. 21 • Map F2 • (089) 33 088 738 • Open 6pm–1am daily • €–€€*

### Arabesk
**5** Arabian-Lebanese cuisine at its best. Relax with a water pipe after dinner, or sit back and enjoy the belly dancers on weekends. ◈ *Kaulbachstr. 86 • Map M1 • (089) 33 37 38 • Open noon–3pm Mon–Fri, 6pm–1am daily • €€*

### Mykonos
**6** Feel-good Greek restaurant serving up ambitious menus that far surpass the standard fare. ◈ *Kaiserstr. 55 • Map F2 • (089) 33 53 80 • Open 11:30am–1am daily • €€*

### Max-Emanuel-Brauerei
**7** This traditional pub dating to around 1800 serves up standard Bavarian fare. *Prix fixe* lunch menu. Beautiful shaded beer garden and legendary Weiße Feste parties during carnival. ◈ *Adalbertstr. 33 • Map L1 • (089) 271 51 58 • Open 11am–1am daily • €–€€*

### Osterwaldgarten
**8** Family-oriented beer garden with a restaurant in the Englischer Garten offering Bavarian cuisine. Usually crowded. ◈ *Keferstr. 12 • Map G2 • (089) 38 405 040 • Open 11am–1am daily • €*

### Kun-Tuk
**9** Swirling red dragons and lanterns surround you in this upscale Thai eatery. ◈ *Amalienstr. 81 • Map L2 • (089) 28 37 00 • Open 11:30am–5pm, 6pm–1am Mon–Fri; 6pm–1am Sat, Sun • €–€€*

### Casa de Tapas
**10** Fabulous Mediterranean atmosphere and tasty tapas. ◈ *Bauerstr. 2 • Map F2 • (089) 27 31 22 88 • Open 4pm–1am daily • €*

**Note:** Unless otherwise specified, restaurants accept all major credit cards. Many have limited or no wheelchair access.

Left **Müller'sches Volksbad** Centre **Maximilian bridge** Right **Gasteig**

# Along the Isar River

FOUR DISTINCT NEIGHBOURHOODS *flank the east bank of the Isar: Bogenhausen, Haidhausen, Au, and Giesing. Bogenhausen is an exclusive district studded with villas and inhabited by many prominent citizens; lively Haidhausen has the best and most exten-sive bar scene; parts of Au and Giesing, on the other hand, still have a special working-class charm. All were on the "other side" of the Isar from the Old Town and long retained their village character. To the west of the Isar, on the left bank, lie the Englischer Garten, Lehel with its beautiful historic buildings, and the Glockenbach quarter, Munich's gay village. Most sights are found along the right bank, such as Müller'sches Volksbad, Villa Stuck, and – on an island in the river – the Deutsches Museum.*

**Friedensengel**

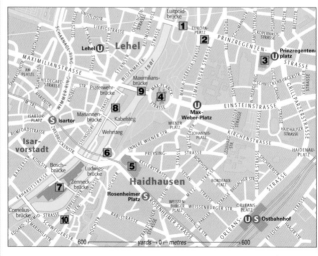

Previous pages **Thai shrine, Westpark**

### 1 Friedensengel

Soaring high above the banks of the Isar, the Friedensengel (Angel of Peace, 1896–99) commemorates the Franco-Prussian war of 1870–71. Based on the Greek goddess Nike, this gilded figure stands 6 m (20 ft) tall. At its foot, two sweeping flights of stairs lead down from the escarpment to a terraced park with fountains on the lower end of Prinzregentenstraße. ◈ *Prinzregentenstr.* • *Map P3*

**Maximilianeum – seat of the Bavarian parliament**

### 2 Museum Villa Stuck

Not far from the Friedensengel is the villa (1897–98) of painter Franz von Stuck, in itself a work of art. A miller's son, Stuck quickly rose to fame and was instrumental in the creation of a Munich style of Art Nouveau – Jugendstil *(see p88)*. The villa has served as a museum since 1968. On view are Stuck's private rooms, a permanent Art Nouveau collection, and changing exhibitions in the studio wing *(see p37)*.

*Die Sünde,* Villa Stuck

### 3 Prinzregententheater

This theatre is one of several monumental buildings on this stretch of Prinzregentenstraße in Bogenhausen *(see p43)*. It was headed by August Everding, whose legacy to the city includes the Bayerische Theaterakademie, a training ground for young stage talents. Next door is Prinzregentenbad, a public bath. Across the street is Feinkost Käfer, a gourmet-food shop. ◈ *Prinzregentenplatz 12* • *Map H4*

### 4 Maximilianeum

This building in Haidhausen by Friedrich Bürklein (1857–74), on the high banks of the Isar, marks the end of Maximilianstraße. The seat of the Bavarian parliament since 1949, Maximilian II built this massive structure as a school for gifted students from poor backgrounds. The school is now housed in the rear building. ◈ *Max-Planck-Str. 1* • *Map P4–P5*

### 5 Gasteig

The site of the former Bürgerspital hospital, and Bürgerbräukeller, where Georg Elser failed in 1939 to assassinate Hitler, it was transformed into the redbrick Gasteig cultural centre between 1978 and 1985. Its facilities include the Munich Philharmonic, the Carl Orff concert hall, the headquarters of the adult education centre (Volkshochschule), and the municipal library. ◈ *Rosenheimer Str. 5* • *Map N6*

**Prinzregententheater**

→ *A plaque mounted on Gasteig commemorates Georg Elser's attempt to assassinate Hitler in 1939.*

**Müller'sches Volksbad**

### 6 Müller'sches Volksbad

Named after Karl Müller – a private citizen who financed the project – this Art Nouveau bathing temple was built from 1897 to 1901 and is based on a design by Carl Hocheder. It was the first public pool in the city and is still one of the most beautiful today. The pool was divided into a men's and a women's area: the men's pool has a barrel vault, the women's a large cupola. It is worth going for a swim just to see the interior and the facilities – which include therapeutic baths and a Roman steam room. Afterwards, drop by Café im Volksbad. ◎ Map N5

### Glasscherben District

Haidhausen used to lie beyond the city boundaries. A poor, rural village, it was referred to as a "Glasscherbenviertel" or "broken glass district." After 1871, French reparation payments launched development in this area, which explains the names of streets in the district – such as Pariser Str., Sedanstr., Bordeau-platz, and Metzstaße.

### 7 Deutsches Museum

Looking diagonally across from the Müller'sche Volksbad, the island seen in the Isar is home to the largest museum of technology in the world. Eighty per cent of the Deutsches Museum was destroyed in World War II; however, the doors to the collection were open again by 1948. Plan at least a full day to see the principal exhibits (see pp8–11).

### 8 Praterinsel & Alpine Museum

Immediately adjacent to the museum island are two other small islands, Praterinsel and Kalkinsel. The Alpine Museum, run by the German Alpine Association, is located on Praterinsel. It documents the history of mountaineering and features special exhibitions throughout the year. A teaching garden displays the various types of rock found in the Alpine regions. Old factories on Praterinsel – in the former Riemerschmid distillery – have been converted into a cultural centre with artists' studios. The ensemble is home to ongoing exhibitions and special events, such as the Comicfest. Tango fans gather in the courtyard on summer nights to enjoy this most sensual of dances. ◎ Map N5

### 9 Isar Bridges

From the bridges that cross the Isar you can enjoy wonderful views of the river and the cityscape. One of the most historically important is the Ludwigsbrücke, between Deutsches Museum and Müller'sches Volksbad. Henry the Lion ordered that the bridge, built in 1157–58 by the Bishop of Freising, be demolished (it was located near today's

For details on the fascinating history of the Praterinsel and its monkish origins, visit www.praterinsel.de

Equipment, c. 1900, Alpine Museum

Oberföhring).This meant the salt road was diverted – effectively usurping lucrative customs fees from the bishopric. Henry then ordered a new bridge built farther to the south – where today's Ludwigsbrücke stands. The new bridge, by which Benedictine monks had settled, was quickly surrounded by a thriving settlement later called München (literally, "near the monks").
◎ Map M6–N6

## 10 Auer-Mühlbach District & Valentin-Haus

In the past, several small creeks ran through Munich, many of which were later filled in with concrete. One of the surviving creeks is the Auer Mühlbach, which is most visible east of the Isar. Just south of Ludwigsbrücke, this creek has formed a small island that is home to a restored ensemble of historic houses. Karl Valentin's birthplace is nearby at Zeppelinstraße 41. The building is not open to the public. ◎ Map N6

Cultural centre, Praterinsel

## A Day on the Isar

### Morning

Setting off from the **Müller'sche Volksbad** after coffee or breakfast at **Café im Volksbad**, turn left at the baths along the Isar to the to the footbridge, which leads to **Praterinsel**. Walk through the teaching garden of the **Alpine Museum** (no entrance fee) and then across the island – making a brief stop at the **cultural centre** – until you reach Maximiliansbrücke, which will take you directly to the **Maximilianeum**. Pass the monument and turn right onto Sckellstr. Follow this street to Wiener Platz, its market stalls, and the **Hofbräukeller**. A narrow lane – An der Kreppe – runs from Wiener Platz to several of the historic inns found in the Glasscherben district. The **Hofbräukeller** offers reasonably priced food and a beer garden in summer.

### Afternoon

Return to Sckellstr., cross Einsteinstr., and walk along Maria-Theresia-Str., flanked by beautiful Foundation Period and Art Nouveau houses. The **Maximilian-Anlagen** is a public park, and perfect for a spot of ambling. Regardless of the route you take, all paths will eventually lead you to the **Friedensengel**. Continue along for a few minutes until you reach **Villa Stuck**, the Art Nouveau museum *par excellence*. For a coffee break, try **Wiener's** (Ismaninger Str. 71a), close to the No. 18 tram stop. Take the tram back to the city centre (Karlsplatz). The ride will take you past some of the most beautiful spots in Munich.

Some 64 beer cellars were located along the Isar between Wiener Platz and Gasteig in the 1860s when the area was a brewery district.

99

Left **Nikolaikirche** Centre **Hofbräukeller** Right **Arched portal of Annakirche**

# Best of the Rest

### An der Kreppe
Restored inns and hostels for day-labourers and brick workers give this corner of Haidhausen a village-like character. ◈ *An der Kreppe (Wiener Platz)* • *Map P5*

### Hofbräukeller
The little brother of the Hofbräuhaus, also serving the famous brew. Set, since 1892, in a neo-Renaissance building, with a popular beer garden *(see p25)*. ◈ *Wiener Platz* • *Map P5* • *www.hofbraeukeller.de*

### Nikolaikirche
This small church, first mentioned in historical records in 1313, is set on the banks of the Isar. The cloister is a mirror image of that at Altötting. ◈ *Innere Wiener Str. 1* • *Map N5*

### Lehel
The Lehel district, part of which is located in the Old Town, boasts many buildings from the Foundation Period. The streets around Thierschplatz are worth a stroll. ◈ *Map M5*

### Sankt Lukas
St Luke's is known for its choral concerts *(see p41)*. ◈ *Mariannenplatz 3* • *Map N5*

### Monastery Church St Anna
This Rococo jewel in the Lehel district was built by Johann Michael Fischer, with ornamentation by the Asam brothers. ◈ *St-Anna-Platz 21* • *Map M4*

### Annakirche (St Anna)
A neo-Romanesque parish church, St Anna (1892) is the result of an architecture competition. ◈ *St-Anna-Platz 5* • *Map N4*

### Upper Maximilianstraße & Maxmonument
The stretch between the old ring road (Altstadtring) and the Maximilianeum is flanked by ornate public buildings, including the Völkerkundemuseum and the Parliament of Upper Bavaria. A monument to Maximilian II stands at the centre of a roundabout. ◈ *Map M4–N4*

### Staatliches Museum für Völkerkunde
Dating from 1859–65, this stately building in the style of the Maximilian era has been home to the Völkerkundemuseum (museum of ethnology) since 1926. The collection comprises over 300,000 objects from cultures beyond Europe *(see p37)*.

### Museums on Prinzregentenstraße
The upper stretch of Prinzregentenstraße is home to the Haus der Kunst, the National Gallery (Nationalmuseum), and the Schack Galerie *(see pp36–7)*.

**Monument to Maximilian II**

*City bus no. 100 runs along the Prinzregentenstraße and stops at several museums.*

Left **Entrance to Feinkost Käfer** Centre **Eltje Rick** Right **Porzellan & Pinselstrich**

# 🏠10 Shops & Markets

## 1 Feinkost Käfer
This delicatessen owned and operated by catering tsar Gerd Käfer is located in upscale Bogenhausen. The city's prominent citizens rub shoulders here as they shop and sample the delicacies.
🔊 *Prinzregentenstr. 73 • Map H4*

## 2 grünermarkt
A massive store selling all kinds of organic products, from "bio-snacks" to environmentally friendly cosmetics and gifts.
🔊 *Weißenburgerstr. 5 • Map P6*

## 3 Markt am Wiener Platz
Permanent kiosks on Wiener Platz are open daily and complemented by stalls set up by travelling vendors. The pretty town square is a perfect spot for a quick coffee break. 🔊 *Wiener Platz • Map P5*

## 4 Teeladen
A tea specialist for the past 20 years, Teeladen sells more than 300 varieties from the best tea gardens in the world.
🔊 *Pariser Str. 27 • Map P6*

## 5 Eltje Rick
Made-to-measure and ready-to-wear fashion by a Munich designer known for unusual cuts and fabrics. 🔊 *Steinstr. 57 • Map P6*

## 6 Candle-Light
Large selection of candles and wonderful gifts. If you love *feng shui*, this is the place for you. 🔊 *Metzstr. 13 • Map P6*

## 7 Porzellan & Pinselstrich
Wonderful stock of fired, unglazed porcelain. Try your hand at painting and decorating one, and take home a very special souvenir. 🔊 *Sedanstr. 18 • Map P6*
• *www.porzellanundpinselstrich.de*

## 8 Esoterischer Buchladen
This esoteric bookshop carries books, tarot cards, salt crystals from the Himalayas, aromatic oils, and other accessories. 🔊 *Sedanstr. 29 • Map P6*

## 9 Liquid
Liquids of all kinds, including fine oils and vinegars from the barrel, open liqueurs, brandy, fine wines, along with brandy tumblers, espresso cups, and accessories. 🔊 *Pariser Str. 36 • Map P6*

## 10 Weißenburger Straße
Haidhausen's main shopping street bustles with shoe and eyewear shops, a variety of boutiques, greengrocers, and supermarkets. There is also a department store nearby, on Ostbahnhof. 🔊 *Map P6*

➤ *For more details on shopping districts* See pp66–7

Left **Café im Volksbad** Right **Café Wiener Platz**

# Cafés & Bars in Haidhausen

### 1 Café im Hinterhof
Hidden in a rear courtyard, this is a café with Art Nouveau atmosphere. Large breakfast menu and generous selection of newspapers make for a relaxing morning. Small meals at lunchtime. ⊗ *Sedanstr. 29 • Map P6*

### 2 Café Wiener Platz
Hip meeting place with a large breakfast selection available well into the night. Patio tables in summer. ⊗ *Innere Wiener Str. 48 • Map P5*

### 3 Café Mondial
Inexpensive lunch menu and delicious desserts, such as Venetian doughnuts. You can also enjoy afternoon coffee on the patio, or cocktails at night. ⊗ *Pariser Str. 34 • Map P6*

### 4 Café Fortuna
Intimate, Italian-style neighbourhood café with a few outdoor tables. Delicious hot chocolate. ⊗ *Sedanstr. 18 • Map P6*

### 5 Café im Volksbad
Attractive Art Nouveau café with a glass roof in Müller'sches Volksbad. Tables are set out in the forecourt in summer. Italian lunch and dinner menu. ⊗ *Rosenheimer Str. 1 • Map N5*

### 6 Eiscafé Venezia
A real old-timer – one of the gradually disappearing Italian ice cream parlours with a 1970s air, and a patio. ⊗ *Pariser Platz • Map P6*

### 7 Maria Passagne
This salon bar opens fairly late in the evening. Small and cosy, it serves exclusively sushi. Be sure to reserve a table (089-48 61 67); the doorman won't admit any more patrons once all the tables are taken. ⊗ *Steinstr. 42 • Map P6*

### 8 Teatro
Bar and dining room with a large selection of tapas at the long counter. The comfortable atmosphere includes Mediterranean scenes projected onto the walls. ⊗ *Balanstr. 23 • Map G6*

### 9 Lissabon Bar
Unpretentious neighbourhood bar reminiscent of those in Portugal. Large portions (mostly fish), excellent selection of port, and, of course, cocktails. ⊗ *Breisacher Str. 22 • Map H5*

### 10 Julep's
Rustic American bar with dining room (Tex-Mex and American dishes). Bartenders mix some 200 different cocktails *(see p60).*

*For more bars and cafés, gay and lesbian venues, fine restaurants, and Bavarian pubs and beer gardens See pp24–5, 50–51, 58–65.*

**Price Categories**

For a three-course meal for one with a glass of wine or beer (or equivalent meal), taxes, and service charges.

| | |
|---|---|
| € | under €30 |
| €€ | €30–40 |
| €€€ | €40–50 |
| €€€€ | €50–60 |
| €€€€€ | over €60 |

Left **Cô-Dô** Right **Rue des Halles**

# 🔟 Restaurants in Haidhausen

### 1 Le Faubourg
Bistro atmosphere with small tables and the daily menu listed on a blackboard. Excellent wine selection and a few patio tables. ◈ *Kirchenstr. 5 (Johannisplatz) • Map P5 • (089) 47 55 33 • Open 6:30pm–1am; closed Sun • €€–€€€*

### 2 Rue des Halles
Oldest French establishment in the French quarter. The plain and unpretentious interior conveys the air of a bistro in the market halls of Paris. Creative French cuisine *(see p65)*.

### 3 Le Bousquérey
Small, intimate restaurant specializing in French cuisine, known for its fish dishes. ◈ *Rablstr. 37 • Map G5 • (089) 48 84 55 • Open 6pm–11:30pm daily • €€–€€€*

### 4 Cô-Dô
Possibly the best Far Eastern food in the city – specialties from the Imperial cuisine of old Vietnam. Tip for vegetarians: try the tofu pâté or soybean quark wrapped in aromatic leaves. ◈ *Lothringer Str. 7 • Map G6 • (089) 448 57 97 • Open 6pm–11:30pm daily • No credit cards • €*

### 5 Zum Kloster
Trendy pub offering good home-made dishes. It feels rural here and in summer there are seats outside under the trees. ◈ *Preysingstr. 77 • Map P5 • (089) 447 05 64 • Open 10am–1am daily • €*

### 6 Vinaiolo
Fine Italian cuisine paired with excellent wines. ◈ *Steinstr. 42 • Map P6 • (089) 48 950 356 • Open noon–3pm & 6:30pm–1am Tue–Sun, 6:30pm–1am Mon • €€–€€€*

### 7 Unions-Bräu Haidhausen
Authentic Bavarian inn with its own brewery. ◈ *Einsteinstr. 42 • Map P5 • (089) 47 76 77 • Open 11am–11:30pm Mon–Sat, 10am–4pm Sun • €*

### 8 Il Cigno
Inexpensive but good Italian eatery with a patio. ◈ *Wörthstr. 39 • Map P6 • (089) 448 55 89 • Open 11:30am–11:30pm daily • €*

### 9 Hofbräukeller
Traditional-style pub serving Bavarian cuisine with a beer garden set among chestnut trees *(see p25 & p100)*.

### 10 Bella Italia
Pizzas to satisfy those with supersized cravings, plus a patio. ◈ *Weißenburger Str. 2 • Map P6 • (089) 48 61 79 • Open 11am–midnight daily • No credit cards • €*

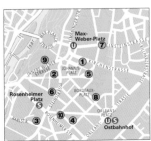

**Note:** *Unless otherwise indicated, all restaurants accept major credit cards. Many have limited or no wheelchair access.*

103

Left **Tierpark Hellabrunn** Centre **Ceiling fresco, Schloss Nymphenburg** Right **Castle Grünwald**

# South & West

$S$OUTH AND WEST OF THE CENTRE, *Munich has a suburban and exclusive residential character, with the exception of the Westend and Neuhausen districts. The latter, which lies to the north, includes Rotkreuzplatz – a square surrounded by beautiful tree-lined streets and bordered by late-19th-century buildings. In recent years, a vibrant bar and restaurant scene has evolved here. Multicultural Westend is far more colourful, and some sections, especially near the Alte Messe, are becoming trendy. Affluent residential areas lie in the south, in Harlaching and above all in Grünwald, where tram No. 25 offers a scenic ride through forests studded with impressive villas. Munich's Isar has been reclaimed in the south and once again follows its natural, meandering route. Beautiful paths beckon walkers alongside the river. You will find Munich's Isar beach, Flaucher, next to the popular Flaucher beer garden, and Tierpark Hellabrunn, the city's superb zoo.*

Chapel, Blutenburg

## 🔟 Sights

1. Bavaria
2. Alte Messe & Verkehrszentrum
3. Westend
4. Westpark
5. Neuhausen
6. Schloss Nymphenburg & Schlosspark
7. Botanischer Garten
8. Schloss Blutenburg
9. Tierpark Hellabrunn
10. Grünwald

*For information on the transportation museum, visit* **www.deutsches-museum.de**

### Bavaria

Munich's tallest "female," Bavaria stands 18.5 m (59 ft) high. She holds an oak wreath in her hand, while a lion, Bavaria's heraldic beast, lies at her feet. Designed by Ludwig Schwanthaler and cast by Ferdinand von Miller, the statue (1840–50) was a masterpiece of technological achievement at the time, incorporating an observation platform in the head *(see p23)*. Klenze's Ruhmeshalle, with busts honouring famous Bavarians, stands behind the colossal statue.
*Theresienhöhe 16 • Map D5 • Open Apr–mid-Oct: 9am–6pm daily (during Oktoberfest to 8pm) • Adm*

### Alte Messe & Verkehrszentrum

Since the trade fair moved to Riem, the site of the Alte Messe (old fair) on Schwanthalerhöhe has been imaginatively developed. Elegant residences have been built on the former fairgrounds, and many of the fomer exhibition halls have been converted to cultural uses. The Verkehrszentrum, Deutsches Museum's excellent branch museum of transport, is housed here in three halls *(see p11)*. Bavariapark, which lies nearby, was created by Ludwig I *(see p39)*.

Asian garden in Westpark

### Westend

The many Turkish, Greek, and other ethnic stores and bars contribute greatly to the appeal of this area, which – at 40 per cent – has the largest foreign population in the city, fertile ground for the vibrant arts scene emerging here. More and more galleries and advertising agencies are setting up shop here every year. *Map D5*

### Westpark

A smaller, west-end version of the Englischer Garten, Westpark was created for the fourth International Garden Show in 1983 and offers landscaped lawns and gardens, as well as picnic and barbecue facilities. Especially pretty is the Asian section with its Japanese garden, Thai pagoda, and other highlights *(see p38)*.

Ruhmeshalle with Statue of Bavaria, Theresienwiese, in the foreground

*Westpark exemplifies the city's dedication to environmental protection: many rare species thrive in its humid biotopes.*

### Palmenhaus

An ideal sanctuary on a rainy day, this historic glass-and-iron greenhouse in the Botanical Gardens makes you feel as though you have been transported to a tropical paradise. Tall, slender palm trees overgrown with deep green vines create a jungle-like atmosphere.

### Neuhausen

Rotkreuzplatz is the centre of this, Munich's second-largest urban district. Countless bars and restaurants line the streets surrounding the square. The many old but well-preserved low-rise apartment buildings found here make this a popular residential area. The adjacent Nymphenburg is more exclusive, with its large single-family homes and villas. Expansive green zones – the Botanical Gardens, Nymphenburg Park, and the Hirschgarten, which has the city's largest beer garden – enhance the quality of life in this district. ✎ Map C3–D3

Porcelain parrot, Nymphenburg

### Schloss Nymphenburg & Schlosspark

When Adelaide of Savoy gave birth to the heir to the throne, Max Emanuel, in 1663, her husband, Elector Ferdinand, celebrated the event both by donating funds to build the Theatinerkirche (see p40) but also by presenting his wife with their future summer residence at Schloss Nymphenburg. Built by the architect Barelli from 1664 onward, the Schloss ensemble underwent many expansions – in the end, the main building achieved an impressive length of 650 m (2,150 ft). The park, originally a small decorative garden, evolved into a large landscaped park, interspersed with several pavilions: Badenburg, Pagodenburg, Amalienburg, and Magdalenenklause. For a special coffee break, visit the Schlosscafé in the exotic Palmenhaus (see pp12–13).

### Botanischer Garten

The Botanischer Garten (Botanical Gardens) were laid out beside Nymphenburg Park at the start of the 20th century. Over 14,000 plant species are cultivated here. Highlights include the Alpinum, an Alpine rock garden, the Arboretum, a spectacular display of rhododendron blossoms, the fern glen, and the greenhouses (see p38).

### Schloss Blutenburg

A path with lovely views leads from Nymphenburg Park to Schloss Blutenburg. Situated amid meadows and fields, this former royal hunting lodge, built between 1435 and 1439 on an island in the Würm River by Duke Albrecht III, is rural in character.

Interior, Schloss Nymphenburg

For details on a walk through the park at Nymphenburg and a cycling tour to Schloss Blutenburg See pp70–71

**Chapel, Schloss Blutenburg**

A late Gothic chapel was added in 1488. Today, Blutenburg houses the Internationale Jugendbibliothek. The castle café is perfect for a coffee break. ◈ Map A2

**Tierpark Hellabrunn**
When Munich's Tierpark was founded in 1911, it was the first zoo in the world that arranged animal enclosures and pavilions according to continents and geographic origins. Highlights include a large aviary, a jungle tent with lions and tigers, and a new tropical forest and aquarium pavilion, where monkeys, snakes, and fish inhabit a jungle and coral-reef habitat. ◈ Tierparkstr. 30 • Map E6
• Open in summer 8am–6pm daily, in winter 9am–5pm daily • Adm
• www.tierparkhellabrunn.de

**Grünwald**
This exclusive villa district lies to the south of the city. The 13th-century Castle Grünwald houses an archaeological collection that includes Roman artifacts. Geiselgasteig and Bavaria-Filmstadt are also located in this district (see p54). ◈ Map S2

## A Day in Westend

### Morning

Begin at the **Bavaria** (see p105). Climb up to the statue's head and enjoy the glorious view across Theresienwiese. Behind the Ruhmeshalle is the attractive **Bavariapark**. Walk through to its northern end and visit the impressive collection of the **Verkehrszentrum** (see p11), a branch museum of the Deutsches Museum, housed in three historic fair halls. Cross Heimeranstr. and follow Ganghoferstr. until it intersects with Tulbeckstr. Here, **Kao Kao** is a good choice for a coffee break (Tulbeckstr. 9). Stroll and browse in the multicultural district from Tulbeckstr. to Ganghoferstr., and then on to Gollierstr., which ends at Gollierplatz. For lunch, try **Rüen Thai** (Kazmairstr. 58), one of the best Thai restaurants in the city.

### Afternoon

Ganghoferstr. and Pfeuferstr. will take you over a S-Bahn track bridge into the eastern section of **Westpark**. Stroll westward, past the mysterious "floating" granite sphere, to the marshland ponds and try to spot the frogs. Walking across a bridge over a major city motorway takes you into the western section of the park and its Thai pagoda, Japanese garden, rose garden with over 2,000 roses, and a manmade lake complete with stage at its centre for open-air music, theatre, and film in summer. For coffee or a pint of beer, stop in at the **See-Café** or the restaurant set in the tranquil surroundings of the rose garden.

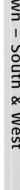

For more information on the Botanical Gardens, visit
**www.botanik.biologie.uni-muenchen.de**

Around Town – South & West

Left **Flaucher** Centre **Bavaria Filmstadt** Right **Großhesseloher Bridge**

# 🔟 Best of the Rest

### 1 Flaucher
Munich's Isar beach *par excellence*. Every summer, sun worshippers flock to the gravel banks along the southern Isar, and many stop in at the pretty beer garden of the same name *(see p24)*.

### 2 Floßlände
River rafts full of merry revellers land here in summer. Downstream, the Isar is being restored to its natural state as gravel islands, canal walls, and artificial embankments are removed. The waves and rapids at the Floßlände are a paradise for surfers, and an alternative to the frigid Eisbach near the Haus der Kunst. Nearby is the Floßlände pub and beer garden (Zentralländstraße 30), and the Asam-Schlössl.

### 3 Asam-Schlössl
Cosmas Damian Asam acquired this 17th-century building in 1724 and decorated the façade with frescoes. The small castle houses a restaurant with a beautiful garden. ◎ *Maria-Einsiedel-Str. 45*

### 4 South Isar Banks & Großhesseloher Bridge
Wonderful paths along the right banks of the Isar River are ideal for walking. To the south, the Großhesseloher Bridge leads across the Isar to the Waldwirtschaft pub and beer garden (Großhesselohe, Georg-Kalb-Straße 3). Farther along the river is a pub in the old Isartal train station (Großhesselohe, Kreuzeckstr. 23).

### 5 Marienklause
In 1865 Martin Achleiter, the lock-keeper at Auer-Mühlbach, built this timber chapel to give thanks for having survived floods and falling rocks in the gorge.

### 6 Gutshof Menterschwaige
This 1803 manor house with beer garden – once the love nest of Lola Montez and Ludwig I – is an ideal destination at the end of a day's excursion. ◎ *München-Harlaching, Menterschwaigstr. 4*

### 7 Geiselgasteig & Bavaria Filmstadt
Called "Hollywood on the Isar," Geiselgasteig is a historic film-studio complex, where productions for television and the big screen are made. Enjoy guided tours and stunt shows at Bavaria Filmstadt *(see p54)*.

### 8 Schäftlarn Monastery
Founded in 762, this monastery with Baroque church is located between Grünwald and Wolfratshausen and has a popular small pub with beer garden. ◎ *Map S2*

### 9 Hirschgarten
Largest beer garden in the city, near Nymphenburg palace, with deer pens *(see p24)*.

### 10 Nymphenburg
A beautiful residential neighbourhood, with villas flanking both sides of the boulevard leading to the palace. ◎ *Map B2–B3, C2–C3*

  *Concerts are held in the church at Schäftlarn monastery on most Saturdays. Call (08178) 34 35 for details.*

Left **Move** Centre **Hussfeld and Zang** Right **Schmuck & Objekte Herzkönig**

# 📑🔟 Shops & Markets

### More & More
Glass, porcelain, home decor, and everything else necessary to make your living space beautiful. Great gift selection, too.
◈ *Blutenburgstr. 93 • Map D3*

### Moma Li Design
One-of-a-kind, deceptively simple, clean-cut garments made by a Munich designer. All pieces are fashioned by hand.
◈ *Bergmannstr. 52 • Map D5*

### Hussfeld & Zang
The emphasis here is on German- and Scandinavian-designed gifts, textiles and soft furnishings. Items are made from natural materials. ◈ *Blutenburgstr. 81 • Map D3*

### Move
This store stocks a large selection of running shoes, from Diesel to Nike. Fans will be thrilled to discover much-sought-after special models. ◈ *Nymphenburger Str. 156a • Map C3*

### Nymphenburger Keramik
If you are looking for decorative tiles for your bathroom, this is the place to go. Large selection of natural stone tiles. ◈ *Nymphenburger Str. 131 • Map C3*

### Moulin
The jewellery created by Christian Mühlbauer – seductive precious stones and quality jewellery in elegant settings – are true pieces of art. Or create your own design and have a piece made to order. ◈ *Leonrodstr. 47 • Map D3*

### Who's Perfect
Top-of-the-line items for office and home with barely perceptible defects. Everything is half price. There is also an interesting designer furniture exhibition. ◈ *Landsberger Str. 350 • Map B4*

### Schmuck & Objekte Herzkönig
Jewellery as art – art as jewellery. This store sells perfect examples of goldsmithing and all manner of *objets d'art*. Creations range from earrings to wedding rings. ◈ *Blutenburgstr. 39 • Map D4*

### Perlerie
Glass pearls, stones and all the accessories needed to create your own jewellery. ◈ *Volkartstr. 17 • Map C3*

### Corsetterie
Actresses, opera divas, and stars looking for that perfect shape shop here for made-to-measure corsets. ◈ *Sprunerstr. 11 • Map D2*

⮞ *For details on shopping districts* **See pp66–7**

Left **Stragula** Centre **Wassermann** Right **Ruffini**

# Cafés & Bars

### Stragula
A mixed crowd frequents this down-to-earth pub, a popular night-time destination for a beer. Bavarian-Italian food is served at reasonable prices, and there are a few patio tables in summer.
Ⓢ *Bergmannstr. 66 • Map D5*

### Café Westend
Part café, part bar with food menu. Bowling lanes and pool tables are in the basement.
Ⓢ *Ganghoferstr. 50 • Map D5*

### Marais Ladencafé
Located in what was once a haberdashery, this café still has all the shop's furnishings and fittings in place. It is a great spot for a coffee. Ⓢ *Parkstr. 2 • Map D5*

### Café Neuhausen
An attractive café with an ornate stucco ceiling. Three lunch specials are offered daily, and brunch is available on Sundays. A garden patio is open in summer. Ⓢ *Blutenburgstr. 106 • Map D3*

### Wassermann
Café, bar, and restaurant rolled into one. Daily lunch specials. In summer, enjoy a patio table under the walnut trees. Live music occasionally.
Ⓢ *Elvirastr. 19 • Map D4*

### Café Freiheit
Café, bar, and restaurant with a 25-year history at this location on Leonrodplatz. Patio.
Ⓢ *Leonrodstr. 20 • Map D3*

### Cafégarten
Breakfast in the morning, pastas at lunch, and cocktails at night. In summer, a tree-shaded patio provides relief from summer heat. Ⓢ *Nymphenburger Str. 92 • Map D3*

### Ruffini
A prototype for many Munich eateries, the Ruffini was the city's first alternative organic-food café. Absolutely scrumptious are the whole-grain breakfasts and bread from the in-house bakery. The roof patio is popular. Author readings on some evenings.
Ⓢ *Orffstr. 22 • Map D3 • Closed Mon*

### Sarcletti
The best Italian-style ice cream in the city. Founder Paul Sarcletti sold ice cream as far back as 1879. The parlour on Rotkreuzplatz was established in 1921.
Ⓢ *Nymphenburger Str. 155 • Map C3*

### Hide-Out
Bar with live music. International and local bands.
Ⓢ *Volkartstr. 22 • Map C3 • Closed Mon*

For more bars and cafés, gay and lesbian venues, gourmet restaurants, Bavarian pubs, and beer gardens See pp24, 50, 58–65

**Price Categories**

| | | |
|---|---|---|
| For a three-course meal for one with a glass of wine or beer (or equivalent meal), taxes, and service charges. | € | under €30 |
| | €€ | €30–40 |
| | €€€ | €40–50 |
| | €€€€ | €50–60 |
| | €€€€€ | over €60 |

Above **Acetaia**

# TOP10 Restaurants

### 1 Acetaia
Gourmet Italian restaurant, where Balsamic vinegar is a prominent feature – even in desserts. ◈ Nymphenburger Str. 215 • Map C3 • (089) 13 929 077 • Open noon–3pm & 6pm–1am; closed Sat lunch • €€€–€€€€

### 2 Broeding
Haute cuisine in a minimalistic ambience offering a five- or six-course menu served with fine Austrian wines. ◈ Schulstr. 9 • Map C3 • (089) 16 42 38 • Open 7pm daily; closed Sun & Mon • €€€–€€€€

### 3 Romans
Elegant atmosphere and romantic patio for fine-weather dining. Perfect choice if you love fine Italian cuisine. ◈ Romanstr. 1 • Map C3 • (089) 168 98 98 • Open 10am–1am daily • €€–€€€

### 4 Zapata
Tex-Mex restaurant with a waterfall as the focal point. Usually packed to the rafters. ◈ Schulstr. 44 • Map C3 • (089) 166 58 22 • Open 5pm–1am daily • €

### 5 Zauberberg
Top German and Mediterranean cuisine. Non-smoking restaurant. ◈ Hedwigstr. 14 • Map D3 • (089) 18 99 91 78 • 7pm–1am Tue–Sat, 6pm–1am Sun; also noon–2pm Tue–Thu • €€–€€€

### 6 Marbella
Tapas bar with a bodega atmosphere serving good food and offering excellent value for money. There is a garden patio in summer. ◈ Horemansstr. 30 • Map D3 • (089) 12 779 753 • Open 6pm–1am daily • No credit cards • €

### 7 Löwengarten
Comfortable, relaxed atmosphere. Inexpensive dishes are served in the garden in summer. ◈ Volkartstr. 32 • Map C3 • (089) 16 13 73 • Open 5pm–1am Mon–Fri, 10am–1am Sat & Sun • No credit cards • €

### 8 Rüen Thai
Hot and spicy Asian food in Westend. This is arguably Munich's best Thai restaurant. ◈ Kazmairstr. 58 • Map D5 • (089) 50 32 39 • Open noon–2:30pm Mon–Fri, 6pm–midnight Mon–Sun • €–€€

### 9 San Marino
Pizza and house wines at good prices – in summer also on the patio. ◈ Westendstr. 161 • Map C5 • (089) 50 26 000 • Open 11:30am–2:30pm & 6pm–11:30pm Mon–Sat • €

### 10 Augustinerbräustuben
Authentic Bavarian brewery pub and restaurant located in former beer cellars and horse stables (see p51).

**Note:** Unless otherwise specified, all restaurants accept major credit cards and are wheelchair accessible.

# DAY TRIPS & EXCURSIONS

TOP 10 MUNICH

Left **Neues Schloss, Schloss Schleißheim** Centre **Ammersee** Right **Town hall, Landsberg am Lech**

# 🔟 Around Munich

### 1 Schloss Schleißheim

Maximilian II Emanuel, the Elector, wanted to rival Versailles with the Neues Schloss (New Palace). Begun in 1701 based on plans by Enrico Zuccalli and completed in 1719 by Joseph Effner, the complex includes a hunting lodge and Schloss Lustheim, a small summer palace on the eastern edge of the Baroque park (see p39), also designed by Zuccalli. The latter houses an important collection of early Meißner porcelain. Oberschleißheim is home to the Flugwerft Schleißheim (see p11). ✪ Map S2 • Open Apr–Sep: 9am–6pm Tue–Sun; Oct–Mar: 10am–4pm Tue–Sun (both castles) • Adm

### 2 Freising

The historic seat of a bishopric, the town is dominated by the cathedral and the bishop's residence, situated on a hill known as the Mons Doctus – Learned Mount. Designed as a Roman basilica with five aisles, the cathedral was completed in 1205 and

**Dachau concentration camp**

embellished from 1723 to 1724 by the Asam brothers, with stucco and stained-glass windows. Not to be missed are the Romanesque crypt and its famous Bestiensäule, a column elaborately carved with fabled beasts. Near the cathedral lies the former Benedictine monastery, Weihenstephan. Today, it is a brewery – arguably the oldest in the world – with a wonderful beer garden. ✪ Map T1

### 3 Dachau

Set in the foothills along the Amper River, some 15 km (9 miles) north of Munich, Dachau is a small town built around a prominent palace – part Renaissance, part Baroque – which has an excellent restaurant. In 1933, the first Nazi concentration camp was set up here, now a place of remembrance – the KZ Gedenkstätte – one of the most frequented in Europe today. Refurbishment of the exhibition at the adjacent museum was completed in 2003. ✪ Schloss Dachau, (081 31) 879 23 • Map S2 • Open Apr–Sep: 9am–6pm daily; Oct–Mar: 10am–4pm Tue–Sun • Adm • KZ-Gedenkstätte Dachau, Alte Römerstr. 75, (081 31) 66 99 70 • Open 9am–5pm Tue–Sun • free

### 4 Herrmannsdorfer Landwerkstätten

Near Glonn, 30 km (19 miles) southeast of Munich, the Hermannsdorfer Landwerkstätten complex was completed in 1986. The centre produces, processes, and sells organic food products,

*In 1957, Stanley Kubrick shot scenes for his film* Paths of Glory *in Schloss Schleißheim.*

and features a gourmet restaurant and beer garden. Take the time for a walk to view works of art such as chimes and sculptures placed throughout the grounds. ✎ *Map T2*

### Kloster Andechs

Situated on the eastern shore of Ammersee on a hill rising to a height of 200 m (650 ft), this monastery with its lovely Rococo church is one of the most important pilgrimage sites in Germany. Many, however, journey here to sample the famous monastery beer, served in the beer garden and pub. ✎ *Map R2*

### Fürstenfeldbruck

Lining its elongated town square, Fürstenfeldbruck boasts a town hall and historic houses in the Baroque and neo-Classical style, and a Baroque abbey by Antonio Viscardi. Its stunning interior includes work by the Asam brothers, among others. ✎ *Map R2–S2*

### Wolfratshausen & Rafting on the Isar

Wolfratshausen lies some 30 km (19 miles) south of Munich on the River Loisach and has a long central market street flanked by 17th- to 18th-century Upper Bavarian gabled town houses. This small town is the starting point for river-rafting tours to Munich, which launch at the Loisach bridge. These are cheerful excursions accompanied by music, picnics, and beer, down the rafting chutes of the Isar to the central landing area near Tierpark Hellabrunn. During the six-hour ride, passengers experience the largest chute in Europe with an 18-m- (60-ft-) drop in altitude. ✎ *Map S3*
• www.isarflossfahrten.de; www.schrall.com

Bayertor, Landsberg

### Ammersee

Bavaria's third-largest lake, Ammersee lies in a glacial basin from the Ice Age surrounded by forested moraines. Under clear skies, there is a glorious view of the Alps. Its shoreline is studded with many small towns, offering activities such as sailing, rowing, surfing, cycling, hiking, and much more. ✎ *Map R2*

### Osterseen

South of Lake Starnberg near Seeshaupt, travellers will find the delightful Osterseen, a group of some 20 small moorland lakes that are among the warmest in Bavaria. This is a perfect spot to go for swimming and peaceful walks in a nature reserve. ✎ *Map S3*

### Landsberg am Lech

This is a city straight out of a picture book. Lining the triangular market square are beautiful town houses and a stunning stucco town hall. It was built around 1700 by the famous building master Dominikus Zimmermann, who also served as mayor of Landsberg (1749–54). The 36-m- (125-ft-) high Bayertor, dating from around 1425, is one of the most impressive medieval city gates in Bavaria. ✎ *Map R2*
• Town Hall: Open 8am–8pm in summer, 9am–4pm in winter

Gothic Madonna, Fürstenfeldbruck

Oberschleißheim, Freising, Dachau, Fürstenfeldbruck, Wolfratshausen, and Ammersee (Herrsching) are on the S-Bahn lines.

Left **Zugspitzplatt** Centre **Painted façade in Oberammergau** Right **Eibsee**

# Garmisch-Partenkirchen & Zugspitze

DEEP GREEN MEADOWS, snow-capped mountains, steep gorges carved out by streams, ancient monasteries, and old houses with colourful painted façades – in this region, Bavaria looks like a picture postcard come to life. Germany's highest peak, the towering Zugspitze (2,950 m/9,700 ft), soars into the sky here. Locals also refer to the region encompassing Garmisch-Partenkirchen, Oberammergau, and Murnau – set in the Alps and the foothills against the impressive backdrop of the Wetterstein massif – as Werdenfelser Land. The Alpine foothills of Bavaria offer cultural highlights, such as King Ludwig II's Schloss Linderhof, and Münter house in Murnau, as well as awesome natural beauty, in places such as Eibsee, Part-nachklamm, and Murnauer Moos. The full spectrum of attractions awaits summer and winter visitors. Excellent ski resorts around Garmisch and on Zugspitz itself draw hordes of visitors in winter. A day excursion by car is the most comfortable way of exploring this area. However, there are excellent links by rail and bus between Munich and the main attractions in the Zugspitz region.

**The Zugspitz region**

## Attractions

1. Garmisch-Partenkirchen
2. Zugspitze
3. Eibsee
4. Partnachklamm
5. Höllentalklamm
6. Kloster Ettal
7. Schloss Linderhof
8. Oberammergau
9. Murnau am Staffelsee
10. Murnauer Moos

*The name "Werdenfelser Land" comes from Fortress Burg Werdenfels near Garmisch. The fortress ruins are still visible.*

Garmisch, Zugspitz massif in the background

### Garmisch-Partenkirchen

Located at the base of the Wetterstein massif and the Zugspitze, the capital of Werdenfelser Land is one of the most popular tourist attractions in Germany. Garmisch-Partenkirchen, which has a population of 30,000, is chiefly known as a winter sports resort. The Winter Olympics were held here in 1936. In summer, the town draws just as many visitors as a spa town and is an ideal base for mountain hiking and excursions into the region. ◈ Map R4

### Zugspitze

One of the best ways to enjoy Zugspitze is to take a round trip from the base of the mountain on the mountain train and cable cars. In Garmisch, the journey begins on a funicular, which takes you to the Schneeferner glacier on the Zugspitzplatt. Here you switch to a cable car, which ascends to the summit (2,950 m/9,700 ft). The observation platform affords a spectacular panoramic vista – in clear weather, all the way to the Dolomites in Italy. Take the Eibsee cable car on your return trip down to the valley – you'll be treated once again to wonderful views of Eibsee, Garmisch-Partenkirchen, and Werdenfelser Land. ◈ Map R4

### Eibsee

Embedded in the rocky landscape of the Zugspitz massif, the deep blue waters of Eibsee lie nearly 1,000 m (3,300 ft) above sea level. The lake formed after a powerful rock avalanche created a deep crater. A walk around the lake takes roughly two hours. The shore is dotted with many scenic bays and idyllic beaches, which are perfect for taking a break or – in summer – a dip in the lake. ◈ Map R4

### Partnachklamm

One of the most impressive gorges in the Bavarian Alps, the Partnachklamm is some 700 m (2,300 ft) long; the rock face along its sides reaches a height of nearly 100 m (330 ft). A short walk from the Olympic ski-jump stadium in Garmisch will take you to the entrance to the gorge. ◈ Map R4 • open year-round

### Höllentalklamm

Located near Garmisch at Grainach, this gorge is entirely different in character to Partnachklamm. The Hammersbach stream tumbles through a one-km- (half-mile-) long gorge down into the valley. Challenging hiking paths lead through lit tunnels. Hiking boots and surefootedness are absolutely essential for an excursion in this gorge. ◈ Map R4 • closed Nov–May

Partnachklamm near Garmisch-Partenkirchen

### Königshaus am Schachen

A post-and-beam house was built on the Schachenalm, a lovely mountain pasture 1,900 m (6,200 ft) above sea level, in 1869 to serve as a refuge for Ludwig II during his mountain excursions. The ground floor is panelled in knotty pine, while the entire upper floor is given over to the Maurische Saal, a Moorish banquet hall: its colourful stained-glass windows, candelabra, and peacock feathers reflect the fascination with the Orient typical of the era.

### Kloster Ettal

Founded by Emperor Ludwig the Bavarian in 1330, the abbey now houses a boarding school. The domed structure of the abbey church was reconstructed in Bavarian Rococo style after a fire. Ettal monastery produces famous herbal liqueurs – dry (green in colour), sweet (amber), and bitter (brown). ◈ Map R4

**Kloster Ettal**

### Schloss Linderhof

Located in the Graswangtal on a beautiful tributary of the River Ammer, Schloss Linderhof lies 10 km (6 miles) outside Ettal (see p30). ◈ Ettal, Linderhof 12 • Map R4 • (0 88 22) 9 20 30 • Open Apr–Sep: 9am–6pm; Oct–Mar: 10am–4pm • Adm • www.linderhof.de

### Oberammergau

This historic spa town is world-renowned for its passion plays – lay theatre performed by locals. Most of Oberammergau's population participates in mounting the event once a decade. This picturesque town is also noted for its façade frescoes. Franz Seraph Zwinck (1748–92), Germany's most famous façade frescoe painter, was born here. ◈ Map R4 • Next passion play performance in 2010

### Murnau am Staffelsee

Painters Wassily Kandinsky (1866–1944) and Gabriele Münter (1877–1962) and writer Ödön von Horváth (1901–38) worked and lived in this picturesque town. Follow in the footsteps of the Blue Rider art group – the Münter-Haus

**First edition of Blue Rider**

and Schlossmuseum, in particular, are highly recommended. There is a beautiful walking path around the idyllic Staffelsee. ◈ Münter-Haus: Kottmüllerallee 6 • Map R3 • (0 88 41) 62 88 80 • Open 2pm–5pm Tue–Sun • Adm • Schlossmuseum: Schlosshof 4–5 • (0 88 41) 47 62 01 • Open 10am–5pm Tue–Sun (Jul–Sep: to 6pm Sat & Sun) • Adm

### Murnauer Moos

At 32 sq km (12 sq miles), the Murnauer Moos is the largest continuous fenland in Bavaria. It is home to several thousand animal species and more than 900 plant species, many of which are threatened with extinction and have been placed under protection in this conservation area. Signposted paths through the fen provide beautiful hiking opportunities in all seasons. ◈ Map R3–R4

*The Königshaus am Schachen is only accessible on foot (3–4 hours); guided tours Jun–Sep at 11am, 1pm, 2pm, and 3pm.*

**Price Categories**

For a three-course meal for one with a glass of wine or beer (or equivalent meal), taxes, and service charges.

| | |
|---|---|
| € | under €30 |
| €€ | €30–40 |
| €€€ | €40–50 |
| €€€€ | €50–60 |
| €€€€€ | over €60 |

Left **Griesbräu zu Murnau** Right **Gasthof Zum Rassen**

# 🔟 Cafés & Restaurants

### 1 Kreut-Alm
A restaurant featuring typical Bavarian cuisine, the beer garden affords a glorious view of Kochelsee and the surrounding mountains. ⊗ *Kreut-Alm/Großweil • Map S3 • (0 88 41) 58 22 • www.kreutalm.de • €*

### 2 Griesbräu zu Murnau
Traditional pub in the centre of Murnau, with home-brewed beer and Bavarian delicacies served in a rustic atmosphere. Check out the fermenting vats.
⊗ *Murnau, Obermarkt 37 • Map R3 • (0 88 41) 14 22 • www.griesbraeu.de • €*

### 3 Schlosscafé Murnau
Take a break from your visit to the museum and enjoy excellent coffee and homemade cake. ⊗ *Murnau, Schlosshof 5 • Map R3 • (0 88 41) 622 12 • www.murnau.de • €*

### 4 Alpenhof Murnau
Fine Bavarian and international cuisine, with a panoramic view of the Alps. ⊗ *Murnau, Ramsachstr. 8 • Map R3 • (0 88 41) 49 10 • www.alpenhof-murnau.com • Not wheelchair accessible • €€€*

### 5 Restaurant Sonn Alpin
Located at an elevation of 2,600m (8,500 ft) on the Zugspitzplatt, the Sonn Alpin is Germany's highest restaurant. The large terrace offers spectacular views and seats 800.
⊗ *Map R4 • www.zugspitze.de • €*

### 6 Hotel "Ludwig der Bayer"
Beer brewed at the monastery and world-famous Ettal liqueurs accompany the international and Bavarian cuisine served here. ⊗ *Ettal, Kaiser-Ludwig-Platz 10-12 • Map R4 • (0 88 22) 91 50 • www.kloster-ettal.de • €*

### 7 Schlosshotel Linderhof
Enjoy a meal next door to a fairy-tale castle: Bavarian and international cuisine. ⊗ *Ettal, Linderhof Nr. 14 • Map R4 • (08822) 790 • www.schlosshotel-linderhof.com • €*

### 8 Gasthof zum Rassen
This traditional inn is home to Bavaria's oldest folklore theatre – and, of course, authentic Bavarian cuisine. ⊗ *Garmisch-Partenkirchen, Ludwigsstr. 45 • Map R4 • (0 88 21) 20 89 • www.gasthof-rassen.de • €*

### 9 "Das Restaurant" in Eibsee-Hotel
Fine regional and international cuisine in an elegant atmosphere with a view of the picturesque Eibsee. ⊗ *Grainau, Am Eibsee 1–3 • Map R4 • (0 88 21) 9 88 10 • www.eibsee-hotel.de • €€*

### 10 Parkhotel Sonnenhof
At the foot of the Kofel, Oberammergau's mountain, the chef prepares traditional Bavarian as well as international dishes. Elegant setting.
⊗ *Oberammergau, König-Ludwig-Str. 12 • Map R4 • (0 88 22) 91 30 • www.parkhotel-sonnenhof.de • €*

 **Note:** *Unless otherwise specified, all restaurants accept major credit cards and are wheelchair accessible.*

Left **Herzogstand and Kochelsee** Centre **Kloster Benediktbeuren** Right **Dießen, Ammersee**

# Baroque & Rococo in Pfaffenwinkel

PFAFFENWINKEL IS A CLASSIC ALPINE foothill region. *Gently sloping hills and verdant pastures alternate with forests, fens, and small lakes. Geographically, the region is bounded by the Lech, Ammer, and Loisach rivers, and by the southern end of Ammersee and Starnberger See, reaching all the way to the Ammergauer mountains. It is known for its abundance*

*of Baroque monasteries and Rococo churches, such as Benediktbeuren and Wieskirche, characterized by the style developed at the world-renowned stucco school at Wessobrunn. The name of the region comes from the words "Pfaffen," which is local dialect for priest, and "Winkel" for corner. Natural beauty abounds in Pfaffenwinkel, with its gorges such as Ammerschlucht, romantic mountain lakes such as the deep, dark blue Walchensee, high mountains with lovely vistas, and lonely fens. By car, the region is reached from Munich via motorway A95 or regional roads B2 and B11. There are also excellent rail and bus links.*

Stuccoed ceiling, Kloster Wessobrunn

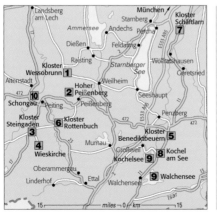

For information on Pfaffenwinkel, visit **www.pfaffenwinkel.de** or **www.pfaffenwinkel.net**

**Rococo interior, Kloster Wessobrunn**

### Kloster Wessobrunn

In the 17th and 18th centuries, Wessobrunn was the centre of the art of stuccowork. Masterbuilders of monasteries and master stuccoworkers trained here, including Joseph Schmuzer (1683–1752) and Dominikus Zimmermann (1685–1766), who went on to build and decorate many of the monasteries and churches in southern Germany in the Baroque manner. Wessobrunn stucco became famous around the world through the work of the Schmuzer and Zimmermann families. Part of the monastery, including the gallery in the Fürstentrakt and Tassilo hall, is open to the public.

One of the oldest German-language manuscripts, the *Wessobrunner Prayer,* dating to around 800, was once held in the monastery's library. It is now part of the Bayerische Staatsbibliothek's collection in Munich. ✆ *Map R3 • (0 88 09) 9 21 10 • Open Mar–Oct: 10am–3pm & 4pm Tue–Sat, 3–4pm Sun; Nov–Feb: 3pm Tue–Sat, 3pm & 4pm Sun • www.kloster-wessobrunn.de • free*

### Hoher Peißenberg

At an elevation of nearly 1,000 m (3,300 ft), the Hohe Peißenberg is not only the geographical centre of Pfaffenwinkel, it also affords one of the most beautiful panoramic vistas in the Alpine foothills – the entire mountain range and the gently rolling hills and sparkling lakes at the foot of the Alps lie before you. Meteorological data have been recorded on the Hohe Peißenberg since 1781 – at first by Augustine choirmasters from nearby Rottenbach monastery *(see p122)*. Refreshments are available at the Bayerischer Rigi café, which features a large terrace. ✆ *Map R3 • www.bayerischer-rigi.de*

### Kloster Steingaden

In 1147, the Premonstratensians built this monastery and abbey under Duke Welf VI. It was the most important centre of monastic life in Bavaria during that era. Surviving elements include the Romanesque cloisters with late Gothic vaulting and a Romanesque basilica, whose exterior form has been preserved. The abbey's interior is highly ornamented in the Rococo style. ✆ *Map R3 • (0 88 62) 2 34 • Open 8am–6pm daily in summer, 8am–5pm daily in winter) • www.steingaden.de • free*

**Romanesque cloister, Kloster Steingaden**

*The Wessobrunner Prayer is engraved on a boulder in front of the local inn, the Gasthaus zur Post.*

Ornate Rococo interior of Wieskirche

### Wieskirche

Known simply as the Wieskirche, the pilgrimage church Zum Gegeißelten Heiland in der Wiese near Steingaden (1746–54) is renowned as a prime example of German Rococo. It represents the work of Dominikus Zimmermann, the famous architect and stuccowork master from Wessobrunn, at his peak. UNESCO listed the church as a World Heritage Site in 1984. ⊗ Map R3
• (0 88 62) 93 29 30 • Open in summer 8am–7pm daily, in winter 8am–5pm daily • www.wieskirche.de • free

### Kloster Benediktbeuern

Benediktbeuren (739) is one of the oldest monasteries in the foothills of the Alps. Karl the

### Wessobrunn Stuccowork

In the 17th and 18th centuries, the most important stuccowork masters came from around the monastery at Wessobrunn. Johann Schmuzer (1642–1701) is regarded as the founder of the Wessobrunn school. The Schmuzer, Zimmermann, and Feichtmayr families spread its fame throughout Europe. Stucco masterpieces are found in the monasteries and abbeys of Wessobrunn, Ettal, Rottenbuch, Weingarten, Zwiefalten, Ottobeuren, Bad Wörishofen, and Steingaden.

Great's acquisition of the arm relic of St Boniface elevated the monastery to the most important cult site of the saint in German-speaking countries. Built between 1669 and 1679, the Baroque monastery is still intact today. Kaspar Feichtmayr of Weilheim built the church with twin towers in the Italian late Baroque style. Famous in its time, the holdings at the monastery library included the Carmina Burana – the most important collection of medieval minstrel songs. The manuscript dates back to the 13th century and is now housed at the Bayerische Staatsbibliothek.

Following secularization, the monastery complex was used for a time as a glassworks. At the beginning of the 19th century, it housed an institute for optics led by the famous optician and physician Joseph von Fraunhofer (1787–1826), who discovered the waves in the solar spectrum that were named after him. Today, the monastery accommodates institutes of pedagogy and theology of the Silesian Order. ⊗ Map S3 • (0 88 57) 880 • Kloster: Open 9am–5pm daily • www.klosterbenediktbeuern.de • Glashütte: Open 9am–6pm daily • free

### Kloster Rottenbuch

Founded in 1073 by Duke Welf IV, this monastery for Augustine Canons survives to this day. It features a rare blend of Romanesque, Gothic, and Rococo architectural styles. In the mid-18th century, Joseph Schmuzer and his son decorated the interior with lavish stuccowork. ⊗ Map R3
• (0 88 67) 10 08 • Open 8am–6pm daily (to 7pm in summer) • free

Munich composer Carl Orff (1895–1982) set parts of the medieval Carmina Burana to music in 1937.

### 7 Kloster Schäftlarn

Benedictine monks founded a monastery at this site as far back as 762. The buildings seen at Schäftlarn today were built in 1702–07 after designs by Giovanni A Viscardi. Consecrated in 1760, the abbey is considered a masterpiece of Bavarian Rococo. Much of the stucco decoration is the work of the famous Zimmermann family. The beautiful beer garden attached to the monastery is perfect for a small repast. ◈ Map S3
• www.abtei-schaeftlarn.de • free

View of Walchensee near Kochel am See

### 8 Kochel am See

At the centre of this popular lakeside resort stands a monument to the legendary blacksmith Balthes, a hero of the Bavarian peasant uprising against Austria in 1705. This was also where the painter Franz Marc lived and worked in the early 20th century. His home has been converted into a museum of his works and those of his friends in the Blue Rider group. ◈ Map S3 • (0 88 51) 71 14
• Mar–mid-Jan: 2pm–6pm Tue–Sun
• www.franz-marc-museum.de • Adm

Romanesque font, Michaelskirche

### 9 Kochelsee & Walchensee

About half of Kochelsee is surrounded by steep hills. Covering an area of just under 6 sq km (2.5 sq miles), the lake is 66 m (215 ft) deep in some parts. Excellent hiking paths run along its shores. A short distance to the south, and some 200 m (655 ft) higher, lies the blue-green Walchensee. Covering 16 sq km (6.5 sq miles) and with a depth of up to 190 m (650 ft), it is the largest and deepest mountain lake in Germany and, in summer, a wind-surfer's paradise. A cable car affording a glorious view of both lakes runs up to Herzogstand (1,750 m/5,700 ft).

◈ Map S4 • Herzogstandbahn (cable car): Walchensee • (0 88 58) 2 36

### 10 Schongau

This picturesque town is located on a hill on the river Lech. A historic town wall with walkways, towers, and gates gives Schongau a medieval air. Altstadt, 3 km (2 miles) to the north, was previously Schongau's old centre before the town spread. It boasts the Michaelskirche, the finest Romanesque vaulted basilica in Upper Bavaria. Containing, among other treasures, a carved Romanesque font, the church was built in 1200. ◈ Map R3 • www.schongau.de

### Freilichtmuseum Glentleiten

Upper Bavaria's largest open-air museum opened in 1976 in the beautiful foothills of the Alps between Murnau and Kochel. An old Bavarian village has been set up here – with original farmhouses, mills, a pottery, workshops, and other farm buildings. There's also a restaurant with beer garden.
Open Apr–Nov: 9am–6pm Tue–Sun, except Jul–Aug: 9am–6pm daily. Adm.
www.glentleiten.de

The canyon-like Ammerschlucht (between Saulgrub and Peißenberg) is a rafter's paradise. The Schleier waterfalls is a highlight.

Left **Frauenchiemsee monastery on Chiemsee** Right **Spa, Bad Tölz**

# Lakes & Towns in Upper Bavaria

WITH ITS GENTLE MORAINE HILLS *and rugged mountains created during the Ice Age, peaceful moor lakes and rapid mountain streams, and picturesque towns and villages, the sub-Alpine region of Upper Bavaria is full of natural beauty. This is especially true of Tölzer Land and the Chiemgau, both of which are true havens for holiday-makers. For sports enthusiasts there is skiing, hiking, cycling, and windsurfing in places such as Reit im Winkl and on Spitzingsee. Culture buffs can visit ancient monasteries and Baroque churches, among them Frauenchiemsee and Hohenaschau. !Weekend-trippers have an abundance of excursions to choose from – for example Kloster Reutberg or Tegernsee – and spa-lovers can recuperate and relax in the therapeutic Kneipp water treatments offered at spa towns such as Bad Tölz. From Munich, Tölzer Land and Chiemgau are reached by car via A8 and regional roads B318 and B472; there are also excellent rail and bus links to the region.*

## Sights

1. Bad Tölz
2. Kloster Reutberg
3. Tegernsee
4. Schliersee
5. Spitzingsee
6. Lenggries
7. Wendelstein, Bayrischzell
8. Chiemsee
9. Reit im Winkl
10. Schloss Hohenaschau

**Traditional painted wardrobe, Heimatmuseum, Bad Tölz**

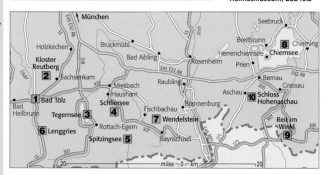

*The Deutsche Alpenstraße, a panoramic motorway through beautiful landscapes, runs through parts of this region.*

### 1 Bad Tölz

Located where the Isar River surfaces from an Alpine valley and flows into the sub-Alpine foothills, Bad Tölz is a popular spa and winter resort. On the right side of the river lies the picturesque old town, with its impressive Markt-straße lined with ornate stucco-work façades, mottos, and frescoes. Alpamare, one of Germany's largest waterparks, is favoured by spa guests and fun-seekers alike. A big annual attraction is the Leonhardifahrt, on 6 November, a procession in honour of St Leonhard, patron saint of horses. It is one of the largest processions in traditional costume in Upper Bavaria.
ⓢ Map S3 • Alpamare, Ludwig-str. 14 • (0 80 41) 50 99 99
• www.alpamare.de

Leonhardifahrt procession in Bad Tölz

### 2 Kloster Reutberg

Situated atop a small hill near Bad Tölz, this monastery was founded by the Sisters of the Franciscan Order in the 17th century. The Baroque abbey is open to the public. It is also worth a trip for the spectacular view of the Alps from the monastery's beer garden. For a pleasant stroll head to the romantic Kirchsee nearby, a good spot for summer swimming.
ⓢ Sachsenkam • Map S3 • free

Virgin Mary, Bad Tölz

### 3 Tegernsee

Framed by wooded mountains, Tegernsee is one of the largest mountains lakes in Upper Bavaria, with an area of 9 sq km (3.5 sq miles) and a length of 6 km (3.5 miles). Its beautiful setting and easy accessibility – it is only 50 km (30 miles) from Munich – have made the lake one of the most popular excursion and holiday destinations since the notion of taking summer breaks began in the 19th century. Tegernsee, Bad Wiessee, and Rottach-Egern form a picturesque chain of towns on the shores of the lake and attract visitors in both winter and summer. Bad Wiessee is home to one of the few casinos in Bavaria. ⓢ Map T3 • Bayerische Spielbank Bad Wiessee Winner 1 • (0 80 22) 9 83 50

### 4 Schliersee

Although less famous than Tegernsee, Schliersee, on the edge of the Alps, is just as attractive a lake. Its appeal lies mainly in the beauty of the surrounding mountains. One of the principal sights in the spa town of Schliersee is the St Sixtus church, with its 18th-century frescoes by Johann B Zimmermann. For an attractive country walk, take the 7 km (4 mile) path around the lake. ⓢ Map T3

Town of Schliersee, viewed from the lake

Bad Tölz is a relatively new spa; the iodine-rich natural springs were only discovered in 1946.

On the Brauneck ridge path near Lenggries

### Spitzingsee

**5** Wildly romantic, the Spitzingsee (1,100 m/3,600 ft) attracts mountain hikers in summer. In winter, skiers enjoy 30 km (19 miles) of groomed ski runs, serviced by 18 cable cars and ski lifts. This is Germany's largest continuous ski region. ✎ *Map T4*

### Lenggries

**6** Located on the Isar River in the Isarwinkel area, Lenggries is a health and winter resort. It is a perfect departure point for excursions into the mountains, such as to Brauneck's summit, which can be reached by foot or by cable car. ✎ *Map S3 • Bergbahn • (0 80 42) 50 39 40 • www.brauneck-bergbahn.de*

### Wendelstein near Bayrischzell

**7** From the summit of the Wendelstein, hikers enjoy one of the most beautiful views in the region. In good weather, the Großglockner is clearly visible. There is a weather station and observatory, and Wettersteinhaus, a traditional mountain inn. Serviced by the oldest rack-railway (1912) in the Alps, the summit has also been linked by cable car since 1970. ✎ *Map T3 • Wendelstein Bergbahnen • www.wendelsteinbahn.de*

### Chiemsee

**8** Popularly thought of as "Bavaria's Ocean," Chiemsee is Bavaria's largest lake, with an area of 80 sq km (31 sq miles). Highlights include the islands Herrenchiemsee, with the Altes- and Neues Schloss *(see p30)*, and Frauenchiemsee, with an 18th-century monastery. ✎ *Map U3*

Lake Chiemsee, known as "Bavaria's Ocean"

### Reit im Winkl

**9** This resort near the Austrian border lies in a snowbelt, and so offers some of the best skiing in the Bavarian Alps. Excellent ski runs are maintained near the Winklmoosalm (1,150m/3,800 ft), home of Olympian skier Rosi Mittermaier. ✎ *Map U3*

### Schloss Hohenaschau

**10** Castle Hohenaschau dates from the 12th century. Renaissance (16th century) and late Baroque (17th century) additions are the chapel and the charity house – Prientalmuseum.
✎ *Aschau • Map U3 • Apr & Oct: 9:30am, 10:30am, 11:30am Thu only; May–Sep: 9:30am, 10:30am, 11:30am Tue–Fri • Guided tours only • Adm*

---

**Altes Schloss, Chiemsee**

Around 1130, an Augustine Canons' seminary was built on the foundations of an eighth-century Benedictine abbey at Herrenchiemsee. Renovated in the Baroque style, it closed in 1803. Ludwig II purchased the island in 1873, built the Neues Schloss, and converted the seminary into private apartments – the Altes Schloss. An exhibit in the seminary documents the constitution of the German Federal Republic, signed and ratified here in 1948.

---

**Price Categories**

| | |
|---|---|
| For a three-course meal for one with a glass of wine or beer (or equivalent meal), taxes, and service charges. | € under €30 |
| | €€ €30–40 |
| | €€€ €40–50 |
| | €€€€ €50–60 |
| | €€€€€ over €60 |

Gasthof Terofal, Schliersee

# Cafés & Restaurants

### 1 Gasthof Grünerbräu
Rustic Bavarian inn serving draught beer brewed in Bad Tölz. Try *Gansjung* (goose) or the dumpling dishes. ◈ *Bad Tölz, Marktstr. 8 • Map S3 • (0 80 41) 60 91 • www.gruenerbraeu.de • €*

### 2 Kloster-Bräustüberl Reutberg
Bavarian cuisine complemented by monastery-brewed beer. The glorious view of the Alps is an added bonus. ◈ *Sachsenkam, Am Reutberg 2 • Map S3 • (0 80 21) 86 86 • www.klosterbrauerei-reutberg.de • €*

### 3 Schlossgaststätte Tegernsee
Traditional pork roast and cool beer served on the large terrace of the beer garden, with its fabulous view across the lake. ◈ *Tegernsee • Map T3 • (0 80 22) 45 60 • www.schlossgaststaette.de • €*

### 4 Panoramarestaurant Wallberg
Opened in 1998, the restaurant lies 100 m (330 ft) below Wallberg's summit (1,700 m/5,650 ft). Spectacular view of the Alps and Tegernsee. ◈ *Rottach-Egern, Am Wallberg 1 • Map T3 • (0 80 22) 68 00 • www.wallberg-restaurant.de • €*

### 5 Landgasthof Reindlschmiede
Country inn near Bad Tölz. Homemade cakes and Bavarian delicacies. ◈ *Bad Heilbrunn, Reindlschmiede 8 • Map S3 • (0 80 46) 2 85 • www.reindlschmiede.de • €*

### 6 Berggasthof Obere Firstalm
Solid Bavarian cuisine at reasonable prices. ◈ *Spitzingsee • Map T4 • (0 80 26) 97 79 44 • www.hotel-firstalm.de • €*

### 7 Winklmoosalm
Where downhill ski prodigy Rosi Mittermaier spent her childhood, hikers can now enjoy coffee and homemade pastries on a large, sun-drenched patio. ◈ *Reit im Winkl, Winklmoosalm • Map U3 • (0 86 40) 9 74 40 • www.winklmoosalm.com • €*

### 8 Inselhotel Zur Linde
This is a traditional hotel with a 600-year history. It is famous for its homemade cakes and, of course, excellent Bavarian cuisine. ◈ *Fraueninsel im Chiemsee • Map U3 • (0 80 54) 9 03 66 • www.inselhotel-zurlinde.de • €*

### 9 Schlosshotel Herrenchiemsee
Bavarian and international cuisine, and a glorious view of the Chiemsee. ◈ *Herrenchiemsee • Map U3 • (0 80 51) 6 90 30 • www.schlosshotel-herrenchiemsee.com • €€*

### 10 Gasthof Terofal
A traditional Bavarian hotel and 500-year-old restaurant located in the centre of Schliersee. Good traditional Bavarian fare. A folklore theatre is built onto the inn. ◈ *Schliersee, Xaver-Terofal-Platz 2 • Map T3 • (0 80 26) 92 92 10 • www.hotelterofal.de • €*

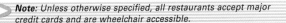

**Note:** Unless otherwise specified, all restaurants accept major credit cards and are wheelchair accessible.

Left **Castle at Burghausen** Centre **Kapellplatz, Altötting** Right **Schloss Amerang**

# 🔟 Along the Inn River

### 1 Rott am Inn

Perched high on the banks above the Inn River is the abbey of Sts Marinus und Anianus, a masterpiece of Bavarian Rococo. Between 1758 and 1763 Johann Michael Fischer rebuilt the chuch, incorporating the Romanesque east towers into his design. The soaring interior is impressive with its daring spatial design and fine decoration. ◈ *Map T2*

### 2 Schloss Amerang

Situated on a rise surrounded by deep natural ditches, the palace lies just south of the town of the same name. From the outside, the palace looks like a medieval fortress. Its large cloistered courtyard dates from the second half of the 16th century. Noted for its excellent acoustics, the courtyard is a regular venue for summer concerts. ◈ *Map U2*
• *Open Easter–mid-Sep: 10am, 11am, noon, 1pm, 2pm Tue–Sun*
• *Adm* • *www.schlossamerang.de*

**Gothic town hall in Wasserburg**

### 3 Kloster Attel

Built in 1715, this Baroque church belonging to the Benedictine abbey is well worth a visit. A Roman memorial stone from AD 204 is incorporated in the imposing church entrance. Limburg, the seat of the Hallgrafen dynasty, was formerly located near the monastery. By relocating its principality to Wasserburg in 1137, the family caused the cultural flowering of that town. ◈ *Map T2*

### 4 Wasserburg

Wasserburg benefits from its location on a spoon-shaped promontory in the Inn River. Typical of the Inn region, the old town is distinguished by wide, open squares lined with arcaded, leafy walkways. Its streets are lined with old houses with colourful painted façades, pretty bay windows, and stepped gables. All these elements give Wasserburg an Italian air. For a stunning view of the old town, head to the *Schöne Aussicht* (beautiful vista) lookout on the opposite side of the river. A wonderful path lined with works of art runs along this stretch of the Inn. ◈ *Map U2*

### 5 Gars am Inn

This former Augustine Canons' seminary, with its early Baroque abbey, was built by Gaspare and Domenico Zucalli between 1661 and 1690. The interior is decorated with lavish stuccowork. ◈ *Map U2*

 *The entries on these two pages are arranged in geographical order, providing an itinerary for a tour through the region.*

### Au am Inn

The Au monastery, founded by the Augustine Canons in the 12th century, occupies an idyllic spot on a bend in the Inn River. It was reconstructed after a fire in the 18th century. The former library, decorated with frescoes, is a highlight of the complex, which is now also home to a restaurant with an attractive beer garden. ✎ Map U2

### Mühldorf

This picturesque town, which lies on a peninsula in the Inn River, was an important trading post during the Middle Ages. The old town is defined by the 500-m- (1,650-ft-) long market square flanked by houses typical of towns along this river – those with romantic arcades and stepped gables. City gates mark the ends of the square. The Nagelschmiedturm, with its Romanesque basement, is worth seeing. ✎ Map U2

**Guardian Angel, Burghausen**

### Altötting

Bavaria's oldest pilgrimage site, Altötting lies on a hill near the right bank of the Inn River. A small, octagonal chapel with a central aisle, the Holy Chapel dates from 750. It was subsequently expanded by a nave. In the interior, a silver tabernacle set into a shell-lined niche on the eastern end contains the votive image of "Our Dear Lady of Altötting" – a revered Black Madonna (c.1300) carved from linden wood. Another feature of interest is the panorama re-creating the view from Golgotha in Jerusalem at the time of the Crucifixion, which is located in a domed structure east of the town centre. This is a monumental depiction of the Passion of Christ, with life-life figures in the foreground representing the stations of the cross. ✎ Map V2

### Burghausen

Burghausen experienced its heyday in the Middle Ages when it was a centre of the salt trade and, occasionally, the Wittelsbachs' second seat of government. The enormous castle, one of Germany's largest, is fascinating. Built in 1255, it was added to and became a fortress at the end of the 15th century. Other highlights include the Gothic Jakobskirche, the 16th-century town hall, and the 18th-century Schutzengelskirche, all on the market square. ✎ Map V2 • Castle: Open Apr–Sep: 9am–6pm daily; Oct–Mar: 10am–4pm daily • Adm

### Tittmoning

This is one of the most beautiful small towns in eastern Bavaria. After the salt trade collapsed, the town succeeded in preserving its historic image. Two city gates lead to a trapezoidal town square with stuccoed houses. A 13th-century castle set on the hill above the town gives a fine view of the surrounding countryside. ✎ Map V2 • Castle: Open May–Sep: 2pm Fri–Wed • Adm • www.tittmoning.de

# STREETSMART

TOP 10 MUNICH

Left **Munich-area motorway** Right **Lufthansa airplane**

# Planning Your Trip

## When to Go
Munich is worth visiting any time of year. The city shines in spring, summer, and autumn, but winter also offers many delights, such as cultural events and, of course, the ski slopes in the Alps.

## Climate
January can bring glorious blue skies to Munich; April is often fickle, and May can be either summery and warm, or quite cold. Beer garden season officially begins in May. The many lakes near Munich are warmest in August. Autumn often has summer-like temperatures, perfect for walks in the countryside.

## Information
The official tourist offices are excellent sources of information, both in Munich and in towns such as Garmisch-Partenkirchen. They mail information on request.
๏ www.muenchen.de
• www.garmisch-partenkirchen.de • www.bad-toelz.de

## Internet
Most Munich attractions, institutions, and events are posted on the Internet. Simply enter a subject word into a search engine of your choice, add the specificatio "Munich."

## Travel Insurance
EU members should carry with them an EHIC slip from their insurance company, which may entitle them to free or reduced-cost medical treatment. Before travelling, ask your insurance agent what is covered; you may wish to purchase additional insurance. Visitors from non-EU countries are advised to have comprehensive insurance in place before travelling. This should cover accidents, illness, and theft. Cancellation insurance may also be worthwhile.

## Visas & Passports
Citizens of countries belonging to the European Union, and of Canada, Australia, New Zealand, and the US do not require a visa to visit Germany as long as their stay does not exceed 90 days. Visitors from South Africa will need a visa. Citizens of many EU countries do not require a passport, just a national identity card with photograph to enter Germany. Given heightened security measures over the past few years, it is a good idea to carry photo identification at all times when travelling in Germany.

## Customs
Visitors from non-EU countries who are 17 years and older may import up to 200 cigarettes and one litre of spirits or two litres of wine. The importation of firearms is prohibited. For EU citizens there are no customs restrictions if the goods are for personal use.

## Maps
Free city maps of Munich are available at the local tourist bureaus. Maps of the surrounding region, including southern Bavaria, are available at bookshops, downtown department stores, and petrol stations.

## Driving Licence
EU citizens and visitors from Western countries need only their national driving licences; citizens from other countries will require an international driving licence.

## Planning Your Stay
The main sights of Munich can generally be seen in one week. Plan for a longer stay if you wish to make excursions to Neuschwanstein, the Alps, or the picturesque towns and lakes in Upper Bavaria.

### Consulates

**British Consulate-General**
Bürkleinstrasse 10
80538 München
• (089) 21 10 90
• info.munich@
fco.gov.uk
• www. britischebot
schaft.de

**Consulate General of the United States**
Königinstraße 5
80539 München
• (089) 288 80 • http://
munich.usconsulate.
gov/service.html/

*For information on both Munich and Germany, visit*
**www.muenchen.de** *and* **www.auswaertiges-amt.de**

Left **Munich's Hauptbahnhof**   Right **Airport coach (central railway station)**

# 10 Arriving in Munich

## 1 Munich Airport

Franz-Joseph-Strauß Airport, recently expanded with the addition of Terminal 2, is a major air-travel hub. Most international and domestic airlines pass through here. It features a business and restaurant complex, doctors' offices, a MediCare centre, and the nearby AirportClinic M, a small hospital. ◈ *Flight info: (089) 97 52 13 13 • www.munich-airport.de*

## 2 Airlines & Ticket Prices

Terminals 1 and 2 of Franz-Joseph-Strauß Airport house the offices of over 100 airlines. For regular tickets and special fares, check the websites of the individual airlines. ◈ *Air Berlin: (01 80) 573 78 00 • www.airberlin.com • Deutsche Lufthansa: (01 80) 583 84 26 • www.lufthansa.de*

## 3 Connections into the City

Munich airport, located on A92, lies 28 km (17 miles) outside the city. The S-Bahn, whose lines S1 (rear carriages marked *Flughafen*) and S8 provide direct access to and from the airport, will take you to Marienplatz in 37 minutes, while an airport coach to the central railway station takes about 45 minutes, as does a taxi.

## 4 Arriving by Train

Whether you are arriving from Berlin, Paris, Amsterdam, Rome, or Budapest – trains arriving from all directions pull in to the Hauptbahnhof, Munich's central railway station. There are as many as three daily direct rail links to the major European capitals. Southern Bavaria is well served by an extensive railway network. ◈ *www.hauptbahn hof-muenchen.de*

## 5 German Trains

German trains and railway lines are operated by the Deutsche Bahn AG. Long-distance routes are served by InterCity Express trains (ICE), InterCity (IC) and EuroCity (EC) trains; the network also runs Interregio (IR) and Regional Express (RE) for shorter distances. The S-Bahn, the suburban trains, link the city to towns and communities within a radius of about 50 km (30 miles). If you decide to travel by rail, you can save considerably by booking ahead. ◈ *www. bahn.de*

## 6 Ostbahnhof

Some InterCity (IC) and EuroCity (EC) trains stop at the Ostbahnhof. This railway station is also the departure point for trains to the south and east, and for car trains to northern Germany and Italy. ◈ *www.reiseauskunft. bahn.de • www.autozug.de*

## 7 Arriving by Coach

Many long-distance coaches depart and arrive at the central coach terminal, Zentralen Omnibusbahnhof (ZOB) next door to the Hauptbahnhof. The most popular routes are operated by Eurolines and Deutsche Touring GmbH. Tourist centres in Upper Bavaria (and some out-of-the-way destinations) are well served by an extensive network of coach routes. ◈ *www. eurolines.com • www deutsche-touring.com • www.rvo-bus.de*

## 8 Arriving by Car

Six motorways lead into Munich from six directions (A8 Salzburg, A96 Lindau, A8 Stuttgart, A9 Berlin, A95 Garmisch-Partenkirchen, and A92 Deggendorf). The Autobahn ring road enables you to bypass Munich in part. If you want to drive into the city, you will need to take two additional ring roads: the Mittlerer Ring, and the Altstadtring.

## 9 Rental Cars

All major rental car operators – including Avis, Europcar, Hertz, and the Munich firm Sixt – have offices at the airport or the central railway station. ◈ *www.avis.de • www.europcar.de • www.hertz.de • www.sixt.de*

## 10 Rules of the Road

Speed limits within Munich city limits are 50 km/h (30 mph). Seat belts must be worn at all times, and children under 12 must travel in the back seat.

Left **Logo of the S-Bahn suburban railway** Right **MVV bus**

# Getting Around Munich

### 1 U-Bahn
The underground rail network, U-Bahn, runs modern and comfortable cars. Nearly all U-Bahn stations are wheelchair accessible. Eight lines are currently in operation within city boundaries. U-Bahn line U6 to the new Allianz Arena in Fröttmaning is now in full operation. When boarding a train, check the direction panel as well as the destination to ensure you board the correct train.

### 2 S-Bahn
Radiating in all directions from the city centre, the suburban rail network, S-Bahn, is ideal for excursions to towns, lakes, and other destinations in the surrounding countryside. The S-Bahn is also an important urban network: its central stretch from Hackerbrücke to Ostbahnhof (via Hauptbahnhof, Stachus, and Marienplatz) offers transfer points to the U-Bahn, buses, and trams. The S-Bahn (S1 and S8) also links the city centre and the airport. Most S-Bahn stations are wheelchair accessible.

### 3 Tram
Usually less crowded than S- and U-Bahn trains, the trams are an attractive alternative because they allow passengers to see the city as they travel. Route Nos. 18 and 19, running through Old Town, are good choices for inexpensive sightseeing. The

No. 25 route to Grünwald is particularly scenic. Most tram cars have ramps for wheelchair access.

### 4 Bus
The city's buses are suitable when travelling short distances. Most provide links to S- and U-Bahn stations. Bus No. 100 runs past several museums (see p36). Specially marked buses have ramps for wheelchair access.

### 5 Tickets
All public transit operated by the MVV (Munich Traffic and Tariff Association) use the same tickets, which can be bought at dispensers at U- and S-Bahn stations, and on trams and buses. The city and its environs are divided into four zones; ticket prices depend on how many zones you travel through. There are several kinds of tickets: multi-ride (Streifenkarten), single-ride (Einzelkarten), and day (Tageskarten). Weekly and monthly passes are also available. Visitors can take advantage of special rates, for example the CityTourCard (www.city tourcard.com), which allows visitors to use all public transport and includes reduced entry to some museums and theatres. It is available for either one or three days, and for either central Munich or the entire area. Before boarding the train, you must stamp your ticket in a franking

machine, usually located at the top of the stairs down to the platform.

### 6 Car
Driving in Munich can be harrowing. Street parking is difficult to find and car parks are expensive. Only cars approved as green (most rentals included) are allowed within the Mittlerer Ring. Drivers must buy a badge online. ✆ www.umwelt-plakette.de

### 7 Bicycle
Munich is a bicycle-friendly city, with many cycling paths. Bicycles can be rented at a reasonable price. ✆ Call a Bike, (07 00) 05 22 55 22 • Mike's Bike Tours, (089) 25 54 39 87

### 8 On Foot
Exploring Old Town is best done on foot. Other areas easy to explore on foot are Schwabing, Haidhausen, the Isar banks, Westend, and Neuhausen.

### 9 Taxis
You can book a taxi by telephone, hail one in the street, or catch one at taxi stands throughout the city. ✆ Taxi-Ruf, (089) 1 94 10 bzw. 2 16 10 • IsarFunk, (089) 45 05 40

### 10 Weißblaue Flotte
The Bavarian Seenschifffahrt runs excursion boats on Ammersee and Lake Starnberg. ✆ (0 86 52) 96 360 • www. seenschifffahrt.de

Left **Sightseeing bus** Centre **Boats operated by the Weißblaue Flotte** Right **Newsstand**

# 🔟 Information & Guided Tours

### 1 Tourist Offices

Munich's tourist office, Tourismusamt München, has three information kiosks: in the town hall on Marienplatz, at the Hauptbahnhof, and at the airport. Here, visitors can obtain information and special services – from city maps to room reservations. 🅢 www. muenchen.de

### 2 München Ticket

München Ticket pre-sells tickets for most major performances and events, including theatre, concerts, and festivals. Offices are located at the town hall, Gasteig, the tourist office at the central railway station, and Info-Pavillon Olympiapark. 🅢 (089) 54 81 81 81
• www.muenchenticket.de

### 3 Bavarian Castle Administration Bureau

Bayerische Schlösserver-waltung, the Bavarian Castle Administration Bureau, provides informa-tion on Bavarian castles and palaces, parks, and lakes. The bureau also offers a variety of guided tours. 🅢 Bayerische Verwaltung der staatlichen Schlösser, Gärten, und Seen, (089) 179 08 444 • www. schloesser.bayern.de

### 4 Transit Maps

Free maps of the Munich transit system are available at the Haupt-bahnhof and Marienplatz,

or can be downloaded from the MVV (Munich Transport and Tariff Asso-ciation) website. Each zone is indicated on the map by a different colour. 🅢 www.mvv-muenchen.de

### 5 Sightseeing Tours

Various operators offer city sightseeing tours and daytrips with tour guides who speak different languages. Most tours set off from the Hauptbahnhof. 🅢 Münchner Stadt-Rund-fahrten, (089) 55 02 89 95 • Panorama Tours, (089) 54 90 75 60 • www.city-sightseeing.com

### 6 Special City Tours

Several operators offer interesting guided theme tours (such as Art Nou-veau in Munich, Jewish history in Munich, beer, and district tours), as well as tram tours, cycling tours, and tours for disabled travel-lers. 🅢 Stattreisen München, (089) 54 40 42 30, www.stattreisen-muenchen.de • Weis(s)er Stadtvogel München, (089) 29 16 97 65, www. weisser-stadt vogel.de • Spurwechsel, (089) 6 92 46 99, www.spurwech-sel.info

### 7 City Magazines

There are several free city magazines, usually available in pubs, bars, and boutiques. Most list cinema and theatre events, and information on current events. In München is the longest

running and most inform-ative; another established city magazine is Prinz.

### 8 Media

Munich is said to be second only to New York City in publishing; it is also an important media centre: many radio and television stations – public and private – are headquar-tered here. The largest daily newspapers, the Süddeutsche Zeitung (SZ) and the Münchner Merkur, print local news and events sections, as does the popular press, AZ (Abendzeitung) and TZ (Tageszeitung). Bayerische Rundfunk, the local pub-lic broadcasting station, broadcasts on five chan-nels; several private stations broadcast news, and music.

### 9 Internet Information

🅢 www.muenchen.de
• www.munichtoday.de
• www.entdecke-muenchen.info • www. ganz-muenchen.de
• www.munichx.de
• www.muenche.citysam. de (for maps)

### 10 Information for Gays & Lesbians

The SUB (acronym for Gay Communications and Cul-tural Centre) is the central information service offer-ing a café, advice, and events. 🅢 SUB, Müllerstr. 43, Map K5–K6, (089) 2 60 30 56 • Münchner AIDS Hilfe e.V., (089) 54 33 30 • LeTra Lesbentelefon, (089) 725 42 72

Left **Bayerische Landesbank, Brienner Straße** Centre **Letterbox** Right **ATM**

# Banking & Communications

## 1 Banks

Most German and many international banks have branches in Munich. Banks are generally open from 8:30am to 4pm Monday to Friday, although hours can vary depending on the day of the week. The main branches of the larger German banks are as follows: Bayerische Landesbank, Brienner Straße 18; Commerzbank, Maximiliansplatz 19; Deutsche Bank, Promenadeplatz 15; Dresdner Bank, Promenadeplatz 7. Two Reisebank branches, one at the Hauptbahnhof and one at the airport, have longer opening hours.

## 2 Exchange

For visitors from other European countries, the days of currency exchange are a thing of the past. All non-EU travellers can exchange foreign currency into Euros at exchange bureaus, for example, at the railway station, or banks. Several currency exchange machines are available downtown. A note of caution: fees and exchange rates vary, tending to be highest at hotels.

## 3 ATMs

Bank machines are widely available throughout the city, and even in smaller towns. You can withdraw money by credit card with your PIN, or by using any card showing a global banking symbol, such as Cirrus. ATMs are accessible 24 hours.

## 4 Credit Cards

All hotels, with the exception of small bed-and-breakfast establishments, most department stores, and boutiques, as well as restaurants accept major credit cards. Cash is still required in smaller establishments and most beer gardens. Posted outside the entrances to restaurants and stores are the logos of the credit cards accepted within.

## 5 Travellers' Cheques

Travellers' cheques are a safe method of payment, although they are only accepted at large hotels and major department stores. Otherwise, you can exchange travellers' cheques for cash at a bank.

## 6 Payphones

Deutsche Telekom operates all public payphones, which accept coins, phone cards, and sometimes credit cards, although coin pay phones are being phased out. At some high-tech telephone booths you can make phone calls, surf the Internet, and send and receive e-mail. Phone cards are sold at post offices, tobaconists, and in some supermarkets.
- Directory enquiries: Germany, 11 833; Outside Germany, 11 834
- Country dialling codes: 0043 (Austria), 0044 (United Kingdom), 01 (US and Canada), 0039 (Italy)
- Within Munich: 089 or 89

## 7 Mobile Phones

T-Mobile, Vodafone, and O2 provide service through most of Bavaria. A note of caution: reception may still be difficult in some remote areas. The use of mobile phones on all public transit is allowed, although reception may not be good. Check with your mobile phone provider before leaving home to find out if your phone can be used in Germany.

## 8 Post Offices

Most post offices are open from Monday to Friday, 8am to 6pm, and Saturday from 8am to noon. You can also buy stamps at automated dispensers and in some stationery shops. The yellow letterboxes have two letter slots – one for mail within the city and the other for outbound mail.

## 9 Internet

All museums, and many hotels and restaurants are listed on the Internet. Major hotels, and some smaller hotels, offer Internet access to their guests, but there is often a fee.

## 10 Internet Cafés

In Munich you will find many Internet cafés, including one that caters to gays and lesbians (see p63). The easyInternet-Café at Bahnhofplatz 1, across from the central railway station is open 24 hours.
- easyInternet-Café, Bahnhofplatz 1, Map J4

*A list of Internet cafés can be found on the website*
**www.easyeverything.com/germany**

Left **Ambulance** Centre **Pharmacy logo** Right **Police car**

# 🔟 Security & Health

### 1 Emergency Numbers

The emergency number for fire, rescue, or ambulance is 112. For police emergencies, dial 110. In addition, there are the following emergency and help lines:
✆ *Emergency doctors: (0 18 05) 19 12 12 • Poison information: (089) 1 92 40 • Women's emergency help line: (089) 76 37 37 • Addiction help line: (089) 28 28 22 • Religious help line 0800-111 0111 (Evangelical) 0800-1 11 02 22 (Catholic)*

### 2 Hospitals

If you are visiting from the EU (European Union), paramedic, hospital, and doctors' services are generally covered by your national health insurance. If you are visiting from other countries, it is advisable to take out travel insurance before starting your trip.

### 3 Doctors & Dentists

For everything other than acute emergencies, visitors are advised to consult doctors or dentists during standard clinic hours. Addresses of doctors and specialists are listed in the *Gelbe Seiten* (yellow pages). Services are covered for EU citizens upon presentation of the EHIC insurance form.

### 4 Pharmacies

Pharmacies are identified with a large red "A" – which stands for the German word for pharmacy (*Apotheke*). Most are open until 7pm or 8pm. After 8pm, every pharmacy posts the name and address of the nearest pharmacy that is open late. You can also call the pharmacy emergency line. ✆ *(089) 59 44 75*

### 5 Crime

Munich has one of the lowest crime rates not only in Germany but in all of Europe, and Bavaria has the highest rate of crime-solving in Germany. In other words, you can feel perfectly safe during your vacation in Munich; simply observe standard precautions such as avoiding parks or outlying areas at night, especially on your own.

### 6 Pickpockets

Crowds are magnets for gangs of pickpockets everywhere, and the same is true in Munich. Be vigilant in crowded U-Bahn or S-Bahn cars, or when walking through crowded areas such as the pedestrian zone – and especially the Oktoberfest.

### 7 Lost & Found

If you lose your belongings, try one of the numbers listed below:
✆ *Lost-and-found, City of Munich: (089) 23 39 60 45 • Lost-and-found at the Deutschen Bahn, Munich: (089) 13 08 66 64 • Lost-and-found at Flughafen München: (089) 97 52 13 70*

### 8 Mountain Safety

If you are making an excursion into the mountains, be sure to have appropriate footwear and clothing. For hikes, you should obtain precise route and weather information ahead of time. You should avoid hiking alone. In winter, it is vital to pay attention to avalanche warnings. The emergency number 112 is also used for the Alps throughout Europe – mobile phone reception is usually good.
✆ *Ambulance transport and mountain assistance service (Bergrettung) Bayern: 19 222*

### 9 Road & Traffic Information

The local public radio station Bayern 3 broadcasts current information on traffic conditions. Information on road conditions is also available from the ADAC, the German Automobile Association. ✆ *Emergency assistance, ADAC: (01 80) 2 22 22 22*

### 10 Women Travelling Alone

Women travelling on their own will feel perfectly comfortable and safe in Munich if they observe normal precautions. Ask for a room near the elevator in your hotel if you are safety-conscious, and do not let strangers into your hotel room. Some parking lots have reserved, well-lit, parking spots for women.

➤ *If you need towing assistance, call (089) 747 1000 (Abschleppdienst).*

Left **LEGOLAND Germany** Centre **Hiking in Tölzer Land** Right **Parking spot for the disabled**

# 🔟 Families, Seniors & the Disabled

## 1 Discounts

Families with children are entitled to a number of discounts. Entrance fees to many sights and for sports events at Olympiapark are reduced for both children and seniors. The CityTourCard covers all travel by public transit in the city and up to a 50 per cent discount for many tourist attractions. One- and three-day cards are sold at the tourist office's information kiosks at Marienplatz, Hauptbahnhof, and the airport.

🌐 *www.citytourcard.de; www.muenchen.de*

## 2 Children's Programmes

Munich's tourist office, the Tourismusamt München, will provide you with information on the many children's summer programmes offered by the city. Castle tours are arranged by the Bayerische Schlösserverwaltung (Bavarian Castle Administration) for a flat fee of 1 Euro. These guided tours include the Residenz, Schloss Nymphenburg, Schloss Schleißheim, and other sights.

🌐 *Tourismusamt München, Sendlinger Str. 1, (089) 23 39 65 00 • Bayerische Schlösserverwaltung, (089) 17 90 84 44*

## 3 Family-Friendly Restaurants

Many Munich restaurants are equipped with booster seats and offer smaller portions for children or even separate children's menus. Be sure to enquire in advance *(see p69)*.

## 4 Seniors

Seniors enjoy many discounts as well as a wide variety of special sporting and hiking activities, guided tours, excursions, and social events.

🌐 *www.seniorenbuero.de*

## 5 Cobblestones

Several areas in Munich still feature original cobblestone paving, which may be a challenge for wheelchair users.

## 6 Public Transit (MVV)

Most S- and U-Bahn stations have been made wheelchair accessible, as have most trams. Special low-axle buses are marked with a disabled sign to indicate that they are equipped with a ramp for access. Easy-access public toilets are found most readily in public transit stations. Details are provided in the MVV brochure *Barrier-free*, available at MVV ticket kiosks.

## 7 Guided Tours for the Disabled

City tours for the hearing impaired, with guides trained in international sign language, are organized by the Fremdenverkehrsamt München. Operators such as the *Weis(s)e Stadtvogel* and *Stattreisen München e.V.* also offer tours for the disabled. 🌐 *Tourismusamt München, Sendlinger Str.1, (089) 23 39 65 00 • Weis(s)er Stadtvogel München, (089) 29 16 97 65 • Stattreisen München e.V., (089) 54 40 42 30*

## 8 Organizations for the Disabled

The *Club Behinderter und ihrer Freunde* (CBF, the Club for the Disabled and Friends), provides information on cinemas, theatres, and museums with access for people with disabilities. Additional information, advice, and wheelchair rentals are available from VDK Bayern. 🌐 *CBF, (089) 3 56 88 or 3 56 88 08, www.cbf-muenchen.de • VDK Bayern, (089) 21 17 400*

## 9 Easy-Access Hotels

Unfortunately, there are few hotels in Munich that are truly equipped for the needs of wheelchair users. Many hotels occupy historic buildings, which are difficult to retrofit. Be sure to check ahead when booking a room.

## 10 Information for the Disabled

The brochure *Munich for Tourists with Disabilities* lists easy-access hotels, museums, pools, and other venues. It is available at the Marienplatz and Hauptbahnhof information kiosks; the tourist office will also mail it on request.

🌐 *tourismus@muenchen.de*

*The Association for the Hearing Impaired, Lohengrinstr. 11, (089) 99 26 98 0, is a good source of information.*

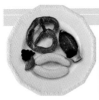

Left **Weißwurst platter** Centre **Rush hour in Munich** Right **Oktoberfest crowd**

# 🔟 Useful Information

### 1 *Weißwurst* after 12 Noon

In the past, *Weißwurst* was eaten as a late or second breakfast. Highly perishable, these white veal sausages were kept in large pots of boiling water from early morning until noon. This led to an unspoken rule: never eat *Weißwurst* after noon. Although this is no longer necessary thanks to modern cooking methods, the old tradition is still observed by many locals.

### 2 Bockbeer

Beer temptations can reach a peak during the *Starkbier* (bockbeer) season, but you should remember that *Starkbier* has an alcohol content ranging from 6.5 to over 7.5 per cent. Enjoy the tasty brews – just be sure not to overindulge.

### 3 Bavarian Words

Even if you know German, the local dialect is still quite a challenge. There are a few key expressions: rolls, called *Brötchen* elsewhere, are called *Semmeln* here; *Weizenbier* (wheat beer) is called *Weißbier*, and a *Radler* could be either a cyclist or a shandy, a mixture of beer and lemonade.

### 4 Cyclists & Rollerbladers

Munich is a wonderful city for cyclists, and many locals jump on their bikes in summer. Unfortunately, there are always a few bad apples. As a pedestrian, you should watch out for cyclists barrelling along pavements, sometimes even going in the wrong direction down a one-way street, or turning sharp corners quickly. The same is true of some rollerbladers.

### 5 Alcohol at the Wheel

It goes without saying that beer is very tempting in Bavaria. However, you should remember that the blood-alcohol limit is 0.5 per cent and that Munich's police force carries out regular spot-checks. After drinking, it is best to leave the car behind and take a taxi.

### 6 Rush Hour

Aside from the difficulty of finding parking in the inner city, driving within the boundaries of the *Altstadtring* (ring road) during rush hour is no fun. Take public transit; it will get you to your destination with greater speed and far less aggravation.

### 7 Pickpockets

Munich is a safe city. However, some caution is advised at certain tourist centres and crowded sights. Here, as elsewhere, there are gangs of pickpockets. Be especially vigilant on crowded platforms, in S- and U-Bahn stations and train cars, at large open-air events such as Oktoberfest, and in the pedestrian zone.

### 8 Parking Infractions

It is best to adhere to all parking rules. Parking attendants patrol the streets, especially in the inner city, and issue tickets when cars are illegally parked or when parking is unpaid. Rental car agencies will present you with any tickets when you return your car, and unpaid fines are collected throughout the European Union. In some areas, parking is restricted to residents with parking permits. If your car has been tagged and towed, call the police for information on where you can collect it – and pay the horrendously steep fines.

### 9 Taxis during Oktoberfest

There are two times of year when taxis are extremely hard to come by – New Year's Eve and Oktoberfest, which is usually held the last two weeks in September. Near Theresienwiese during Oktoberfest, taxi drivers may refuse to carry passengers who appear intoxicated.

### 10 Hotels during Oktoberfest

Munich hotels, even luxury hotels, tend to be fully booked during Oktoberfest. If you are planning a stay at this time, reserve well in advance and make sure to notify the hotel if you are arriving after 5pm so that your room will be held for you.

Left **Stadtmuseum** Centre **Kebab kiosk in Westend** Right **Flea market**

# Munich on a Budget

### 1 Free Museum Admission

On Sundays, admission is free to all state and municipal museums, including the Bayerische Nationalmuseum and the Münchner Stadtmuseum *(see p36)*. Free admission is only applicable to the permanent collections.

### 2 Cheap Eats

Many ethnic eateries in Munich are tasty and inexpensive choices for quick snacks, take-aways and meals. Pizza and kebabs are widely available, and small Turkish or Asian kiosks offer quick meals, some even have small tables or counters. Highly recommended is the *Suppenküche* (soup restaurant) in the Viktualienmarkt.

### 3 Cheap Restaurants

Traditional pubs with Bavarian cuisine tend to be quite inexpensive. Most restaurants have *prix fixe* menus at lunch, which are considerably less expensive than the evening menus. This is also true for some of the top restaurants where, if you have time to enjoy a four-course meal at lunch, you're in for a treat.

### 4 Accommodation

Hotels in Munich can be expensive. Consider staying in the surrounding areas for less costly accommodation. One alternative is to rent an apartment through one

of several agencies – apartments are available for stays as short as a few days or long as a few months *(see p149)*. Camping is another viable alternative in summer.
⊗ *Campingplatz München-Thalkirchen*
• *Zentralländstr. 49*
• *(089) 7 23 17 07*
• *www.camping-muenchen.de*

### 5 Admission Discounts

In the evening just prior to the start of the performance, box offices at theatres, concert halls, and other venues offer discounted admission for students and seniors.

### 6 Public Transport

Visitors to Munich can benefit from a wide range of discounted tickets for public transportation, for both the city centre and outlying areas. The CityTourCard is a combined travel-and-admission pass that is sold at tourist information kiosks, as well as at MVG kiosks and ticket vending machines at metro, tram, bus and train stations. With the day pass you can travel all day without restrictions. Three-day passes are best for weekend trips, while partner passes, for up to five people, are a family-friendly option. Children under six travel free; children over six and youth pay reduced fares.
⊗ *www.citytourcard.com*

### 7 Flea Markets

Flea markets and the three Auer Dulten *(see p52)* are an inexpensive way to spend a fun day strolling and browsing. Prices are usually low and real treasures can sometimes be found.

### 8 Free Concerts

The concert marathon at the Theatron in Olympiapark is free every summer. Students at the *Hochschule für Musik* (music conservatory), located at Arcissstr. 12, also put on excellent free concerts.
⊗ *Programmes and times: (089) 289 27 442*

### 9 Cheap Sightseeing

Board an eastbound tram No. 18 or No. 19 at Stachus. These routes travel through some of the most beautiful areas of Munich.

### 10 Open Houses & Long Nights

Nearly all attractions and institutions have an open house each calendar year. Ask at the Munich tourist office to find out when these events, usually free of charge, will take place. The *Lange Nächte* (long nights) are especially popular. These are extended-hour opening nights for museums, theatres, music, and more – all for a flat fee. Buses shuttle between dozens of participating venues during these events.

*For information on free outdoor events and festivals, visit*
**www.umsonst-und-draussen.org**

Left **Traditional** *Lederhose* Centre **Nymphenburg porcelain** Right **Glass painting**

# 🔟 Things to Buy

### 1 Nymphenburger Porzellan

Be it a porcelain figurine or a dining set – all the pieces at the porcelain manufacture at Schloss Nymphenburg *(see p12)* are based on historic models. These pieces are of high artistic value and hence quite expensive. ✪ *Porzellanmanufaktur Nymphenburg, Odeonsplatz 1 • Map L3*

### 2 Chocolates by Elly Seidl

If you have a sweet tooth, the hand-made chocolates and other sinful sweets at Elly Seidl's shop are just for you. Connoisseurs swear that Elly's concoctions surpass those of her Swiss or Belgian competitors. Try the champagne truffles. ✪ *Maffeistr. 1 & Am Kosttor 2 • Map L4 & M4*

### 3 Folk Dress

Classic folk dress – and their contemporary versions – make good souvenirs. Accessories, such as belts, hats, and fringed scarves are also available. These are fashioned from fine materials such as leather, linen, wool, and loden, and are correspondingly expensive. Hard to beat are *Lederhose*, traditional Bavarian leather knickerbockers, which never wear out and get more and more beautiful with age. ✪ *Loden Frey, Maffeistr. 7–9 • Map L4 • Angermaier, Rosental 10 • Map L4*

### 4 Reproductions in Museum Shops

As in New York, Rome, and Berlin, the shops in Munich's museums sell fine reproductions of works of art, limited editions, posters, and reproductions of designer pieces from both their own collections and those of other musuems.

### 5 Beer Mugs

Simple beer mugs and glasses or more elaborate ones with decorated zinc lids and painted designs are available in most antique shops, in the department stores lining the pedestrian zone, and behind Frauenkirche. If you happen to be in a traditional Bavarian pub and really like the brewery mugs or glasses, you can ask whether you may purchase one.

### 6 Special Toys

The museum shop at the Deutsches Museum carries an outstanding selection of unique toys, from building sets to robots – enthusiastically received by children and adults alike. A subsidiary of the museum shop has opened at Marienplatz. *(see pp8–9).*

### 7 Delicacies and Kitchenware

Allois Dallmayr is a Munich institution where you can see live lobsters and crabs in the fountain. The shop is not huge, but has sections dedicated to coffee, cakes, olive oil, kitchen utensils and crockery *(see p83).*

### 8 Oskar Maria Tableware

A perfect souvenir for those who love German literature, Dukatz cups and saucers are inscribed with humorous and subtle quotes by Bavarian author Oskar Maria Graf. They are for sale at Oskar Maria café. ✪ *Oskar Maria, Salvatorplatz 1 • Map L3*

### 9 Glass Painting & Religious Art

Much *verre églomisé* (painting on glass, often with religious motifs) originates in the Murnau region. Traditional crib figures are created in the town of Oberammergau, a centre for woodcarving. Antique and specialty shops carry a wide range of religious and folk art.

### 10 Soccer Memorabilia

The shops of Munich's two opposing soccer clubs are located nearly opposite one another next door to the Hofbräuhaus. They carry everything that a true fan's heart desires. Other shops nearby sell typical Munich souvenirs such as postcards, posters, beer mugs and knick-knacks. ✪ *FC-Bayern-Shop, Orlandostr. 1 (at Platzl)* • *Fan-Shop TSV München 1860, Orlandostr. 8 (at Platzl) • Map M4*

*You can sometimes find real treasures at the Auer Dulten (popular fairs in the Au district) or at flea markets See pp52–3*

Left **Dallmayr** Centre **Sales at Karstadt department store** Right **Hieber am Dom**

# TOP 10 Shopping Tips

### 1 Opening Hours

Most stores in the city are open 9am to 8pm Monday to Saturday. Government offices, banks, and post offices close earlier, usually at 4pm, 5pm, or 6pm. On Christmas Eve and New Year's Eve, most stores close at noon. Stores in small towns outside Munich keep shorter hours, often closing at 5pm weekdays, at noon on Saturday, and on Wednesday afternoons. Hours may well be extended in the near future, as the legal retail closing hours are currently the subject of lively debate.

### 2 Sales/Discounts

End-of-summer and -winter sales have been undermined for some time now by special sales events all year long. Just keep your eyes open for *Rabatt* (discount) or *Sonderverkauf* (special sale) signs. Price labels on merchandise are non-negotiable in most stores. At wholesalers, in some boutiques, and at flea markets, you can try your hand at bargaining for a reduced price.

### 3 Payment by Credit Card

Most city-centre stores accept all major credit cards. Outside the city and in smaller boutiques, credit cards might not be taken, with the exception of the Maestro card, which is accepted virtually everywhere.

### 4 Consumer Protection

The Landratsamt of Munich (regional and municipal affairs office) is responsible for food and consumer goods. If you have any problems, such as exchanging a purchase, contact them or the Munich subsidiary of the Bavarian Consumer Protection Agency. ⬥ *Landratsamt München, Mariahilfplatz 17, Map F6–G6, (089) 62 21-23 28 bzw. 62 21-28 17 • Verbraucherzentrale München, Mozartstr. 9, Map E5, (089) 53 98 70*

### 5 Sales Tax

In Germany, sales tax (*Mehrwertsteuer*) is 16 per cent and included in the marked price. Travellers from non-EU countries can apply for a refund with the relevant documents from Global Refund either at the airport or by mail from home. The Customs official has to see the goods purchased and stamp the sales receipts when you leave Germany.

### 6 Exchange

Full-price items have limited warranties and can be exchanged if they are damaged or otherwise unsatisfactory; in some cases, you will get a full cash refund. Note: there is usually no exchange policy for discounted items.

### 7 Fashion

Fashion boutiques are located chiefly in the main shopping districts, especially the pedestrian zones, Sendlinger Straße, Maximilianstraße, Theatinerstraße, and in Schwabing on Leopoldstraße and around the university *(see p66)*.

### 8 Music

In addition to the large chains such as WOM, Saturn, Media-Markt, and the CD sections of department stores, you'll find an interesting selection in independent stores, such as Hieber am Dom (Liebfrauenstr. 1), which also carries a large collection of sheet music. Ludwig Beck am Rathauseck *(see p83)* offers excellent jazz, worldbeat, blues, and classics, both modern and traditional.

### 9 Books

Munich's principal bookseller is Hugendubel department store, whose flagship store is located on Marienplatz. Many small independent bookshops, including those selling foreign-language books, are located in the university district. If you have a passion for antiquarian books, be sure to visit Kitzinger *(see p91)*.

### 10 Factory Outlets

Factory outlets have now come into fashion in Munich. Many are located outside the city in commercial districts. Your best bet is to check on the Internet. ⬥ *www.factory-outlet-shop.de • www.wekacityline.de/mshow*

Left **Ratskeller** Right **Hotel Residenz**

# Hotel and Restaurant Tips

**Room Reservations**
You can book hotel rooms by phone, fax, or e-mail. The Munich tourist office also offers a free booking service from 8am to 7pm Monday to Friday, and from 10am to 6pm Saturday. ◐
*Tourismusamt München*
• *(089) 23 39 65 00*

**Hotel Categories**
The number of stars indicates the quality of a hotel – and its price. Most room prices in Munich hotels include breakfast. Prices vary depending on the season – with Oktoberfest being the most expensive – and room comfort. Many hotels offer special weekend packages or reduced prices at low season. Check the Internet for online specials, too.

**Choosing a Hotel**
Munich hotel prices are generally higher than those of hotels in the rest of Bavaria. The prices indicated in the various sections of this guide *(see p144)* are average prices only. However, even in Munich there are less expensive alternatives; such as small hotels, bed-and-breakfast establishments, hostels, and short-term rental apartments *(see p148)*.

**Restaurant Reservations**
It is advisable to reserve tables at all gourmet and popular restaurants, and whenever you are dining in a group, especially at weekends. If there are just one or two of you, finding a seat at a table in a traditional pub is easy – just walk in and sit down at a free table or at empty seats at a larger table (first asking if the seats are free). Keep in mind that these pubs always have a number of tables reserved for regular patrons, often with a sign hanging over them saying *Stammtisch* (table reserved for regulars).

**Tipping**
Service (about 12 per cent) and food tax (about 7 per cent) are included in restaurant bills but it is customary to round out the bill and give a tip of up to 10 per cent.

**Dining Hours**
Most restaurants open for lunch, although some are only open from 6pm. Establishments that are open at lunch sometimes close for a few hours in the afternoon. Evening restaurants are open until midnight or later. Beer gardens in the city close at 11pm. Most restaurants post their menus – including daily specials – on pavement boards or at the door.

**Bavarian Cuisine**
True Bavarian cuisine is best experienced in the traditional pubs or brewery-operated restaurants *(see p50)*. Try *Weißwurst* (poached white veal sausage) with sweet mustard and a pretzel, *Schweinshaxn* (grilled pork knuckle) or *Schweinsbraten* (roast pork), served with potato dumplings and red cabbage. Fresh fish such as *Forelle* (trout) or *Renke* (whitefish from mountain lakes) are usually served whole and are excellently prepared, even in small country restaurants. *Brotzeit* – cold cuts, cheese, and radish served with bread – is especially popular in beer gardens.

**Other Cuisines**
Like most large cities, Munich has a wide variety of ethnic restaurants – from Middle Eastern to Polynesian. Local residents are especially fond of Italian cuisine.

**Gourmet Dining**
Munich is home to an impressive array of top-notch restaurants and expensive, fashionable establishments. Some of the city's gourmet restaurants are among the very best in Europe *(see p64)*.

**Dress Code**
Your attire should be at least as elegant as the restaurant. For men, this means a jacket or blazer – with or without a tie – and appropriate footwear (no running shoes and no shorts). Otherwise, the dress code is generally casual and relaxed, especially in beer gardens.

Left & Centre **Königshof room and lobby** Right **Bayerischer Hof**

# Luxury Hotels

### 1 Mandarin Oriental

First-class service and historic ambience near the Maximilianstraße. This five-star hotel has 53 rooms and 20 suites, as well as banquet and conference facilities. The rooftop patio with pool affords fabulous views. Onsite restaurants include Mark's and Mark's Corner. ◈ *Neuturmstr. 1 • Map M4 • (089) 29 09 80 • www.mandarinoriental.com • €€€€€*

### 2 Le Méridien

New deluxe hotel at the central railway station with 381 rooms and suites. Modern comfort, exquisite service, and luxurious accommodations. Onsite facilities include a restaurant, bar, and a wellness/fitness centre. ◈ *Bayerstr. 41 • Map J4 • (089) 242 20 • €€€€€*

### 3 Dorint Sofitel Bayerpost

This new five-star hotel has been created behind the historic façade of a former postal building: an elegant setting for banquets and conferences, accommodating up to 750 participants. Large spa area. ◈ *Bayerstr. 12 • Map J4 • (089) 59 94 80 • www.dorint.com • €€€€€*

### 4 Kempinski Hotel Vier Jahreszeiten

The recent renovation of this grande dame of the Maximilianstraße means that comfort and luxury are evident in each of the individually furnished rooms, which still retain their 1858 elegance. A top-notch restaurant and bar are found on-site, as well as a wellness centre and business facilities. ◈ *Maximilianstr. 17 • Map M4 • (089) 212 50 • www.kempinski-vierjahreszeiten.de • €€€€€*

### 5 Königshof

This elegant hotel is centrally located overlooking the lively Stachus square. Luxuriously furnished with great attention to detail, the establishment offers 74 rooms and 13 suites. The restaurant is among the very best in the city. ◈ *Karlsplatz 25 • Map J4 • (089) 55 13 60 • www.geisel-privathotels.de • limited wheelchair access • €€€€€*

### 6 Maritim Hotel

A first-class hotel at the central railway station with 339 lavishly appointed rooms and 11 elegant suites. Nine conference rooms are available for gatherings of up to 550. ◈ *Goethestr. 7 • Map E5 • (089) 55 23 50 • www.maritim.de • €€€€€*

### 7 Bayerischer Hof

An institution among hotels worldwide and now in the hands of the fourth generation, this family-owned luxury hotel features 395 rooms and suites, each with its own style. Three restaurants (a garden restaurant, Palais Keller, Trader Vic's) and Falk's bar, plus a nightclub, piano bar, rooftop patio with pool, and a business centre round out the services. ◈ *Promenadeplatz 2–6 • Map K4–L4 • (089) 2 12 00 • www.bayerischerhof.de • limited wheelchair access • €€€€€*

### 8 Excelsior

The interiors of this hotel near Hauptbahnhof and the pedestrian zone are reminiscent of an idyllic country retreat. Geisel's vinothèque is a must for all wine lovers. ◈ *Schützenstr. 11 • Map J4 • (089) 55 13 70 • www.geisel-privathotels.de • €€€€€*

### 9 Hilton Munich Park

Centrally located right at the Englischer Garten, this quiet hotel boasts 461 rooms and suites that offer the highest level of comfort. The Tivoli restaurant offers theme buffets. The hotel also has facilities for conferences for up to 1,600 participants. ◈ *Am Tucherpark 7 • Map G3 • (089) 384 50 • www.hilton.de • €€€€€*

### 10 Palace

Small, first-class hotel near the Prinzregententheater with 74 rooms and suites furnished with a French flair. Garden, restaurant, and bar, as well as fitness area and rooftop patio. ◈ *Trogerstr. 21 • Map H5 • (089) 41 97 10 • www.daspalace.de • €€€€€*

 **Note:** *All hotels accept major credit cards. Unless otherwise stated, they are not equipped for wheelchair access.*

**Price Categories**

| For a standard, double room per night (with breakfast if included), taxes, and extra charges. | |
|---|---|
| € | under €60 |
| €€ | €60–100 |
| €€€ | €100–150 |
| €€€€ | €150–200 |
| €€€€€ | over €200 |

Left & Right **Hilton Munich City exterior and interior**

# Business Hotels

### 1 Hilton Munich City

First-class hotel with 481 luxuriously appointed rooms, of which 20 are suites and one is a presidential suite. Located next door to the Gasteig. All rooms are equipped with Internet access and fax machines. Conference rooms with a capacity for 500 people. ⊗ *Rosenheimer Str. 15 • Map N6 • (089) 480 40 • www.hilton.de • €€€€–€€€€€*

### 2 Holiday Inn Munich – City Centre

Across from the Gasteig, this hotel boasts 580 rooms (12 suites) and a beautiful view of the city from the high banks of the Isar River. Event facilities for 2,000 participants and 16 conference rooms. ⊗ *Hochstr. 3 • Map N6 • (089) 480 30 • €€€€–€€€€€*

### 3 Arabella Sheraton Grand Hotel

Twenty-two floors with 643 rooms (31 suites) and a view all the way to the Alps. Fine dining is guaranteed at the gourmet restaurant, Ente vom Lehel. There is a spa with an indoor pool and a fitness room. Three floors are reserved for conference facilities, accommodating groups ranging from five to 1,250. ⊗ *Arabellastr. 6 • (089) 926 40 • www.arabellasheraton.com • €€€–€€€€€*

### 4 Holiday Inn München City-Nord

Traditional upmarket chain hotel with 365 comfortable rooms and conference rooms holding up to 600 people. ⊗ *Leopoldstr. 194 • Map G2 • (089) 38 17 90 • www.munich-citynorth-holiday-inn.de • €€€–€€€€€*

### 5 Marriott Hotel München

Established conference hotel with 348 rooms and 13 conference rooms catering to business clients. Wireless connections in all conference areas. ⊗ *Berliner Str. 93 • Map G1 • (089) 36 00 20 • www.marriott.com • limited wheelchair access • €€€–€€€€€*

### 6 Eden-Hotel-Wolff

Located directly at the Hauptbahnhof, this established four-star hotel offers 240 function rooms as well as 10 conference rooms, each with a 250-person capacity. ⊗ *Arnulfstr. 4 • Map E4 • (089) 551 11 50 • www.ehw.de • €€€€– €€€€€*

### 7 InterCityHotel München

Four-star hotel in a heritage-protected railway building with 198 sound-proofed and comfortable rooms. All conference rooms are equipped with wireless connections. ⊗ *Bayerstr. 10 • Map J4 • (089) 44 44 40 • www.intercityhotel.de • limited wheelchair access • €€€–€€€€€*

### 8 NH München Neue Messe

This new hotel at the Munich fair offers 253 comfortably furnished rooms and nine conference rooms for up to 300 participants. Wheelchair-accessible facilities, laundry service, car park, fitness facilities, plus room amenities including safes and wireless connections. ⊗ *Eggenfeldener Str 100 • (089) 99 34 50 • www.nh- hotels. com • €€€–€€€€€*

### 9 Kempinski Hotel Airport München

A highlight of this hotel is the palm atrium with 20-m- (65-ft-) tall palm trees and a view of the airport runways – a perfect setting for receptions, exhibitions, or presentations. The 389 rooms are well equipped with amenities for business travellers. ⊗ *Terminalstr./ Mitte 20 • (089) 978 20 • www.kempinski-airport.de • wheelchair accessible • €€€€–€€€€€*

### 10 Mövenpick Hotel München-Airport

Ultramodern, four-star conference hotel just a few minutes drive from the terminals at Munich's international airport. It boasts 165 sound-proofed rooms and 17 conference rooms. ⊗ *Hallbergmoos, Ludwigstr. 43 • (0811) 88 80 • www.moevenpick-munich.com • wheelchair accessible • €€€–€€€€€*

*For information on easy-access hotels* **See p138**

Left **Hotel Astor** Centre & Right **Hotel Königswache**

# Mid-Range Hotels

## 1 Hotel Euro-päischer Hof

This 148-room hotel, at the upmarket end of the mid-range scale, is located directly across from the central railway station. Non-smoking rooms, breakfast buffet, underground car park. There are special packages for children, and pets are permitted. In-house Italian restaurant. ⊗ *Bayerstr. 31 • Map J4 • (089) 55 15 10 • www.heh.de • €€€–€€€€*

## 2 Alpen-Hotel-München

This upscale three-star hotel offers a welcome oasis from the bustle of the nearby pedestrian zone. All rooms have Internet access and the highest three-star standards. The onsite Stefans Gasthaus serves Bavarian and international cuisine. ⊗ *Adolf-Kolping-Str. 14 • Map J4 • (089) 55 93 30 • www.alpenhotel-muenchen.de • limited wheelchair access • €€–€€€€*

## 3 Hotel Astor

With 46 rooms, this hotel near the central railway station offers the amenities found in a four-star hotel, including modem connections in every room. The in-house Italian Bistro Nozzi has a cosy lounge with an open fireplace, and a wine cellar. ⊗ *Schillerstr. 24 • Map J5 • (089) 54 83 70 • www.hotel-astor.de • limited wheelchair access • €€–€€€€*

## 4 Hotel Einhorn

Occupying a beautiful Art Nouveau building, the Einhorn offers 110 rooms equipped with all the comforts of a three-star hotel. Public transport and S-Bahn are within five minutes walking distance. ⊗ *Paul-Heyse-Str. 10 • Map E5 • (089) 53 98 20 • www.hotel-einhorn.de • limited wheelchair access • €€€–€€€€*

## 5 Hotel Senefelder

A comfortable hotel near the central railway station. Its 70 rooms are furnished in a modern style. Breakfast is served until 11am; parking is available. ⊗ *Senefelderstr. 4 (near Bayerstr.) • Map J4 • (089) 55 15 40 • www.hotel-senefelder.de • €€–€€€*

## 6 Hotel Leopold

This traditional hotel in the heart of Schwabing has a classic style and an idyllic garden that reflect the ambience of a family-run operation. All 75 rooms offer three-star comfort. Non-smoking rooms and special beds for allergy sufferers are available on request. ⊗ *Leopoldstr. 119 • Map G2 • (089) 36 70 61 • www. hotel-leopold.de • limited wheelchair access • €€€–€€€€*

## 7 Hotel Königswache

This small hotel is close to the three Pinakotheken. Nearby U-Bahn connections provide easy and quick access to the city centre. All rooms are three-star rooms and are equipped with Internet access. ⊗ *Steinheilstr. 7 • Map J2 • (089) 542 75 70 • www. koenigswache.de • €€€*

## 8 Cosmopolitan

Just a few steps off Leopoldstraße, the Cosmopolitan offers rooms with Lignet Roset's signature clean, modern interior design. Breakfast buffet until 11am. ⊗ *Hohenzollernstr. 5 • Map F2 • (089) 38 38 10 • www. geisel-hotels.de • €€€*

## 9 Hotel Herzog

A good-value choice for the central location – right next to the U-Bahn station Goetheplatz. The Herzog's 80 tastefully furnished rooms are modern and comfortable. Most rooms have balconies overlooking the picturesque courtyard garden. ⊗ *Häberlstr. 9 • Map E6 • (089) 59 99 39 01 • www.hotel-herzog.de • €€–€€€*

## 10 Ibis München Messe

Located at the Neue Messe, this efficiently run hotel offers 100 simple yet modern rooms with Internet access. Parking is available, pets are permitted, and there is a restaurant and bar on site. ⊗ *Feldkirchen, Otto-Lilienthal-Ring 2 • (089) 93 92 90 • www.ibis-hotel.de • wheelchair accessible • €€–€€€*

*All hotels accept major credit cards. Unless otherwise stated, they are not equipped for wheelchair access.*

**Price Categories**

| | |
|---|---|
| For a standard, double room per night (with breakfast if included), taxes, and extra charges. | € under €60 |
| | €€ €60–100 |
| | €€€ €100–150 |
| | €€€€ €150–200 |
| | €€€€€ over €200 |

Left **Courtyard at the Hotel Opéra** Right **Bar at the Cortiina**

# 🔟 Hotels with Flair

### 1 Advokat

A design hotel with an elegant, minimalist style in soothing earth tones. The beautiful rooftop patio affords spectacular views of Old Town. With its city centre location, this hotel is the ideal departure point for sightseeing and shopping. ⊗ *Baaderstr. 1 • Map M5 • (089) 21 63 10 • www.hotel-advokat.de • €€€€*

### 2 Anna Hotel

A gem in an ideal location. This new boutique hotel, which has been styled from top to bottom, is operated by the Geisel family, who have a tradition as hoteliers in Munich (with Hotel Königshof). Another popular feature is the hip in-house restaurant-bar Anna. ⊗ *Schützenstr. 1 • Map J4 • (089) 59 99 40 • www.geisel-hotels.de • limited wheelchair access • €€€€–€€€€€*

### 3 Hotel Opéra

A pretty and charming hotel in an imposing palais in the Lehel district. Each of the attractive rooms is furnished in a unique and palatial manner. For aperitifs and much more, guests gather in the glorious neo-Romanesque courtyard. At Gandl, the restaurant next door, you can enjoy an excellent dinner. ⊗ *St-Anna-Str. 10 • Map N4 • (089) 210 49 40 • www.hotel-opera.de • €€€€–€€€€€*

### 4 Hotel Gästehaus Englischer Garten

Attractive boutique hotel in a heritage building in the Englischer Garten with 25 tastefully appointed rooms. Breakfast is served on the cosy terrace, surrounded by the greenery of the park. ⊗ *Liebergesellstr. 8 (Ecke Keferstr.) • Map G2 • (089) 3 83 94 10 • www.hotelenglischergarten.de • €€€*

### 5 Prinzregent am Friedensengel

Notable for its Bavarian ambience, the Prinzregent offers elegant rooms that are individually furnished with antiques. ⊗ *Ismaninger Str. 42–44 • Map P4 • (089) 41 60 50 • www.prinzregent.de • €€€€–€€€€€*

### 6 Ritzi

The rooms and suites at this hotel, located near the Maximilianeum, are furnished with a tremendous sense of style, and based on themes (Africa, Bali) or colour concepts. Elegant Art Deco flourishes and an in-house restaurant add to the appeal. ⊗ *Maria-Theresia-Str. 2a • Map P4 • (089) 4 19 50 30 • www.hotel-ritzi.de • €€€€–€€€€€*

### 7 Prinz

Small, elegantly appointed hotel near the Gasteig, high above the Isar. Most rooms afford a wonderful view of the city. Works by local artists are often on display. ⊗ *Hochstr. 45 • Map N6 • (089) 441 40 80 • www.hotel-prinz.de • €€€–€€€€*

### 8 Romantikhotel Insel Mühle

Set in a converted 14th-century mill, the Romantik-hotel boasts cosy, rustic rooms panelled in light wood. Dinner at the hotel restaurant is served on the beautiful patio to the sound of the nearby burbling stream. ⊗ *München-Untermenzing, Von-Kahr-Str. 87 • (089) 8 10 10 • www.weber-gastronomie.de • limited wheelchair access • €€€–€€€€*

### 9 Splendid-Dollmann

This hotel in an elegant 19th-century manor house features paintings and antiques in the guest rooms. Many cultural venues and the Maximilian-straße are within walking distance. ⊗ *Thierschstr. 49 • Map N4 • (089) 23 80 80 • www.splendid-muc.de • €€€–€€€€*

### 10 Cortiina Hotel

This stylish boutique hotel with an individual sense of style opened in 2001. The interiors of the 33 rooms are designed with natural wood and stone, linen, and leather, yet accommodate modern guestroom technology. The bar is a hip meeting place at night. ⊗ *Ledererstr. 8 • Map L4 • (089) 2 42 24 90 • www.cortiina.com • €€€–€€€€*

➡ *For information on easy-access hotels* **See p138**

147

Left & Centre **Hotel Jedermann** Right **Hotel Blauer Bock**

# Budget Hotels

### Hotel Stefanie

A family-run hotel with a long tradition in the Maxvorstadt. The 33 modest but comfortable rooms have telephones and TV. Parking is available, and pets are permitted.
Ⓢ *Türkenstr. 35* • *Map L2*
• *(089) 288 14 00*
• *www.hotel-stefanie.de*
• *€€€*

### Hotel Eder

This charming, family-operated budget hotel is located on a quiet side street near the central railway station. Telephone and TV are found in all 30 rooms, which have polished wood panelling and rustic details.
Ⓢ *Zweigstr. 8* • *Map J4*
• *(089) 55 46 60*
• *http://hotel-eder.de*
• *€€–€€€*

### Hotel Blauer Bock

This family-run hotel near the Stadtmuseum places personal service high on its list of priorities. Telephone and TV in 75 rooms. Non-smoking rooms are available. Parking is also available, and pets are welcome.
Ⓢ *Sebastiansplatz 9 (St-Jakobs-Platz)* • *Map K4–L4*
• *(089) 23 17 80* • *€€–€€€*

### Hotel Pension Flora

This pension occupies a heritage-protected, restored turn-of-the-19th-century building in the city centre. The 35 rooms are appointed with practical yet individual furnishings; some retain their original plaster details. There are no telephones in the rooms. Pets are permitted.
Ⓢ *Karlstr. 49* • *Map K3*
• *(089) 59 70 67*
• *www.hotel-flora.de* • *€€*

### Hotel Jedermann

The Jenke family has owned and operated this centrally located hotel for over 40 years, and their dedication shows in the level of service enjoyed by their guests, making it one of the most popular hotels in Germany. Most of the 55 rooms overlook a bright courtyard; those facing the street have soundproof windows. Many rooms are equipped with Internet connection.
Ⓢ *Bayerstr. 95* • *Map E4–E5* •
*(089) 54 32 40* • *www.hotel-jedermann.de* • *€€–€€€*

### Hotel Eisenreich

A small budget hotel near the Neue Messe. Easy and convenient access to downtown from the nearby U-Bahn station. Rooms are equipped with cable TV and telephone. Free Internet access is available.
Ⓢ *Baumkirchner Str. 17*
• *(089) 43 40 21*
• *www.hoteleisenreich.de*
• *€€–€€€*

### Hotel Olympia

A three-star hotel in the south of Munich, convenient to the Forstenrieder Park leisure area. Telephone and TV in all 34 modern rooms. Parking is available, and pets are welcome.
Ⓢ *Maxhofstr. 23*
• *(089) 75 40 63*
• *www.hotel-olympia-muc.de*
• *€€*

### Hotel Aurora

Three-star hotel in a convenient location near the A8 and A99. By S-Bahn, you can reach downtown in 15 minutes. All 20 rooms are comfortably furnished and have cable TV, a radio, and a direct-dial telephone. PCs are available for use on request.
Ⓢ *Limesstr. 68a* • *(089) 89 73 69 30*
• *www.hotel-garni-aurora.de* • *€€*

### Hotel Lämmle

A good budget-conscious hotel choice, located near Westpark. The 24 rooms are simple and modern in style; all have cable TV. Parking is available; pets are permitted.
Ⓢ *Friedenheimerstr. 137* • *Map B5* • *(089) 57 15 29* •
*www.hotellaemmle-muenchen.de* • *€€*

### Hotel Royal

This centrally located hotel has a good soundproofing system, meaning that you can be at the heart of the action and still get a good night's sleep in one of the 40 elegantly furnished rooms.
Ⓢ *Schillerstr. 11a* • *Map J4*
• *(089) 59 10 21* • *www.hotel-royal.de* • *€–€€*

 **Note:** All hotels accept major credit cards. Unless otherwise stated, they are not equipped for wheelchair access.

**Price Categories**

For a standard, double room per night (with breakfast if included), taxes, and extra charges.

| | |
|---|---|
| € | under €60 |
| €€ | €60–100 |
| €€€ | €100–150 |
| €€€€ | €150–200 |
| €€€€€ | over €200 |

Left & Right **Bar and bunk bedroom in 4you München**

# 🔟 B&Bs, Hostels & Apartments

## 1 Pension Am Kaiserplatz

A lovely pension with just 10 rooms, in a quiet location in the heart of the Schwabing district. Most rooms have showers but no WC. Be sure to book early, as the rooms are often reserved months in advance. 🔎 Kaiserplatz 12 • Map F2 • (089) 34 91 90 • €

## 2 Hotel Mona Lisa

A small hotel near Englischer Garten, in the Lehel district. Seven rooms, each with telephone, TV, minibar, and unique furnishings. The Mona Lisa team goes out of its way to provide personal service. 🔎 Robert-Koch-Str. 4 • Map N4 • (089) 21 02 83 80 • www.hotelmonalisa.de • €€

## 3 Pension Greiner

Located between Leopoldstraße and Englischer Garten, this small pension offers nine cosy rooms, most with shower and WC. A generous breakfast buffet is served. Pets are welcome. 🔎 Ohmstr. 12 • Map M1 • (089) 380 18 80 • www.pensiongreiner.de • €€

## 4 Jugendherberge München-Neuhausen

Youth hostel near Rot-Kreuz-Platz, a 10-minute U-Bahn ride to downtown. Shared bathrooms and showers on each floor, breakfast buffet. Full board or dinner-only meal plans are available. Youth hostel pass required. 🔎 Wendl-Dietrich-Str. 20 • Map C3 • (089) 13 11 56 • www.djh.de • €

## 5 Easy Palace International Youth Hostel

A youth hostel located near the central railway station, the Easy Palace offers 62 rooms with WC and shower, plus a bar, restaurant, 24-hour concierge, Internet terminals, bicycle rentals, and free lockers. No age limit and no youth hostel pass required. 🔎 Mozartstr. 4 • Map E5 • (089) 558 79 70 • www.easypalace.de • limited wheelchair access • €

## 6 4you München

Ecologically oriented youth hostel near central railway station with 60 rooms (with and without bath/WC), breakfast buffet; full board or dinner-only meal plans also available. No age limit. In-house childcare available. 🔎 Hirtenstr. 18 (Querstraße der Arnulfstr.) • Map E4 • (089) 55 21 66 0 • www.the4you.de • wheelchair accessible • €–€€

## 7 Hotel-Gästehaus im Forum am Westkreuz

Guesthouse with self-catering flats, located at the S-Bahn station Westkreuz (15-minute ride to downtown). Each flat features a kitchenette and four-piece bathroom. Nearly all units have a balcony or rooftop patio. The Forum complex in which the apartments are located has 28 retail stores and two restaurants. 🔎 Friedrichshafener Str. 17 • (089) 83 99 00 • www.gaestehausimforum.de • €€–€€€

## 8 Maximilian Apartments

These exclusive apartments are located in a building with a heritage-protected façade and a lush courtyard. The welcoming flats are appointed with all the conveniences: cable TV, telephone, kitchen, and eating counter. Weekly cleaning and laundry services are available. 🔎 Hochbrückenstr. 16 • Map M4 • (089) 24 25 80 • www.schaper-apartment.com • €€€

## 9 Bed & Breakfast München

This agency offers a range of apartments and guest rooms with and without breakfast per day, week, or month (commission is charged). 🔎 (089) 168 87 81 • www.bed-breakfast-muc.de

## 10 Mr. Lodge

A wide range of accommodation offered, from furnished bachelor flats to exclusive business suites. All available units are posted online. 🔎 (089) 340 82 30 • www.mrlodge.de

For information on easy-access hotels **See p138**

# Phrase Book

## In an Emergency

| Where is the telephone? | Wo ist das Telefon? | voh ist duss tel-e-fone? |
| Help! | Hilfe! | **hilf**-uh |
| Please call a doctor | Bitte rufen Sie einen Arzt | **bitt**-uh **roof**'n zee ine-en artst |
| Please call the police | Bitte rufen Sie die Polizei | **bitt**-uh **roof**'n zee dee poli-**tsy** |
| Please call the fire brigade | Bitte rufen Sie die Feuerwehr | **bitt**-uh **roof**'n zee dee **foyer**-vayr |
| Stop! | Halt! | **hult** |

## Communication Essentials

| Yes | Ja | **yah** |
| No | Nein | **nine** |
| Please | Bitte | **bitt**-uh |
| Thank you | Danke | dunk-uh |
| Excuse me | Verzeihung | fair-**tsy**-hoong |
| Hello (good day) | Guten Tag | **goot**-en tahk |
| Hello | Grüß Gott | **grooss** got |
| Goodbye | Auf Wiedersehen | owf-**veed**-er-zay-ern |
| Good evening | Guten Abend | goot'n **ahb**'nt |
| Good night | Gute Nacht | goot-uh **nukht** |
| Until tomorrow | Bis morgen | biss **morg**'n |
| See you | Tschüss | chooss |
| See you | Servus | sayr **voos** |
| What is that? | Was ist das? | voss ist duss |
| Why? | Warum? | var-**room** |
| Where? | Wo? | **voh** |
| When? | Wann? | **vunn** |
| today | heute | **hoyt**-uh |
| tomorrow | morgen | **morg**'n |
| month | Monat | **mohn**-aht |
| night | Nacht | **nukht** |
| afternoon | Nachmittag | **nahkh**-mit-tahk |
| morning | Morgen | **morg**'n |
| year | Jahr | yar |
| there | dort | **dort** |
| here | hier | **hear** |
| week | Woche | **vokh**-uh |
| yesterday | gestern | **gest**'n |
| evening | Abend | **ahb**'nt |

## Useful Phrases

| How are you? (informal) | Wie geht's? | vee gayts |
| Fine, thanks | Danke, es geht mir gut | dunk-uh, es gayt meer goot |
| Until later | Bis später | biss **shpay**-ter |
| Where is/are? | Wo ist/sind...? | voh ist/sind |
| How far is it to...? | Wie weit ist es...? | vee **vite** ist ess |
| Do you speak English? | Sprechen Sie Englisch? | shpresh'n zee **eng**-glish |
| I don't understand | Ich verstehe nicht | ish fair-**shtay**-uh nisht |
| Could you speak more slowly? | Könnten Sie langsamer sprechen? | **kurnt**-en zee **lung**-zam-er **shpresh**'n |

## Useful Words

| large | groß | **grohss** |
| small | klein | **kline** |
| hot | heiß | **hyce** |
| cold | kalt | **kult** |
| good | gut | **goot** |
| bad | böse/schlecht | **burss**-uh/**shlesht** |
| open | geöffnet | g'**urff**-nett |
| closed | geschlossen | g'**shloss**'n |
| left | links | **links** |
| right | rechts | **reshts** |
| straight ahead | geradeaus | g'**rah**-der-**owss** |

## Making a Telephone Call

| I would like to make a phone call | Ich möchte telefonieren | ish mer-shtuh tel-e-fon-**eer**'n |
| I'll try again later | Ich versuche es später noch einmal | ish fair-zookh-uh es **shpay**-ter nokh ine-mull |
| Can I leave a message? | Kann ich eine Nachricht hinterlassen? | kan ish **ine**-uh nakh-risht hint-er-**lahss**-en |
| answer phone | Anrufbeantworter | an-roof-be-**ahnt**-vort-er |
| telephone card | Telefonkarte | tel-e-**fohn**-kart-uh |
| receiver | Hörer | **hur**-er |
| mobile | Handy | han-dee |
| engaged (busy) | besetzt | b'zetst |
| wrong number | Falsche Verbindung | falsh-uh fair-**bin**-doong |

## Sightseeing

| entrance ticket | Eintrittskarte | ine-tritz-**kart**-uh |
| cemetery | Friedhof | **freed**-hofe |
| train station | Bahnhof | **barn**-hofe |
| gallery | Galerie | **gall**-er-ree |
| information | Auskunft | **owss**-koonft |
| church | Kirche | **keersh**-uh |
| garden | Garten | **gart**'n |
| palace/castle | Palast/Schloss | pallast/shloss |
| place (square) | Platz | **plats** |
| bus stop | Haltestelle | **hal**-te-shtel-uh |
| free admission | Eintritt frei | ine-tritt fry |

## Shopping

| Do you have/ Is there...? | Gibt es...? | geept ess |
| How much does it cost? | Was kostet das? | voss **kost**'t duss? |
| When do you open/ close? | Wann öffnen Sie/ schließen Sie? | vunn **off'n** zee **shlees**'n zee |
| this | das | duss |
| expensive | teuer | **toy**-er |
| cheap | preiswert | **price**-vurt |
| size | Größe | **gruhs**-uh |
| number | Nummer | **noom**-er |
| colour | Farbe | **farb**-uh |
| brown | braun | brown |
| black | schwarz | **shvarts** |
| red | rot | **roht** |
| blue | blau | **blau** |
| green | grün | **groon** |
| yellow | gelb | **gelp** |

## Types of Shop

| chemist (pharmacy) | Apotheke | appo-**tay**-kuh |
| bank | Bank | **bunk** |
| market | Markt | **markt** |
| travel agency | Reisebüro | **rye-z**er-boo-roe |
| department store | Warenhaus | **vahr**'n-hows |
| chemist's, drugstore | Drogerie | droog-er-**ree** |
| hairdresser | Friseur | freezz-**er** |
| newspaper kiosk | Zeitungskiosk | tsytoongs-kee-osk |
| bookshop | Buchhandlung | **bookh**-hant-loong |
| bakery | Bäckerei | beck-er-**eye** |
| butcher | Metzgerei | mets-ger-**eye** |
| post office | Post | posst |
| shop/store | Geschäft/Laden | gush-**eft**/**lard**'n |
| film processing shop | Photogeschäft | **fo**-to-gush-**eft** |
| clothes shop | Kleiderladen, Boutique | klyder-lard'n boo-**teek**-uh |

### Staying in a Hotel

| | | |
|---|---|---|
| Do you have any vacancies? | Haben Sie noch Zimmer frei? | harb'n zee nokh **tsimm**-er-fry |
| with twin beds? | mit zwei Betten? | mitt tsvy bett'n |
| with a double bed? | mit einem Doppelbett? | mitt ine'm **dopp**'l-bet |
| with a bath? | mit Bad? | mitt **bart** |
| with a shower? | mit Dusche? | mitt **doosh**-uh |
| I have a reservation | Ich habe eine Reservierung | ish **harb**-uh ine-uh rez-er-**veer**-oong |
| key | Schlüssel | shlooss'l |
| porter | Pförtner | **pfert**-ner |

### Eating Out

| | | |
|---|---|---|
| Do you have a table for…? | Haben Sie einen Tisch für…? | harb'n zee tish foor |
| I would like to reserve a table | Ich möchte eine Reservierung machen | ish **mer**-shtuh ine-uh rezer-**veer**-oong makh'n |
| I'm a vegetarian | Ich bin Vegetarier | ish bin vegg-er-**tah**-ree-er |
| Waiter! | Herr Ober! | hair **oh**-bare! |
| The bill (check), please | Die Rechnung, bitte | dee **resh**-noong bitt-uh |
| breakfast | Frühstück | **froo**-shtock |
| lunch | Mittagessen | **mit**-targ-ess'n |
| dinner | Abendessen | **arb**'nt-ess'n |
| bottle | Flasche | **flush**-uh |
| dish of the day | Tagesgericht | **tahg**-es-gur-isht |
| main dish | Hauptgericht | **howpt**-gur-isht |
| dessert | Nachtisch | **nahkh**-tish |
| cup | Tasse | **tass**-uh |
| wine list | Weinkarte | vine-kart-uh |
| glass | Glas | **glars** |
| spoon | Löffel | **lerff**'l |
| fork | Gabel | **gahb**'l |
| teaspoon | Teelöffel | tay-lerff'l |
| knife | Messer | **mess**-er |
| starter (appetizer) | Vorspeise | **for**-shpize-uh |
| the bill | Rechnung | **resh**-noong |
| tip | Trinkgeld | **trink**-gelt |
| plate | Teller | **tell**-er |

### Menu Decoder

| | | |
|---|---|---|
| Apfel | **upf**'l | apple |
| Apfelsine | **upf**'l-seen-uh | orange |
| Aprikose | upri-**kawz**-uh | apricot |
| Artischocke | arti-**shokh**-uh-or-ber-jeen-uh | artichoke |
| Aubergine | | aubergine (eggplant) |
| Banane | bar-**narn**-uh | banana |
| Beefsteak | **beef**-stayk | steak |
| Bier | beer | beer |
| Bohnensuppe | bum-en-zoop-uh | bean soup |
| Bratkartoffeln | brat-kar-toff'ln | fried potatoes |
| Bratwurst | brat-voorst | fried sausage |
| Brezel | bret-sell | pretzel |
| Brot | brot | bread |
| Brühe | bruh-uh | broth |
| Butter | **boot**-ter | butter |
| Champignon | **shum**-pin-yong | mushroom |
| Currywurst | **kha**-ree-voorst | sausage with curry sauce |
| Ei | **eye** | egg |
| Eis | **ice** | ice/ ice cream |
| Ente | **ent**-uh | duck |
| Erdbeeren | ayrt-**beer**'n | strawberries |
| Fisch | **fish** | fish |
| Fleisch | flaysh | meat |
| Forelle | for-**ell**-uh | trout |
| Gans | ganns | goose |
| gebraten | g'**braat**'n | fried |
| gegrillt | g'**grilt** | grilled |
| gekocht | g'**kokht** | boiled |
| geräuchert | g'**rowk**-ert | smoked |
| Geflügel | g'**floog**'l | poultry |
| Gemüse | g'**mooz**-uh | vegetables |

| | | |
|---|---|---|
| Gulasch | **goo**-lush | goulash |
| Hähnchen (Hendl) | haynsh'n | chicken |
| Hering | **hair**-ing | herring |
| Himbeeren | him-beer'n | raspberries |
| Kaffee | kaf-**fay** | coffee |
| Kalbfleisch | kalp-flysh | veal |
| Kaninchen | ka-**neensh**'n | rabbit |
| Karotte | car-**ott**-uh | carrot |
| Kartoffelpüree | kar-toff'l-poor-ay | mashed potatoes |
| Käse | **kayz**-uh | cheese |
| Knoblauch | **k'nob**-lowkh | garlic |
| Knödel | **k'nerd**'l | dumpling |
| Kuchen | **kookh**'n | cake |
| Lachs | **lahkhs** | salmon |
| Leber | **lay**-ber | liver |
| Marmelade | marmer-**lard**-uh | marmalade, jam |
| Milch | **milsh** | milk |
| Mineralwasser | minn-er-**arl** vuss-er | mineral water |
| Nuss | **nooss** | nut |
| Öl | **erl** | oil |
| Olive | o-**leev**-uh | olive |
| Pfeffer | **pfeff**-er | pepper |
| Pfirsich | **pfir**-zish | peach |
| Pflaume | **pflow**-me | plum |
| Pommes frites | pomm-**fritt** | chips/ French fries |
| Rindfleisch | **rint**-flysh | beef |
| Rührei | **rhoo**-er-eye | scrambled eggs |
| Saft | **zuft** | juice |
| Salat | zal-aat | salad |
| Salz | **zults** | salt |
| Sauerkirschen | zow-er-**keersh**'n | cherries |
| Sauerkraut | zow-er-krowt | sauerkraut |
| Sekt | **zekt** | sparkling wine |
| Senf | **zenf** | mustard |
| scharf | sharf | spicy |
| Schlagsahne | shlahgg-zarn-uh | whipped cream |
| Schnitzel | **shnitz**'l | veal or pork cutlet |
| Schweinefleisch | **shvine**-flysh | pork |
| Semmel | **tsem**-mel | bread roll |
| Spargel | **shparg**'l | asparagus |
| Spiegelei | shpeeg'l-eye | fried egg |
| Spinat | shpin-art | spinach |
| Tee | **tay** | tea |
| Tomate | tom-art-uh | tomato |
| Wassermelone | vuss-er-me-lohn-uh | watermelon |
| Wein | **vine** | wine |
| Weintrauben | vine-trowb'n | grapes |
| Wiener Würstchen | veen-er voorst-sh'n | frankfurter |
| Zitrone | tsi-trohn-uh | lemon |
| Zucker | **tsook**-er | sugar |
| Zwiebel | **tsvee**b'l | onion |

### Numbers

| | | |
|---|---|---|
| 0 | null | **nool** |
| 1 | eins | **eye'ns** |
| 2 | zwei | **tsvy** |
| 3 | drei | **dry** |
| 4 | vier | **feer** |
| 5 | fünf | **foonf** |
| 6 | sechs | **zex** |
| 7 | sieben | **zeeb**'n |
| 8 | acht | **uhkht** |
| 9 | neun | **noyn** |
| 10 | zehn | **tsayn** |
| 11 | elf | **elf** |
| 12 | zwölf | **tserlf** |
| 13 | dreizehn | **dry**-tsayn |
| 14 | vierzehn | **feer**-tsayn |
| 15 | fünfzehn | **foonf**-tsayn |
| 16 | sechzehn | **zex**-tsayn |
| 17 | siebzehn | **zeep**-tsayn |
| 18 | achtzehn | **uhkht**-tsayn |
| 19 | neunzehn | **noyn**-tsayn |
| 20 | zwanzig | **tsvunn**-tsig |

# General Index

Index

# Acknowledgments

## The Author

Dr. Elfi Ledig has worked for many years as an author and editor of reference books and travel guides. She is currently Editor-in-Chief of a Munich health and wellness magazine and lives in Munich.

At Dorling Kindersley, Munich:
**Publishing Director**
Dr. Jörg Theilacker
**Editors** Gerhard Bruschke, Linde Wiesner
**Editorial Assistant**
Birgit Walter
**Design & Layout**
Dr. Alex Klubertanz
**Additional Text** Brigitte Maier, Georg Ledig
**Additional Photography** Julian Puttins, Georg Ledig, Wendelin Lomeg
**Index** Dr. Bettina Jung

At Dorling Kindersley, London:
**Publisher**
Douglas Amrine
**Publishing Managers**
Helen Townsend, Kate Poole
**Senior DTP Designer**
Jason Little
**Senior Cartographer**
Casper Morris
**Picture Researcher**
Brigitte Arora, Romaine Werblow
**Production Controller**
Louise Daly
**Revisions Coordinators**
Leah Tether, Hugo Wilkinson

At International Book Productions Inc, Toronto:
**Publishing Director**
Barbara Hopkinson
**Translator**
Elisabeth Schwaiger
**Editor** Judy Phillips
**DTP Designer** Dietmar Kokemohr
**Editorial Assistance**
Ken Ramstead
**Proofreader** Sheila Hall

## Picture Credits

t-top; tl-top left; tlc-top left centre; tc-top centre; tr-top right; trc-top right centre; cla-centre left above; ca-centre above; cra-centre right above; cl-centre left; c-centre; cr-centre right; clb-centre left below; cb-centre below; crb-centre right below; bl-bottom left; b-bottom; bc-bottom centre; bcl-bottom centre left; br-bottom right; r-right; ra-right above; rb-right below

Every effort has been made to trace the copyright holders, and we apologize for any unintentional omissions. We would be pleased to insert the appropriate acknowledgments in any subsequent edition of this publication.

The publishers would like to thank the following individuals, companies, and picture libraries for their kind permission to reproduce their photographs:

4 you München: 149tr, 149tl; Allianz Arena: Herzog/de Meuron 72tl; Bavaria Filmstadt GmbH: 55b, 68b, 108tc; Bayerische Landesbank: 136tl; Bayerischer Hof: 59b, 144tr; Blutenburgtheater: 44tr; Club Morizz: 62tc, 62b; Cortiina Hotel: Fabrice Dallanese 147tr; Deutsche Eiche: 62tl; Geisel Hotels: 64tr, 65t, 144tl, 144tc; Griesbräu zu Murnau: 119tl; Hilton Munich City: 145tr, 145tl; Hotel Astor: 146tl; Hotel Jedermann: 148tl, 148tc; Hotel Königswache: 146tc, 146tr; Hotel Residenz Passau: 143tr; Internationales Dokumentarfilmfestival: 54tl; LEGOLAND Deutschland GmbH: 69tl, 69r, 138tl; Lenbach: 64tc, 64b; Mathäser: Jörg Hempel, Aachen 54tr, 55br; Max-Emanuel-Brauerei: 93tl, 93tr; Muffathalle: 58b; Münchener Biennale: 46tr; Münchner Filmfestwochen GmbH: 46b; Pasinger Fabrik: 44tl; Porzellan & Pinselstrich: 101tr; Pusser's: 60b; Ratskeller München: 143tl; Josef Schwab, Starnberg: 32b; Tantris: 64tl; Theater 44: 45t; Weinhaus Neuner: 85t; Zirkus Krone: 68tc.

Fremdenverkehrsamt Mühldorf: 74tc. Fremdenverkehrsamt München: 4–5; Bjarne Geiges 7tr, 25tc; Robert Hetz 1. Kurverwaltung Garmisch-Partenkirchen: 117t, 117b, 119tr, 125c. Tourismusverband Starnberger Fünf-Seen-Land: 7br, 32–33cs, 70b, 73t. Tourist-Information Bad Tölz: 68tr, 74tr, 74b, 75t, 75r, 124tr, 126tl, 138tc.

A1 PIX: 3bl.
ALPINES MUSEUM, MÜNCHEN: 99tl.
ARCHIV WOLFGANG LEHNER/
WENDELIN LOMEG: 45r, 51r, 53tr, 54b,
55tr, 59r, 61tr, 61rb, 65r, 73r, 135tl.
ARTOTHEK: Bayer & Mitko 6clb;
*Schlaraffenland*, 1566, Pieter Brueghel
14–15c, 16tc; Blauel/Gnamm *Raub
der Töchter des Leukippos*, 1618 Peter
Paul Rubens 15tl; *Spiel der Wellen*,
1883, Arnold Böcklin 16tr, 37c, 97c;
Joachim Blauel *Alexanderschlacht*,
1529, Albrecht Altdorfer 14bc; *Willem
van Heythuysen*, 1625–30, Frans Hals
15bl; *Entkleidung Christi*, ca. 1579, El
Greco 15bc; *Frühstück im Atelier*,
1868, Edouard Manet 16bl, 37tl;
Toni/Ott 34tc.
BAR CENTRALE: 84tl.
BAU MUNICH: 63tr.
BAYERISCHE SEENSCHIFFFAHRT: 32tlc.
BAYERISCHE VERWALTUNG DER
STAATLICHEN SCHLÖSSER, GÄRTEN UND
SEEN: 3tl, 6bl, 12br, 20–21cb, 28bc,
29tr, 29tl, 29b, 30tl, 30tr, 31tr, 31cr,
34tl, 71c, 106br, 106br, 107tr.
BAYERISCHES NATIONALMUSEUM: 36tr,
37br.

ALOIS DALLMAYR: 142tl,
DEUTSCHES MUSEUM MÜNCHEN: 6tl, 8tl,
8c, 8cb, 8tr, 9tl, 9tr, 9cr, 9crb, 9clb,
10tr, 10tl, 11cra, 11clb, 10tc, 10b.
DEUTSCHE BAHN AG: 133tl.
DK IMAGES: 74tl, 104tc, 107r, 107br;
Demetrio Carrasco 125tr.
DEUTSCHE PRESSE-AGENTUR GMBH: 2tl;
picture alliance/ Peter Kneffel 3tr; picture alliance/Scholz 116cr.
FLUGHAFEN MÜNCHEN: 132tr, 133tr.
VERA GAUDERMANN: 14cla, 16cl, 17t,
17b, 18–19c, 19cr, 24–25c, 24cr, 25cr,
25b, 27crb, 38tc, 42tc, 44b, 50tl,
50tc, 50tr, 51t, 52tl, 52tr, 54tc, 58tl,
58tc, 58tr, 60tl, 60tc, 60tr, 62tr, 66tl,
66tc, 66tr, 67t, 83tc, 83tr, 84tc, 84tr,
88t, 90tl, 90tc, 91tl, 91tr, 92tl, 92tc,
92tr, 94–95, 99b, 105t, 108tl, 108tr,
109tl, 109tc, 110tl, 110tc, 110tr, 111tl,
138tr, 139tc, 140tl, 140tc, 140tr, 142tc,
142tr, 148tr.
HAUS DER BAYERISCHEN GESCHICHTE, BIL-
DARCHIV: 34tr.
HEIMATMUSEUM BAD TÖLZ: 124cr.
HUSSFELD AND ZANG: 109tc.
IFA-BILDERTEAM: Hollweck 22–23; IFA-
IMAGES: 48–49, 52tc, 53r, 56–57, 80t,
81bl, 81r, 82tc, 130–131.

ÜLANDESHAUPTSTADT MÜNCHEN/ MÜNCH-
NER STADTMUSEUM: 35r, 86cr.
GEORG LEDIG: 103tr, 116tl, 120tl, 120cr,
123t.
WENDELIN LOMEG: 100tc, 101tc, 102tl,
102tr, 103tl, 127t.
WERNER NIKOLAI: 74tl.
PROJECTS UNLIMITED: Christoph Knoch
83tl.
JULIAN PUTTINS: 22l, 22cr, 22bl, 23t,
23cra, 23c, 23bl, 24l, 46c, 47r, 139tr.
HERBERT SCHWINGHAMMER: 97b.
STAATLICHES MUSEUM ÄGYPTISCHER
KUNST, MÜNCHEN: 21cr.
STÄDTISCHE GALERIE IM LENBACHHAUS:
*Entwurf für den Umschlag des
Almanachs Der Blaue Reiter*, Wassily
Kandinsky © ADAGP, Paris und DACS,
London 2005 118cr.
STADTMUSEUM, MÜNCHEN: 89tl.
ODA STERNBERG: 42tl.
ZEFA VISUAL MEDIA: Damm 7crb; San-
tos 26–27tc.
All other images are © Dorling Kindersley
London. For further information see

**www.dkimages.com**

## Special Editions of DK Travel Guides

DK Travel Guides can be purchased
in bulk quantities at discounted prices
for use in promotions or as premiums.
We are also able to offer special editions and personalized jackets, corpo-
rate imprints, and excerpts from all of
our books, tailored specifically to meet
your own needs.

To find out more, please contact:

(in the United States)
**SpecialSales@dk.com**

(in the UK) **travelspecialsales@
uk.dk.com**

(in Canada) DK Special Sales at
**general@tourmaline.ca**

(in Australia) **business.development
@pearson.com.au**

# Selected Street Index